VENGEANCE
HITLER'S NUCLEAR WEAPON: FACT OR FICTION?

VENGEANCE
HITLER'S NUCLEAR WEAPON:
FACT OR FICTION?

PHILIP HENSHALL

ALAN SUTTON PUBLISHING LIMITED

First published in the United Kingdom in 1995
Alan Sutton Publishing Ltd
Phoenix Mill · Far Thrupp · Stroud · Gloucestershire

Reprinted 1995

British Library Cataloguing in Publication Data

A catalogue record for this book is available from the British Library.

ISBN 0-7509-0874-2

Typeset in 11/12pt Erhardt.
Typesetting and origination by
Alan Sutton Publishing Limited.
Printed in Great Britain by
Butler & Tanner, Frome, Somerset.

Contents

Preface

In December 1938 two Germans, Otto Hahn and Fritz Strassman, verified the fission of uranium U.235. After a pause, during which the full implications were digested by the scientific community, discussion centred on the obvious question: the chain-reaction would have the potential to release an unimaginable amount of energy, but to what purpose? The world from Europe to the Pacific was heading inexorably towards war and the talk was not only of the peaceful use of this energy but also the military use, and in Germany in particular it was the military use which had the most appeal.

But to produce an explosive of unprecedented power also requires some means of delivering it to an enemy, and the success of this must, as far as possible, be guaranteed. If the means seems obvious now there is no reason to believe it was not obvious in 1939; Germany had a history of military innovation, and on the Baltic coast the army was developing the essential partner to the nuclear weapon, the ballistic missile. Yet after the war, the archives and the writings of those who directed the rocket and nuclear work make no mention of this partnership. General Dornberger and Wernher von Braun from Peenemünde, and the nuclear physicists kept silent.

However, the rocket facilities built in France tell another story. So, too, does a recently discovered drawing of a modified V2.

Hitler's vengeance weapon was no myth.

ACKNOWLEDGEMENTS

I would like to thank the following: my engineering and scientific friends and colleagues in the aeronautical, defence and nuclear fields; French farmers, postmen, shopkeepers, gendarmes, schoolteachers and others who have provided much help and friendly assistance in my search for the rocket sites, remembering events of many years ago, and in particular Admiral Canonne, Commander of the Cherbourg Naval Base, and members of his staff; those who contributed their own wartime experiences and personal records of the rocket threat, including ex-members of the ACIU and RAF; Professor Jurgen Rohwer for his continuing interest in the U-234 story and Teruaki Kawano of the National Institute for Defense Studies, Tokyo, for his assistance with the Japanese naval history; Greenwood Publishing Group, Inc., Westport, CT, for kind permission to reproduce material from Ermenc, J.J., *Atom Bomb Scientists, Memoirs 1939–1945* (1989), quoted on pages 38 and 147.

Introduction

There is one major question from the start of the Second World War which remains unanswered. The alarm bells were first sounded on 19 September 1939 at the Guildhall in the old port of Danzig, now flying the German flag after 20 years of isolation.

With Hitler's armed forces mopping up the remains of the Polish resistance there were just eight days to go before Warsaw capitulated. The Guildhall was to be the venue for Hitler's first victory speech of the war; in this speech for the first time he referred to a mystery weapon with which Germany would be in an unassailable position.

On 24 April 1939 the German War Ministry had received a letter from an eminent Hamburg professor, Paul Harteck, pointing out that the new science of nuclear physics had the potential to provide explosives of such power that any country possessing them would have an overwhelming advantage over others. This was not the first notification to the German military of one of the potential uses of the new nuclear power and it was clear that such information could not be ignored.

Early in November 1939 a package was delivered by an unknown courier (a German dissident?) to the British embassy in Oslo. It included references to German developments in pilotless aircraft as well as rocket research being carried out on the Baltic coast at Peenemünde. This information ended up in London on the desk of Dr R.V. Jones of MI6, who was given the task of investigating its veracity. But there were other more pressing issues confronting the political and military leaders in London, and the Oslo Report, as it became known, was filed into relative obscurity; talk of secret weapons was becoming commonplace.

However, as 1939 came to an end, at Peenemünde work on rockets was proceeding at an ever-increasing rate, under the leadership of Colonel Walter Dornberger and Wernher von Braun. On 2 October 1942 the first successful launch took place of the A4, later to be known as the V2, and simultaneously a number of records were attained for a manmade object. The A4 achieved the highest and fastest flight, but more importantly it established the basic techniques for all modern rockets, including their use as a long-range weapon capable of delivering a destructive payload over thousands of miles and with an accuracy of within a few feet. (A4 was the Peenemünde project name for the rocket, whereas V2 or *Vergeltung-Waffe* 2 (retribution weapon 2) was its operational name; V1 was the flying bomb.)

Work in the nuclear field was also gathering momentum and compared with rockets, there was a rich vein of talent to draw on.

Hahn and Strassman had demonstrated the fission of uranium in December 1938 and now a whole galaxy of Nobel prize winners was involved in various aspects of nuclear research at the numerous scientific institutions throughout Germany. One of these Nobel winners was already beginning to make his name as the unofficial spokesman for the nuclear scientists; his name was Werner Karl Heisenberg.

This nuclear and rocket work carried on during the early 1940s, even though the German military machine had had successes. By 1943, however, there were signs that the conventional forces were beginning to falter. Defeats for the army in Russia, at Stalingrad in the winter of 1942 and Kursk in 1943, had resulted in huge losses of material and manpower, and these were becoming increasingly difficult to replace. The invincibility of the army was now in question. Furthermore, the Luftwaffe had failed to subdue the British in 1940 and now was unable to stop the ever-increasing air raids on German civilian and industrial targets. German forces at sea were faring no better. The U-boats were suffering unacceptable losses with the constantly improving convoy system and detection methods of the Allies. In response, rocket developments now covered a multitude of projects, including anti-aircraft weapons, aircraft-launched anti-ship missiles and tactical battlefield weapons, not only from Peenemünde but also the other major armaments firms. Priority was still given to the V2 ballistic missile; design work was proceeding to extend its range to 3,500 miles using the A9 (a V2 with swept-back wings) and the A10 (a 200 ton thrust booster) combination. By 1943 the V2 had been developed into a reasonably reliable weapon, capable of carrying a 1 ton payload over a range of 200 miles and plans for its use were well developed. In Northern France a vast complex of rocket facilities was being built, capable of handling all foreseeable developments, from the 46 ft V2 to the 100 ft A9/A10 and the appropriate warheads; just as a modern ballistic missile would be unthinkable carrying only high explosives, the advantages of a nuclear or chemical payload were obvious, especially when considering the 3,500 mile range version.

Germany was being subjected to ever-increasing air raids and a 1 ton high explosive payload paled into insignificance compared to the 2 million tons of bombs that were eventually dropped by the Allies.

Two deadly nerve gases, Tabun and Sarin, had been developed by the chemical giant I.G. Farben and were already in mass production, but there were technical problems with their use including dispersion at the target and antidotes. The nuclear option also had its problems, but these were much more basic.

By 1943, despite what had appeared to be an early lead in nuclear physics, the possibility of producing an atomic bomb within the necessary timescale was rapidly receding. To manufacture a uranium bomb similar to the one dropped on Hiroshima would require several kilograms of highly (70%) enriched uranium, and the technology for producing such a large amount would not be available for years. Similarly, to produce a plutonium bomb such as the one dropped on Nagasaki would require the building of a reactor, since plutonium is an artificial isotope produced in a nuclear reactor. Here, again, there were problems. Under the semi-official lead taken by Heisenberg, reactor technology had progressed only so far and then had apparently become immured in technical and political rivalries to such an extent that they were years behind the Americans. There was, however, one relatively simple solution to the production of a nuclear weapon: it did not necessarily have to be an atomic bomb of either sort. If even a crude reactor could be got working, in a few months it would have produced enough radioactive material to provide an alternative nuclear weapon.

Paul Harteck had been trying to build a zero-energy low-temperature reactor since 1940, but objections from Heisenberg had hampered progress. Now things were changing; the general lack of progress in nuclear technology was being questioned and Harteck now found allies in the government, including the most unlikely establishment, the Post Office. Although slightly (3%) enriched uranium is the more usual material for a reactor fuel, it is possible to use natural uranium oxide with a very efficient moderator (to slow the neutrons down, as the probability of the fission of U.235 by slow neutrons is very high), such as 'heavy' water or pure carbon and it was the latter that Harteck was now working on. The objective was to produce enough highly radioactive material, used with a conventional high-explosive bomb, to spread its lethal particles over a wide area. In *Soviet Atomic Spies* (Robert Hale, 1952) Bernard Newman describes a novel idea in warfare: scattering radioactive dust on the enemy. It was certainly new, but not in 1952; 10 years earlier the idea had been novel.

An Austrian expert Professor Hans Thirling has revealed that a novel kind of war is now feasible. It would depend on by-products of the present atomic piles used for the production of plutonium; these would consist of radioactive isotopes.

These could be used to impregnate fine sand which would then be scattered by air over enemy territory. The powder would cover a wide area with an almost invisible layer of dust, sufficiently radioactive to be lethal over a period of a few weeks.

However, Germany's nuclear weapon would also include plutonium and the radiation would last for years.

Since Hitler's Danzig speech there had been little further mention of secret weapons but from 1943 the German propaganda machine began to make repeated references to a special weapon which would bring retribution to the enemy. This would take the form of a weapon so deadly that all human life would be exterminated within a radius of several kilometres.

Did Paul Harteck build the low-temperature reactor to produce its deadly radioactive package? There was no shortage of uranium oxide or carbon. Certainly the designers at Peenemünde produced drawings of a rocket that could carry such a payload. But time was running out for Hitler's Third Reich and the final players now entered the stage; these were the submarines of Hitler's *Kriegsmarine* and the Imperial Japanese Navy.

U-234 left Kiel for Japan on 25 March 1945, beginning a voyage that should have lasted about 10 weeks. As it happened the war in Europe ended when U-234 was only halfway across the Atlantic and her captain surrendered to a US destroyer. Among her cargo unloaded at Portsmouth, New Hampshire, a few days after she docked on 19 May were a number of lead containers carefully packed in what had been the forward mineshafts.

According to the US authorities, 56 kg of uranium oxide were unloaded from U-234, but uranium oxide emits virtually no radiation; it could be carried in a cardboard box. Was this part of the package from Harteck's reactor and what affect did the discovery have on the war against Japan? Might there have been similar packages already in Japan, waiting to be used? In Japan there were two very special submarines, the largest in any navy, and each was capable of carrying three aircraft. In addition two large submarines had been modified to carry two of the same aircraft, each with a bomb-load capacity of 1,800 lb.

These vessels, I.400, I.401, I.13 and I.14, were kept well out of sight early in 1945, while U-234 should have arrived early in June. Not until the middle of July did all four make their first operational sortie and by then it was clear that U-234 would not be arriving with her very special cargo.

CHAPTER ONE

The Birth of the Weapon

The history of the rocket in Germany dates back to the First World War. The blockade of Germany by the British surface fleet and submarines, and its almost complete isolation from the rest of Europe (only Austria, Bulgaria and Turkey could be classed as Allies), meant that the ability to wage a modern war depended to a large extent on what Germany could produce from its own efforts. It is true that neutral Norway and Sweden still believed in free enterprise and therefore supplies of raw materials, such as nickel, chrome, manganese and copper, for munitions were still getting through, via Holland. However, there was one exception. The Kaiser's army marched on its stomach, but in 1915 food and supplies were conveyed to the battlefield by horsedrawn transport. Hundreds of thousands of horses were used and they needed fodder. This in turn required fertilizer, for which nitrates (also used in explosives) had to be imported from Chile. By 1915, with this supply cut off by the naval blockade of Germany, IG Farben was producing synthetic nitrates and together with Nobel prize winner Emil Fischer it became the 'master of ersatz'.

Twenty-five years later Fischer provided Hitler's Reich with the modern equivalent of horse-fodder: petrol made from abundant Ruhr coal. In spite of the fact that this process provided petrol at twice the current market price, Hitler insisted on the scheme going ahead, and by 1939 2 million tons of this petrol, three-quarters of Germany's requirements at that time, were being produced by this method. Within four years this had risen to 7 million tons.

At the forefront of developments in the armaments industry was the giant Krupp organization. Before the First World War it was producing big guns which were superior to anything in the Allies' possession. Krupp's two secret weapons were Big Bertha and the *Pariskanone* (Paris Gun).

Only 25 miles from the German border stood the Belgian fortress town of Liège. Its defences effectively blocked any German advance through Belgium into France, and this was one of the essential conditions of the Schlieffen Plan. The town had been reinforced and rearmed 35 years earlier with a 30 mile circle of armour-plated forts; these contained the very latest 210 mm (8.3 in) guns, linked together by an underground supply system. It was thought to be impregnable, especially as Port Arthur (China) with inferior defences had withstood a six-month siege by the Japanese a few years earlier.

For years Krupp had been working to perfect the largest artillery piece ever produced: the 420 mm (16.5 in) howitzer Big Bertha. The main difficulties were not its actual production but making its 98 tons transportable, so that it could be fired from several positions without having to be rebuilt each time, and to provide a suitable firing platform. The problems were eventually solved and by 1914, eight Big Berthas, were on the move by rail, each in two sections. Despite a blown-up railway tunnel 20 miles from Liège, in 24 hours the guns had been dragged within range of the northern and eastern line of the forts. Late in the afternoon of 12 August 1914 the first gun opened fire on Fort Pontisse. Its 1 ton armour-piercing projectile with a delayed-action fuse scored a direct hit, and Fort Pontisse disappeared in a cloud of smoke. Minutes later Fort Loncin suffered the same fate, and four days later the last fort had fallen.

The railmounted Paris Gun had a bore of 210 mm (8.3 in), weighed 150 tons and fired a 220–250 lb shell over a maximum range of 81 miles. Originally designed for the navy, it had a crew of 60 seamen plus officers and had a full Admiral in charge. The shells had to be heated before use and after each firing the barrel was lowered and checked for straightness. Every shot increased the bore slightly, so each shell was larger than the one before; the diameters varying between 8.3 and 8.4 in and up to a total weight of 30 lb. Consequently each shell was numbered, and after 65 firings the barrel was replaced. Complicated trajectory calculations were carried out, including atmospheric pressure, air temperature and humidity and the curvature of the earth's surface. During the final countdown a group of thirty surrounding batteries opened fire to mask its position from Allied teams trying to locate it, and a squadron of fighter planes was held in readiness just in case bombers were sent over.

In true ballistic fashion the shell reached an apogee of 26 miles before plunging earthwards – the greatest height achieved by any manmade device up to that time. Over a 20 week period in 1917 more than a thousand Parisians were killed, but at a cost of over 35,000 marks per shell.

This was an expensive way to kill the enemy and 27 years later a similar conclusion was reached about another German long-range weapon, the V2. The V2 was the first manmade device to exceed the Paris Gun's record, and its capabilities were superior in other ways. The Paris Gun was the ultimate development in conventional long-range artillery, but no further progress was possible. The V2, on the other hand, marked the beginning of the rocket and space age, and for the ultimate weapon the only part of the equation missing was the nuclear payload.

Unlike rocketry, nuclear physics was proceeding as a science related to the basic laws of the universe; this was the world of the Nobel Prize and official recognition from the international scientific community. It was a far cry from the crude and often publically ridiculed world of early rocketry.

The 1930s had seen a steady corroboration of some of the basic nuclear theories in laboratories throughout Europe and the US. With the confirmation of the fission of uranium U.235 the door was open for the nuclear age, but circumstances were beginning to dictate how this energy would first be used. In Europe and the Pacific one word was beginning to dominate the news headlines: war.

This then was the breeding-ground for the weapons of the future, which the victorious Allies thought they had extinguished with the Treaty of Versailles, drafted in 1919 and accepted grudgingly by President Hindenburg on behalf of the German people, on 10 January 1920. The treaty, or Diktat, as it was known in Germany, restricted the army to a volunteer force of 100,000 men; it also banned tanks, aeroplanes, submarines and warships over 10,000 tons.

The armaments industry including Krupp, was stripped of all its weapon-making machinery, which had survived the war intact. Krupp ostensibly turned to the manufacture of anything from typewriters and prams to locomotives and rolling-stock, but secretly was buying controlling interests in certain companies abroad, especially in Holland and Sweden, where Krupp owned the majority of the stock in the armaments firm Bofors. The Allies could easily check whether the armaments ban was being upheld, and frequently did so, but checking on design was another matter.

Design groups from the armaments firms moved out of the factories in the Ruhr and into offices around Berlin and once again Krupp provided the inspiration for the new subterfuge; if Krupp could do it so could others. But it was not only in Berlin that the design teams were at work. Offices were set up in South America, Russia, Finland – in fact anywhere that not too many questions would be asked.

By 1921 an American Army team investigating new Krupp patents noticed that 26 were for artillery control devices, 18 for electrical fire-control equipment for heavy guns, 9 for fuses, 17 for field guns and 14 for heavy artillery which could only be moved by rail (echoes of Big Bertha).

One office was in the Potsdamer Platz, virtually next door to the Reichstag Parliament building, where under the harmless-sounding name of Koch und Kienzle(E), some of Krupp's most gifted designers were hard at work on the next generation of weapons. In this case the (E) stood for *Entwicklung* (development) and the heavy tractors came equipped with 75 mm guns; they were designed for transportation on railway wagons through Belgium and France.

In 1927 the German amateur rocket society, Verein für Raumschiffahrt (VfR), had been founded and a small testing ground was established close to Berlin, at Reinickerdorf. Its original members included most of the early rocket experimenters of the day: Hermann Oberth, Max Valier, Willy Ley and Klaus Riedel. Many of the early attempts at rocket flight produced spectacular failures and there was usually a newsreel cameraman on hand to record the event. This, and the fact that the main aim was space travel, led most other countries to regard VfR members as cranks.

Experiments in Germany included work on rocket sledges, cars and mail-carrying rockets, and despite some of the bizarre designs that were produced a wide range of practical and theoretical knowledge was being accumulated.

All this work, however, was essentially being carried out by scientific amateurs; industry was not particularly interested because there did not appear to be a customer for the new technology. Nevertheless, the progress of these rocket pioneers was being followed with discreet interest. The Weapons Department of the army under General Becker, and in particular the Ballistics and Munitions Office, had by 1929 produced a report for the Defence Ministry on the possibility of using rocket propulsion for military purposes. The initial interest was in the simple unguided solid-fuel rocket as a replacement for artillery, but the first step had been taken. In 1930 a 35-year-old captain, Walter Dornberger, joined the Ballistics Office. His first task was to determine what use, if any, the work carried out by the VfR and others might be to the army. Funds were even provided, discreetly, in an attempt to put the work on to a professional footing. Reinickerdorf was visited several times by army staff, including Dornberger, but the VfR seemed incapable of putting their rocket work on to a systematic programme of development; greater concern was shown for producing papers and articles on space travel and flights to the moon.

In 1932 Wernher von Braun joined Dornberger's small team at the Kummersdorf artillery range, 17 miles south of Berlin, where in 1930 the army's first rocket-motor testing facility had been set up.

The eighteen-year-old von Braun had joined the VfR after his technical education in Berlin and his move to Kummersdorf was well timed, as the VfR was closed down by the government in 1933. Various reasons were given, including the misappropriation of funds and complaints from nearby residents, but from this date onwards all rocket research became *Staatsgeheimnis* (a state secret).

By 1933 Dornberger and his superiors were convinced that liquid fuels were the only practicable types of propellant for the rockets that the army was interested in. Solid fuel rockets required heavy steel canisters to hold the propellant, they were uncontrollable once ignited and had limitations on size. From 1933 to 1934, therefore, all the effort at Kummersdorf was directed towards producing a reliable liquid-fuelled motor with a thrust of 650 lb, enough to power the first of the definitive rocket designs from the new organization: the A1.

Dornberger was now gathering together the nucleus of a team, mainly from industry, that a few years later was to manage the huge organization centred at Peenemünde. Apart from von Braun one of the early recruits was Arthur Rudolph, who was also interested in liquid-fuelled rocket motors. He was later to be in charge of V2 production at the underground Nordhausen factory and went on to work for the Americans in a similar capacity on the Apollo moon-landing project.

CHAPTER TWO

The First Rockets

The A1 was completed by the end of 1933. It was 5 ft long, 15 in in diameter and was powered by the now-reliable 650 lb thrust liquid-oxygen- and alcohol-powered motor. To obtain the required stability of what was basically a large shell-like projectile with tail fins, an 85 lb section at the nose of the missile was designed to rotate under the power of a small electric motor. In the event the A1 never left the ground. Static ground tests showed that the rocket was inherently unstable, the centre of gravity being too far forward of the centre of pressure (of the aerodynamic forces).

Dornberger decided that more effort had to be applied to the question of stability and control; a reliable motor was one thing but a successful flight was another, and Dornberger had witnessed too many apparently successful launches by the VfR, only to see disaster strike a couple of hundred feet above the ground. Experts in the gyroscopic fire control of large naval guns were consulted and their advice applied to the A1's successor, the A2. The A2 was a replica of the A1 except that it had a crude gyroscopic stabilizing device located in the middle of the rocket.

By December 1934 two A2s were ready for launch, but the limitations of using the artillery range at Kummersdorf, only a few miles from Berlin, were now becoming apparent. A rapid search was made for a temporary alternative and the A2s were eventually launched from a deserted area on the island of Borkum in the North Sea. Both launches were successful and the rockets reached identical heights of 1½ miles.

The A2 was no larger or more sophisticated than liquid-fuelled rockets launched in America by Dr Robert Goddard, who operated with the help of funding from the Californian Institute of Technology, but without official government support. In Germany, Reinhold Tiling was also launching liquid- and solid-fuelled rockets as large as the A2 and there is evidence that one of his test vehicles may have reached an altitude of 6 miles in 1931. Tiling was killed shortly afterwards when one rocket exploded on launch but as with Goddard no official government help had been forthcoming and consequently progress was limited. Dornberger, on the other hand, received not only official Army backing but also the support of Army officers who had taken part in the First World War and fully appreciated the advantages of new technology in warfare.

General Hans von Seekt had masterminded the rebuilding of the German Army after, and in spite of, the Diktat. As the Commander-in-Chief of the

Weimar Republic's army from 1920 to 1926 he had ensured that all branches of the armed forces, although paying lip-service to the Versailles Treaty, had in fact been planning the most modern offensive fighting-force the world had seen. By the time he retired in 1926, the ground rules had been laid and despite a period of unsettled control in the armed forces when Hitler came to power in 1933, General Werner von Blomberg, as Defence Minister, ensured that support for the radical new army continued.

In 1936 Dornberger, now with a team of 150 engineers and scientists from both military and civilian circles, gave a demonstration at Kummersdorf to an assembled party of Army leaders, including the Commander-in-Chief, General Werner von Fritsch. Dornberger conducted a full tour of the test facilities, workshops and design office, finishing with a demonstration of three rocket motors of 650 lb, 2,200 lb and 3,500 lb thrust. To the uninitiated, the sight of each motor in turn belching out flames and smoke with a thunderous roar, but starting and stopping at the flick of a switch, must have been very impressive. General von Fritsch was evidently impressed because after the tour, when Dornberger raised the question of increased funding and most important, a separate and independent establishment where all the rocket work could be carried out at one location, von Fritsch agreed to provide more money and for Dornberger to look for a suitable site. Wernher von Braun, who was already a rising star in Dornberger's new organization, had been looking for such a site for some weeks. One of the places he visited was the island of Usedom. The northern part of the island was on the Baltic Sea and was a wild and desolate area, covered in pine forests. It faced an uninterrupted stretch of the Pomeranian coast, which provided an ideal firing range, and Dornberger approved of the choice. The area was called Peenemünde.

The next step was to try to get the Air Force interested in rocketry; although General von Fritsch had given his approval for increased funding, Dornberger knew that he probably did not appreciate the likely cost of building the sort of rocket centre that Dornberger had in mind. He need not have worried; with very little persuasion the head of the Development Office in the new Luftwaffe, Colonel von Richthofen, approached General Albert Kesselring, Director of Aircraft Construction, and after various meetings it was agreed that the Luftwaffe would also have a research and development establishment at Peenemünde, complete with airfield. It was to be the world's largest rocket centre, and the whole facility would be built by the Air Force, with costs shared by the Army. Once constructed, the Army would have overall control of the area. Work progressed in haste, and by the end of 1936 the Diktat was already dead and buried.

The German armaments industry under orders from Hitler was getting into top gear. Two 26,000 ton pocket-battleships – 16,000 tons above the Versailles limit – were already under construction; the *Scharnhorst*, *Gneisenau* and U-boats were being transported back from Finland, Holland and Spain for assembly in Germany, for Admiral Raeder's new *Kriegsmarine*.

On 16 March 1935 Hitler had ordered the introduction of compulsory military service. This provided an army of 300,000 men and a completely new organization was set up for the armed forces with a new title, the *Wehrmacht*. On 22 July 1936, Hitler agreed to Franco's request for military assistance in Spain and although the total cost to Germany was over half a billion marks, the Civil War proved to be an excellent testing ground for much of the new military equipment with which the *Wehrmacht* was now being provided. It is not surprising therefore that Dornberger and his team found a willing acceptance of their plans for the rocket weapons of the future.

By now Dornberger's staff had been formed into several specialist departments, and von Braun was his personal assistant. Dr Steuding was in charge of trajectory calculations; Dr Steinhoff instrumentation guidance and telemetry; Dr Herman aerodynamics and windtunnel testing; Dr Thiel motors and Walter Riedel the design office.

The next rocket to be built was the A3. This was 25 ft long, had a diameter of 2½ ft and used a 3,500 lb thrust oxygen- and alcohol-fuelled motor. Static tests were carried out at Kummersdorf late in 1936, and by the winter of 1937/8 it was ready for launch. There was some urgency to launch the first A3, as Hitler's rearmament of Germany was gathering speed and certainly Dornberger did not want the rocket to be left behind in the weapons race.

As Peenemünde was full of construction workers, four A3s were launched from the adjacent island of Greifswalder Oie, but in the event all were failures; after rising a few hundred feet they lost stability and crashed. From the post-launch meetings it was clear that, using the existing technology and methods, the A3 had been too great a leap forward from the 5 ft long A2. For instance, no systematic programme of windtunnel tests had been carried out on models of the A3 to check its control and stability through the various speed ranges expected during flight. Also, no inert free-flight trials had been carried out on A3s launched from an aircraft to confirm the windtunnel results. With no previous experience of rockets as large as the A3 they were in no-man's land from then on.

The embarrassing decision was taken to scrap the remainder of the unlaunched A3s and, with its successor, the A4, already on the drawing board, to go ahead with a much modified A3, using the same basic dimensions and motor but with different control surfaces and a new control system. This time each design step was verified by experimental work and the A5, as the new rocket was eventually called, was subjected to a comprehensive programme of windtunnel and free-flight testing.

To improve the guidance and control system the electrical firm Siemens was approached; the large subsonic windtunnel of Luftschifbau Zeppelin GmbH, Friedrichshafen, and the University of Aachen's small supersonic windtunnel were used for initial design work.

The flight-testing programme started in September 1938, when scale models one-fifth of the actual size were dropped from Heinkel IIIs at heights of up to 20,000 ft; the flights were recorded by cine-theodolite cameras. For the first time, the speed of sound, Mach 1, was exceeded in steep dives below 5,000 ft. These test vehicles had parachutes fitted to aid recovery and some of the rockets were used several times. Due to delays in the manufacture of the new control and guidance system, four full-size A5 test vehicles were launched from the island of

Greifswalder Oie without the systems installed in July and August 1938. The flight test programme carried on through 1938 and into 1939 and included ground-launched scale models with various control surface configurations and powered by a hydrogen peroxide (HTP) and catalyst motor developed by the Kiel firm of Hellmuth Walter. This was the first time Walter had been involved in rocket motors and it was the start of a long and useful association. The results of all this test and development work enabled Dornberger's team to produce a final design and in October 1939 the first two launches took place of full-size A5s, from Greifswalder Oie. These launches were successful and proved the basic configuration.

The next launch included the Siemens control gear in which the vertical axis of the pitch gyroscope was slowly rotated towards the horizontal position, 4 seconds after launch. This axis change was fed back via servo motors to the control surfaces which then applied the necessary movements to bring the rocket's pitch axis into line with that of the gyroscope. This resulted in the rocket following a gradual arc from the vertical until the angle was reached that produced the required range. Neglecting drag, for a ballistic missile an angle of 45° produces the maximum horizontal range. The A5, like its successor the A4 (V2) and the whole family of modern long-range rockets, was a ballistic missile in that after the initial powered and controlled part of flight, the trajectory was unpowered and unguided and followed a natural ballistic trajectory. When viewed from above this takes the form of a straight line.

To ensure the rocket hits the target, great accuracy is required to determine the initial angle of flight and duration of motor operation. Over the next two years, from October 1939 to 1941, with launches now transferred to the operational Peenemünde, 25 A5s were launched without a single major failure; all were recovered by parachute. This programme covered virtually all the aspects of the V2, including radio control using the Giant Würzburg radar situated on the mainland, 5 miles west of Peenemünde.

Apart from its size, the A5 differed in one major aspect from the V2: the fuel system. The A5 like its predecessors had its fuel mixture injected by pressurized nitrogen but this was not suitable for the V2, which used 7.5 tons of fuel per minute. A very powerful fuel pump was required, small enough to fit inside the 5.4 ft maximum diameter of the V2; it also needed to be capable of producing around 5,000 hp. At that moment nothing like it existed anywhere.

With the successful start of the A5 programme in October 1939, Dornberger could feel some satisfaction. On 5 September Dornberger, together with the Chief of the Ordnance Office, General Becker, had reported on progress to the Army Commander-in-Chief, General Walther von Brauchitsch. Fritsch, Brauchitsch's predecessor, had originally given the go-ahead for the rapid expansion in rocket development, but had been sacked by Hitler on a fictitious homosexual charge and Brauchitsch had been appointed on 4 February 1938. Fortunately for Dornberger, the new Commander-in-Chief was equally amenable to the vast sums of money now being spent on rockets in the Army's name.

It is interesting to note the progress Dornberger had made since 1930, when he first took up his appointment at Kummersdorf. Starting out with a handful of enthusiastic engineers, within nine years he had put Germany in an unassailable position as far as rocket development was concerned. The choice of Dornberger was one of those fateful decisions which can mean life or death to a project. His talents were such that he was able to direct the work of highly qualified civilians and at the same time maintain a strict military establishment, at which huge sums of money were being spent.

Although Hitler never visited Peenemünde, in March 1939 he visited Kummersdorf with von Brauchitsch and Becker to see demonstrations of rocket motors, always an impressive sight. At the time the way in which long-range rockets might fit in with his rapidly growing military plans must have seemed remote; nevertheless, Dornberger explained the possibilities of the V2 and Hitler listened in silence.

The work at Peenemünde, meanwhile, was going ahead with some haste. By January 1940 the supersonic windtunnel was in operation, under the control of Dr Rudolf Hermann from the University of Aachen. This windtunnel, which cost the enormous sum of £100,000 at 1939 prices, was the most advanced in the world and the first in which aerodynamic forces could be measured on models at supersonic speeds. The speed range of the 14 in × 14 in working section was Mach 1.2 to 4.5; this was achieved by evacuating the air from a 41 ft diameter sphere at one end of the tunnel and allowing dried and turbulent-free air to rapidly replace the vacuum. Entry nozzles for the working section could be changed in 10 to 15 minutes, and these controlled the different speed ranges of the airflow. The supersonic flow in the working section could be maintained for 20 seconds, after which there was a 3 to 5 minute delay while the vacuum was restored by the six compressors. During its busiest time, between 1940 and 1941, when the V2 design was being finalized, three shifts were working on the tunnel, for an average of 500 hours per month. Actual test work was confined to the hours from 7 a.m. to 2 a.m. in order to obtain the driest possible air.

The windtunnel was also used by the Luftwaffe aerodynamicists. With its own research department, instrumentation laboratory, workshops and design office it was regarded as one of the Peenemünde showpieces, and always figured on the itineries of VIP visitors. The use of this advanced windtunnel by the Luftwaffe ensured that many of the phenomena associated with supersonic flight were known to the German designers early in the 1940s. Always looking to the future, a Mach 10 windtunnel was being planned in 1941, with a working section measuring 3 ft x 3 ft. This was to cater for the larger and faster developments of the V2, but the tunnel never got beyond the planning stage.

Peenemünde also had its own power station, docks and oxygen plant. As well as the usual facilities for a town of 20,000 inhabitants, there was a prisoner-of-war camp for specially selected prisoners, who provided cheap labour. When the last A5 test vehicle was launched in 1941 the first V2 was already well on its way to completion. The amount of data available from tests on the A5, and the fact that the V2 was actually being built at the same time, ensured that the V2 benefited immediately from work on the A5.

The problem of designing a fuel-pump system with the required size and power was solved in 1941 by Walter, which had become a specialist in the use of

HTP-powered motors and other equipment. HTP, when mixed with a suitable catalyst, produces superheated steam at 500°C; Walter used this steam to drive a small turbine which had blades of only a 19 in diameter. This turbine developed around 5,000 hp and powered the pumps for the liquid oxygen and alcohol; these pumps delivered a total of 280 lb of fuel per second to the V2's combustion chamber, a fantastic performance at that time. Significantly the same principal is applied to most if not all modern liquid-fuelled rockets.

While the engineers and scientists were trying to produce the V2 to schedule, Dornberger was also trying to tackle another problem. In wartime the operation of an establishment like Peenemünde depended to a large extent on its priority ratings. Funding was important but unless you had the highest possible priority ratings for all the basic raw materials, and especially the more exotic items, you could not obtain them. In September 1939, at the outbreak of war, Peenemünde was given increased priority for all its requirements. However, the rapid conquest of Poland, the Low Countries and France, followed by the armistice on 17 June 1940, resulted in a hasty reappraisal of all uncompleted weapons projects. Peenemünde was dropped completely from the priority ratings in August of that year.

The next nine months undoubtedly hardened the attitude of Dornberger, von Braun and the other senior members of the team. Hitler stood triumphant over much of Europe and the short-term requirement for a rocket weapon was apparently diminishing. There was a very real possibility that Peenemünde would become nothing more than another research centre, of which Germany had dozens.

The situation changed yet again with the failure of the Luftwaffe in the Battle of Britain, together with the first winter setbacks for the Army in Russia and the declaration of war on America on 11 December 1941. Priority ratings were raised later in 1941, but only enough to ensure that the development of the V2 was maintained at a low level, not enough to produce an operational weapon on a large scale. Brauchitsch, who had been a staunch supporter of Dornberger's plans, had been forced by Hitler to resign as Commander-in-Chief of the Army on 19 December 1941, due to a combination of failing health and Hitler's belief that the Army General Staff were mainly to blame for the defeats in Russia. Hitler himself took over the position and Dornberger realized that the loss of Brauchitsch would be a serious one. Work continued, however, and the first V2 test vehicle was reaching completion; it was to be followed at a fairly casual rate by two more test vehicles, the programme being to launch them at intervals of two months starting on 13 June 1942. This first launch was a very important event; hence senior members from all three branches of the armed forces were there, together with Albert Speer, Minister for Armaments and Munitions.

Despite the extensive pre-launch checks, two seconds after motor ignition V2-001 fell back on to the launch pad and exploded. The fuel pumps had failed because of an electrical fault. Though an embarrassing failure, work proceeded on 002. However, yet another setback occurred. On 16 August, after what appeared to have been a successful launch, the rocket broke up while travelling at Mach 3, 45 seconds into its trajectory. Although the remains of 002 were never recovered it

V2 being prepared for launch from Cuxhaven in a British-controlled exercise in September and October 1945. Each V2 required 8,750 lb of alcohol/water mixture and 11,000 lb of liquid oxygen at −190°C. In the foreground is a tripod-mounted clinometer to confirm the rocket's critical vertical alignment. (Imperial War Museum)

was determined from telemetry records that the structural failure was due to the rapid deceleration which follows a sudden motor stoppage. None of the V2 test vehicles launched from Peenemünde was ever recovered but each one was fitted with a container of coloured dye to indicate in the sea where the impact point was.

It is strange how often 'third time lucky' applies; on 3 October 1942 003 made a perfect launch and flew a faultless 120 miles along the coast, before impacting only 2½ miles from the theoretical target point. The flight of 003 was able to claim a number of firsts in the record books. After 4½ seconds, when the rocket started inclining from the vertical, Mach 1, the speed of sound, was reached at 26 seconds. This was the first time that Mach 1 had been exceeded by a missile with any form of guidance. At 58 seconds the motor was switched off by a radio signal; the rocket, at a height of 110,000 ft and Mach 5, continued its flight, reaching an apogee of 60 miles before it plunged downwards in an arc towards the ground. Re-entering the earth's atmosphere at over 3,000 mph, the outside skin temperature rose to 650°C as friction slowed it down to 2,000 mph, Mach 3; at this speed it hit the sea.

It was almost exactly 25 years since shells from Krupp's Paris Gun had reached a record height of 26 miles and now a new age was dawning. The plotting of the rocket's trajectory was carried out by two radar systems. Five miles directly behind the launch pad on the mainland was a Giant Würzburg radar station. Originally developed by Telefunken as a fighter ground-control and bomber-height-finding radar, it had a 25 ft diameter bowl and had an accuracy of +/– 300 ft at its maximum ranges. The Wurzburg followed the rocket, receiving signals from its own transmitter, until at the required height and speed a signal from the ground shut off the fuel pump's valves, stopping the motor. As the flight progressed, other information was also received from the rocket such as temperatures, accelerations and pressures, via a coded telemetry link. The complete trajectory was followed by a string of Wurzburgs along the Baltic coastline.

With this successful launch Dornberger realized that although the priority ratings were acceptable for a development programme, if the rocket was to be used as a military weapon on a large scale, and with the further developments planned, they would have to have publicity and recognition for the project. Consequently, Dornberger and von Braun circulated eight copies of a report which gave the progress of the rocket programme up to that time, together with all the possible military developments as a long-range weapon. The report was circulated to a restricted list of civilian and military leaders, including the Army High Command and War Department.

Dornberger at this time was still a colonel and the publication of the report generated some resentment from those above him. Nevertheless he was in charge of the largest and most expensive weapons project the Army had ever been responsible for and as such the report could not be ignored. In the report, reference was made to using 4,000 V2s a year, and comparisons were made with the average number of bomber missions flown over Britain; owing to the heavy losses suffered by the Luftwaffe, the rocket was shown in a very good light.

To some extent, this report, was merely an exercise on paper, as it provided no plans for supplying the raw materials required for a launching .programme as large as 4,000 a year. Typically the liquid oxygen requirement would have been 25,000 tons per year. Taking into account losses from evaporation as it was transferred from storage (at –200°C) to the launching point, the actual production requirement was 45,000 tons. The potential impact on the general users of oxygen is indicated by the following comparison: in 1944 Germany was producing 24 million tons of crude steel per year, which required 260 million cubic metres of oxygen; 4,000 V2s would require 25 million cubic metres. Hence, if no additional provisions were made, the manufacture of the V2s would result in a loss of steel production of 2.4 million tons, an unacceptable situation. This does not even take into account the demands of other oxygen users in industry and medicine.

The outcome of the widespread circulation of this report, which was almost a public request for recognition, was a directive from the War Department that development should proceed, but that mass production would be a planning exercise only; all previous memoranda and drawings were to be destroyed, except for three copies of the latter. This was a strange order and being a military establishment there is no doubt it was carried out. The significance of this action will become apparent later in this book.

While Dornberger and von Braun were busy planning the mass production of the V2, the matter was about to be taken out of their hands. On the death of Dr Fritz Todt in a flying 'accident' on 9 February 1942, Albert Speer had taken over all his duties, on direct orders from Hitler. These included the post of Minister of Armaments and Munitions, and Speer decided that he would appoint the mass-production expert at that time sought by Dornberger and von Braun. The person he chose was Gerhard Degenkolb, a dynamic production engineer who had introduced modern mass-production techniques to locomotive construction. In 1941 the two industrial giants Krupp and Henschel had produced 1,900 locomotives by traditional craft techniques. Degenkolb then introduced standardized designs and production rose in 1943 to 5,500 completed locomotives.

Dornberger complained strongly to Speer about what he considered to be interference and the loss of control over part of the project, but to no avail. In fact the V2 was nowhere near ready for mass production and in any case the rocket had not been designed with mass production in mind. The accuracy required for a number of the components during manufacture and assembly meant that very high levels of skill were required in what was a new type of technology. As Degenkolb very quickly discovered, there was a world of difference between heavy engineering and rockets.

Degenkolb set up his V2 production committee in Berlin and in October 1943 produced plans for 300 V2s, rising to 900 per month by December. The facilities chosen were the pre-production works at Peenemünde, originally intended for very small-scale production, the Zeppelin GmbH works at Friedrichshafen, and the Henschel-Rax works at Wiener Neustadt. Speer wasted little time in obtaining as much advice as possible from leading industrialists. Directors from various firms were sent to visit Peenemünde in order to assess the chances of the V2 becoming a production weapon. The feasibility of making Peenemünde a limited company was also considered, to make the project more cost effective.

Apart from the lack of mass-production preparation, there was the problem of modifications. Although several V2s had been launched by now, these tests had shown up a large number of deficiencies in the design, as well as indicating where improvements could be made to the V2's performance. The result was that thousands of modifications were being incorporated, some of them only small, but they still caused delays to the plans.

To emphasize the progress that had been made with the V-weapons Hitler ordered that a demonstration of the V1 and V2 should take place at Peenemünde on 26 May 1943. Hitler himself did not attend but there was a large gathering of military and civilian VIPs. The two V1s crashed soon after launch but both V2s made perfect flights. A successful launch of a large rocket like the V2 would have enormously impressed those who were witnessing it for the first time, especially as they would probably have arrived at the observation bunker just as the countdown was nearing zero. As the successful completion of the last few checks was announced over the loudspeakers, the atmosphere must have been tense; then the dramatic sight and sound of the launch must have been stunning. It was not surprising therefore that two days later Dornberger was promoted from Colonel to Major-General; this was the start of the recognition he had been seeking for some time.

The success of this demonstration was followed by a universal acknowledgement from all sides that rockets, and in particular the V2, had an immense military potential. Test launches were now running at the rate of 25 per month, a fantastic achievement considering that they were still working with quite a low priority rating. In addition, personnel and equipment were being diverted to help Degenkolb to organize mass production.

The turning-point for the whole project came on 7 July 1943. Dornberger and von Braun, together with all the demonstration models, films and other equipment, were ordered to Hitler's Rastenburg headquarters in East Prussia, from where he was directing the Russian campaign. After giving a complete presentation of their work, Hitler told Dornberger that if the V2 had been available in 1939 the war would never have started. The project was immediately given the highest priority rating available, *Dringende Entwicklung* (DE), and at the meeting Hitler told Dornberger that he wanted not 900 but 2,000 V2s a month, the intention being to launch up to 5,000 on one day.

Although 5,000 launches on one day was probably said in the general euphoria of the moment, Hitler must have realized how impractical this was. Still, the message from the top was clear: the rocket had arrived. This is only part of what Hitler told Dornberger and von Braun; the remainder would be for a very restricted group, on a 'need to know' basis.

The date on the drawing of the 'modified' V2 (shown in fig. 1) – the version that was going to provide one half of the V4 weapon system – is also 1943; the day and month are unrecognizable, but that is largely irrelevant. Now, work could also proceed on the V4 version at the DE priority rating, and time was of the essence. Karl Saur, one of Speer's departmental heads and an old party member and confidant, was given the job of ensuring that all the various sub-contractors working on the V2 understood and worked to the new schedules.

CHAPTER THREE

Recognition – the Reasons and the Cost

The rocket was now at a crossroads. On one hand Dornberger, von Braun and the rest of the Peenemünde team had finally received Hitler's official approval of the V2. They had also gained the recognition that here was the basis for a weapon capable of affecting the outcome of the war and in particular it could provide an answer to setbacks which the conventional forces were encountering, especially in Russia. However, to Dornberger the recognition brought ominous portents of the future. The most obvious drawback was that it brought the project under the detailed scrutiny of Hitler and all the other civilian and military leaders who were part of his inner circle; this included the SS.

Himmler had pre-empted Hitler's recognition of the project by visiting Peenemünde in April 1943, a visit for which he gave very little advance notice. It was not one of the usual VIP organized tours, but more of a fact-finding mission for Himmler. The reasons for this sudden change in emphasis may not have been obvious to Dornberger, although he probably had a good intimation of the true military situation from his service contacts. Apart from Hitler and Keitel, not many would know the complete picture of the military situation on land, sea and air. The fact was that 1943 had started badly and was getting worse. On 30 January 1943 the newly promoted Field Marshal Friedrich Paulus had surrendered at Stalingrad with what was left of the 285,000 men of his 6th Army. Hitler's anger reached new heights at a military conference on 1 February, when he berated his Army leaders for what he considered to be a betrayal by Paulus: never before had a German Field Marshal surrendered on the battlefield. On 12 May 1943 the last of the Axis forces in North Africa surrendered in Tunisia with the loss of over 240,000 German and Italian troops. But the worst was yet to come and this time there was no obvious scapegoat.

The Russians had recaptured the city of Kursk and the Kursk salient between Orel and Belgorod during the previous winter, 1942/3. Now by the summer of 1943 they had concentrated huge armoured forces in the area, ready for a campaign to recapture the Briansk/Orel region in the north and to head south into the Ukraine to push the Germans out of the capital Kharkov.

The bulge in the Russian forces was an obvious weakness and to Hitler this seemed like a golden opportunity to repeat one of the classic pincer movements of 1941/2, and destroy the very same Russian armies which had been victorious at Stalingrad, before pushing on towards Moscow in the north and back to Stalingrad in the south. But the Russians had prepared massive defences in depth, for just this eventuality. Under the personal supervision of Marshals Zhukov and Vassilevsky, the defences included unprecedented numbers of anti-tank and anti-personnel mines, trenches, pillboxes and miles of barbed wire, in some areas extending to a depth of 60 miles, and of course thousands of guns.

The importance of this battle to Hitler himself, and eventually to the German Armed Forces, cannot be over-exaggerated. The build-up of German forces had carried on throughout the spring, with a slight hiccup due to the situation in Italy, when Hitler thought Mussolini was about to capitulate; by the end of June, however, the men and equipment were ready.

Facing the front of the bulge, in the west, the 2nd Army under General von Weichs was to hold back any forward movement of the Russians. The actual 'pincers' would be formed by the 9th Army under General Model, which was to push down from the north towards Kursk. This force contained twenty divisions, of which seven were armoured, two motorized and eleven infantry: a total of 1,500 tanks and 3,000 guns. The southern arm of the claw was the 4th Army under General von Hoth, with eighteen divisions, of which ten were armoured, one motorized and seven infantry: a total of 1,700 tanks and 2,000 guns. In addition, air-cover was provided by three air corps of Marshal Richthofen's 4th Air Fleet. In overall command was Field Marshal von Manstein.

As early as 10 March Hitler had flown to Zaporozhe in the Ukraine to brief von Manstein on the new campaign, which was to be called Operation Citadel. At the end of June, all the commanders were flown to Munich where Hitler declared in a stage-managed performance, in front of them and other leaders, that 'this would be a victory to light up the world'. Operation Citadel was to start on 5 July.

In total the battle involved more troops than D-Day, more planes than the Battle of Britain and more tanks than El-Alamein. As far as Hitler was concerned, they were 500,000 of the best fighting troops left in Germany together with the very latest equipment, including the new Tiger tanks, the quality of which would be difficult if not impossible to replace. However, within two days of the start of the battle it was clear that there were problems with the German advance. After four days the bulge had only been dented by ten miles in the north and thirty miles in the south, and the tips of the two German pincers were still one hundred miles apart. The losses on both sides were enormous and it was now obvious that this time the German forces had come up against well-prepared Russian defences; this was not going to be a repeat of earlier victories.

On 12 July the main Russian counter-attacks started as it became clear that the German attack had run out of steam. Orel was recaptured on 4 August and Kharkov on 23 August, starting a momentum initiative that carried the Russian forces up to the end of the war. Operation Citadel caused the German forces heavy losses: 70,000 killed and wounded; nearly 3,000 tanks; over 1,000 guns; 1,400 aircraft and over 5,000 other vehicles.

By the summer of 1943 the U-boats had lost the Battle of the Atlantic, which had been crucial to keeping American aid out of Europe. After the peak of 700,000 tons of Allied shipping sunk in the summer of 1942, long-range air-cover for the convoys, better surface protection and the use of radar spelt disaster for the U-boats. Between April and July 1943, 109 U-boats were sunk for the loss of 550,000 tons of Allied shipping. Admiral Döenitz had no choice but to withdraw his forces from the Atlantic while new tactics were worked out and technical improvements made to the boats. One addition, the *Schnorchel*, enabled the boats to use the diesels and hence recharge the batteries underwater, but it was really only a defensive measure as it forced the boats to spend more time underwater, thereby restricting their speed to 6–8 knots. From September 1943 until the end of the year only 67 Allied ships were sunk against a loss of 62 U-boats, an unacceptable situation and one which gradually deteriorated as the war progressed.

In the air the mass bomber raids had started in 1942. The centres of Lübeck and Rostock were destroyed in March and April, followed on 16 May by Kiel, and Dortmund on 25 May. The first 1,000 bomber raid occurred on 30 May, when the target was Cologne. These raids continued throughout 1943, and on 26 and 29 July Hamburg received particularly heavy raids, which made 750,000 people homeless. Berlin was a regular target, and on the nights of 2 and 3 August and 22 September it was the turn of Nuremberg and Hannover. Even Goebbels wrote in his diary that 'we are facing problems [in Hamburg] of which we had no conception even a few weeks ago.'

It was also obvious that as the great population centres of Germany began to suffer, so the industrial centres would also become targets. Albert Speer reorganized military production to such an extent that in some cases there was an improvement, despite the bombing. Fighter aircraft figures rose dramatically: 1942 – 5,515; 1943 – 10,898; 1944 – 25, 285; but the main problem was the shortage of trained crews. Here the Allies had a distinct advantage, as the training of pilots took place as far afield as Canada and the USA, which remained untouched by the war. Strategic raids on armaments sites had started by August 1943, with the daylight raids by the USAF deep into Germany. Among the first targets were the Schweinfurt ball-bearing factories and the Regensburg Messerschmitt plant, where precision bombing was essential. Albert Speer, as Minister of Armaments and Munitions as well as a member of Hitler's inner circle, was able to ensure that the deteriorating situation, with regard to raw materials and finished items, was well known.

This, then, was the overall military position known to Hitler and a few others, in the summer of 1943. The outcome of the war was not yet a foregone conclusion, but a revolutionary weapon was now needed, and one which would give people hope.

On 7 July, two days after the start of Operation Citadel and when it was apparent there was a major problem with the offensive, Hitler decided that now was the time for 'miracle' weapons. With the use of the V2 in a conventional sense, with a high-explosive warhead, the new production figure of 2,000 V2s per month, together with the problem of Allied bombing, meant that a higher production rate and more secure facilities were required, to give protection from air attack. The site chosen was at Kohnstein, close to Nordhausen in the Harz Mountains, south-west of Berlin. Here the mountain had been tunnelled for mining, and during the war the tunnels were used to store strategic chemicals. To build a bombproof factory for V2 production the tunnels simply needed to be enlarged. At this point the SS came on the scene; in the first instance it would be in charge of security at the new plant. Second, the expansion of the underground workings would require a considerable workforce, which would be provided and managed by the SS. The provision of this labour was assisted by the existence a few miles away of the Buchenwald concentration camp.

Of course Dornberger, von Braun and the other leading members of the Peenemünde team would have to act as advisors, and in some cases become a permanent part of the Nordhausen management. Another problem had suddenly arisen at Peenemünde. After years of uninterrupted work, on the night of 17 August 1943 the RAF bombed the site, with a force of almost 600 heavy bombers. This raid was quickly followed by raids on the Zeppelin and Henschel works, where originally the mass production of the V2 had been planned. The total damage was not particularly serious but in consequence the V2 development programme had to be reappraised. Two weeks after the raids the Army High Command informed Dornberger that in future the majority of launches, including tests of operational V2s, were to take place at an ex-SS training camp, Heidelager, near Blizna in south-east Poland. Security would again be provided by the SS.

Himmler was once again beginning to intrude on the project. He appointed the SS Brigadier Dr Hans Kammler, whose job would be to organize V2 launch teams. In 1942 Dornberger had formed a special Army unit to train other Army units in the servicing and launch of the V2. This unit, Lehr und Versuchs Batterie 444, had obtained its experience at Zinnowitz, 10 miles south of Peenemünde, and now they took over the main part of the launch training programme. By now launches were including live warheads as part of the development work, especially in an attempt to solve the fuse problem. Ideally the V2 should explode just above the ground and that required a very sensitive proximity fuse. But with the V2 travelling at Mach 3 this was a problem that was never solved.

The Army had also started making arrangements for the operational use of the V2 and two experienced artillery officers were appointed to supervise field operations. Lieutenant-General Erich Heinemann was in overall control of both V2 and V1 operations, while Major-General Richard Metz was in charge of the V2. By the end of 1943 the first V2s were coming off the production lines, as originally planned under Degenkolb, from Peenemünde, Friedrichshafen and Wiener Neustadt. At the same time the first batch at Nordhausen was in production, under the direction of Arthur Rudolph, one of Dornberger's original team members from Kummersdorf. However, the problems of mass production had still not been solved. These included premature airbursts several hundred feet above the target, and although the situation was improved by insulating the fuel tank, there were still thousands of modifications coming through from Peenemünde for incorporation in the production versions.

In January and February 1944 a total of 140 rockets were produced, followed by 170 in March and 300 in April. The figure of 2,000 ordered by Hitler had been arranged so that 300 were to come from each of the original facilities and the remainder from Nordhausen. In the event, by May 1944 all production was centred at Nordhausen.

The celebrations of Dornberger, von Braun and the other senior members of the Peenemünde team were tempered by the realization that there was a price to pay for this new 'blessing from above'. There was a POW camp at Peenemünde which housed many of the men used on the menial low-skilled tasks or forced labour around the establishment, but conditions for these workers had been reasonable. Nordhausen, however, was different. For the job of enlarging the tunnels, up to 15,000 prisoners were brought in by the SS and a separate camp was built adjacent to the main tunnel entrance. The workers spent all their time inside the tunnels, as the work carried on for 24 hours a day, 7 days a week, in atrocious conditions. With no proper sanitation or drinking-water, the noise, dust, cold and almost perpetual darkness meant that thousands died before even the prison camp was finished outside the tunnels. The SS records list almost 3,000 dead up to March 1944, and that is obviously an underestimation.

V2 production started in January 1944, and thousands of workers were required. Eventually the workforce totalled 32,000, housed in 31 sub-camps of the main Dora camp. The SS records show that almost 13,000 workers died between September 1943 and April 1945, but again that is likely to be a considerable underestimation. A report by Willy Messerschmitt, who used a considerable number of impressed workers in his factories, stated that the death rate at Nordhausen was 17,000 per year.

After the war the Nordhausen area became part of East Germany and following an unsuccessful attempt by the Russians to blow up all the tunnels they were sealed and a small memorial erected on the site of the Dora camp.

Of those who ran the Nordhausen factory, only one civilian and 18 SS officers were put on trial in 1947 for war crimes. The evidence and investigation leading up to the trial were carried out by the US Army and all the details remained classified until 1978.

In that year President Carter established the Office of Special Investigations (OSI) to search out and prosecute Nazi war criminals living in the USA. One of its young lawyers Eli Rosenbaum, read *Dora: The Hell of All the Concentration Camps*, written by one of Nordhausen's French survivors, Jean Michel. This eventually lead to the removal of restrictions on access to the US files on Nordhausen and a belated investigation into those Germans who had moved to the USA after the war, including those involved in rocketry. But what was the involvement of Dornberger, von Braun and other senior members of the Peenemünde team in the Nordhausen operation? Dornberger in his book *V2* makes only four references to Nordhausen, or Central Works, as it was known at Peenemünde, and the most he has to say about the project is that it was 'a new emergency factory still under construction'.

One of the most enlightening investigations of their true roles at Nordhausen was presented in *The Paperclip Conspiracy*, broadcast by BBC TV on 20 February

1987. The 'paperclip' referred to the American method of indicating which of the rocket and medical experts were to be protected from any war-crime investigations after the war. Over 500 of these people, with their families, were brought into the USA at the end of the war, and those to be safeguarded had a paperclip inserted into their file. In some instances their wartime involvement with the SS or anything that might affect their acceptance into the USA was removed from their file or rewritten.

It is still possible, however, to surmise the agenda of one meeting at Nordhausen. The agenda on 6 May 1944 included obtaining a further 1,800 prisoners from occupied countries for work at the site. The meeting was chaired by George Rickhey, General Manager at Nordhausen, who was later prosecuted and acquitted in the US Army trial after the war. Among those present, and heading the distribution list for the minutes of the meeting was Major-General Dornberger; 14th on the list was von Braun; 51st was Dr Steinhoff and 11 below him was Arthur Rudolph.

Dr Steinhoff was the original instrumentation expert at Peenemünde. Interestingly, his brother, who was the commander of U-511, took part in tests involving the launch of solid-fuel rockets from his submarine, close to Peenemünde, in the summer of 1942. Arthur Rudolph has already been mentioned as one of the original Peenemünde team and he eventually became Production Director at Nordhausen. The Americans made use of his expertise after the war; he was one of the rocket experts transported to the USA and later became Production Director for the Saturn–Apollo moon-landing project, which put Armstrong and Aldrin on the moon on 20/21 July 1969. This moon project eventually employed 376,000 people and had a budget from 1966 to 1967 of six billion dollars. When Eli Rosenbaum's investigations started in 1979, von Braun had already died from cancer but Rudolph was questioned about his involvement at Nordhausen. On 13 October 1982, before any further action could be taken, he relinquished his American citizenship and returned to Germany.

Dornberger had never joined the rest of the Peenemünde team in America, although he did visit von Braun at least once, but as an ex-General in the German Army his presence in the USA after the war would have been a little too embarrassing for even the US Army. Yet he knew too much to be prosecuted, especially about the other experts who were to provide the experience and know-how behind the US long-range ballistic missile (ICBM) and space programmes.

With the abolition of East Germany and with restrictions removed, the underground workings at Nordhausen are now being opened up, 50 years after they were sealed by the Russians. A complete survey is due to be carried out of the internal workings and a new memorial erected at the site.

Of all the rocket and aviation medicine experts who were taken into the USA after the war it is claimed that they saved America 20 years in the space and weapons race. Was the cost justifiable?

CHAPTER FOUR

The Choice

With the German military situation beginning to deteriorate and a crash programme of rocket production initiated, there was still the question of whether the V2 could deliver the goods and turn the balance of the war. The V2 like any other rocket, was only one part of the weapons system. There was also the long-range bomber, and belatedly increased priority was given to its development. The four-engined Messerschmitt Me264 had first flown on 15 December 1942 and the six-engined Junkers Ju390 on 20 August 1943. The most promising, the Ju390, carried out evaluation trials from the Atlantic coast near Bordeaux in February 1944, flying to the east coast of America and back without real problems. But again, time was running out. The chances of producing such a large aircraft in sufficient numbers within the required timescale was even more remote than the rocket programme.

It was now apparent to Hitler and the other leaders that if priority had been given to the rocket project two years earlier, the various problems could have been solved. When Peenemünde was dropped from the priority ratings in August 1940, following the rapid conquest of Poland, the Low Countries and France, work at the site slackened off. The last A5 test vehicle was not launched until September 1941, and it took almost six months to prepare and launch the first three V2s, compared with the launch of 25 V2s a month once the priorities were uprated in 1943. V2s were coming off the production line at Nordhausen, but it was really only a trickle, and it was already the spring of 1944. The figures speak for themselves: January – 50; February – 90; March – 176; April – 250; May – 430; June – 132; July – 100; August – 370; September – 630.

Dornberger and von Braun had written numerous reports and given dozens of presentations on the use of the V2 as a weapon of mass destruction from as long ago as 1940. However, the truth was that the V2 was never designed for such a role. Manufacture and assembly at Peenemünde by a highly skilled workforce was one thing, but expecting the same performance from a workforce that was largely forced labour, and supervised by a harsh regime, was quite another. In addition to the fact that modifications were still coming through from Peenemünde, the quality of the finished product was not up to the required standards.

The build-standard table for the V2 model B, types A, B, C and D, illustrates that this was an operational model fitted with a live warhead. This table is dated 3 May 1944 and lists all the main modifications incorporated into the above variants; it shows that not until production had reached 1,221 was model B, type

D, ready for use, and that was in May 1944. The V2 had stretched technology to its limits and it was a fact that many of the components worked, but only just. The rocket motor was a typical example, with its eighteen brass fuel nozzles and hundreds of tiny holes for injecting cooling alcohol between the double skin of the combustion chamber and exhaust. Any significant loss in the cooling effect resulted in the mild-steel sheet, used for the motor, burning into holes, thereby producing exhaust jets at the side of the motor; this, in turn, led to failure and destruction of the rocket. The problem of premature air-bursts, hundreds of feet above the target had more or less been solved by insulating the alcohol tank and stiffening the instrument bay, situated immediately behind the warhead. But it was not the complete answer; failures still occurred, albeit less frequently.

Impact accuracy was poor, and the rocket rarely landed within a 10 mile radius of the target; in fact Dornberger used to joke that the safest place for observers was at the centre of the theoretical target, as the rocket never ended up there. Target accuracy was to some extent dependent on the quality of the gyroscopes and accelerometers; the integrating accelerometer used later instead of radio signals to control motor shut-off was critical in this respect. The smallest reduction in manufacturing and assembly standards would be difficult to detect but it could seriously affect the performance of the rocket.

As mentioned later, the rocket launches against the United Kingdom and other European targets were carried out using a greatly reduced check-out procedure, and the rockets themselves were not subjected to the extensive inspection and testing before arrival at the launch site, that had originally been envisaged.

The problem of the fusing system was never completely resolved. Ideally the warhead should have detonated 50–100 ft above the ground in order to obtain the maximum blast effect. This required a proximity fuse, either acoustic or pressure, but although they were used on slower missiles, none was able to cope with the V2's Mach 3 impact velocity. The majority of operational V2s were fitted with normal impact fuses which resulted in the rocket expending part of its warhead in digging a 30 ft crater. Nevertheless, with test V2s being launched finally at the rate of one per day (mainly for launch-crew training) the rocket was beginning to approach some degree of operational reliability.

Back at Peenemünde, Dornberger was also working on further developments of the V2. These included the ultimate refined versions of the V2, the A7 and A8, which had an improved motor, larger fuel tanks and improved fuel, and a lighter structure. The next stage, again an intermediate one, was the fitting of a pair of swept-back wings to the A9, which was basically a standard V2.

One A9 was launched successfully, at the second attempt, on 24 January 1945 at Peenemünde. This development was expected to increase the range to 350-plus miles. Since there is a practical limit to the range for one particular rocket design, owing to fuel restrictions, exhaust temperature and pressure, and the fact that it is difficult to obtain a better fuel-to-weight ratio than 0.8, the alternative is two or more stages. At Peenemünde they were working on a development by which the rocket used a large booster to reach the required speed out of the earth's atmosphere; the booster would then be jettisoned, leaving the rocket to carry its payload to the target.

The A10 was a large single-stage booster rocket with a 200 ton thrust. The A10 booster combined with an A9 second stage would have improved the original range of the V2 from 200 miles to 3,500 miles, allowing the USA to be reached with ease. It is interesting to note that the A10 booster was virtually a one-third scale version of one of the five Saturn V boosters used on the Apollo 11 moon rocket and of course designed by von Braun and part of the Peenemünde team.

Although Peenemünde was the centre of all the main rocket design and development, this work resulted in other firms producing rockets for other roles. For example, Henschel, the heavy-engineering firm, was producing a family of air-to-surface missiles from the team's aircraft expertise. The Hs117, 293 and 298 were launched from bombers, and the Hs293 in particular was fairly successful against Allied shipping, as it was visually guided to its target from the parent aircraft. The armaments firm Rheinmetall Borsig produced three major rocket designs. The *Rheinbote* (Rhine messenger) was a 4-stage solid fuel rocket with an 88 lb warhead and a range of 100 miles, unguided and spin-stabilized. The *Rheintochter* (Rhine daughter) was a 20 ft, 2-stage solid fuel anti-aircraft missile and the R111 was a mixed solid/liquid staged anti-aircraft rocket with a 50,000 ft ceiling. Finally, the associate of Krupp, Ruhrstahl AG, produced the first air-to-air guided missile, for the new jet fighter, the Me262. The X4 had a 2 mile range, a BMW liquid-fuel rocket motor, and some versions were equipped with an acoustic fuse, which detonated the 44 lb warhead when its microphone picked up its own sound from the target.

Peenemünde itself also produced a scaled-down version of the V2, called the Wasserfall (Waterfall). This was approximately half the size of the V2, and had a range of 30 miles. It was intended to be able to stand for up to 3 months, with full fuel tanks, ready to launch.

Last but not least, mention must be made of what might be called the Peenemünde red herring. As no mention was ever made either during or after the war of Hitler's real 'miracle weapon', Dornberger and von Braun appeared to be trying to ensure that any references to 'modified' V2s were so bizarre that nothing of the sort would be taken seriously. The modification in question was the project to build a number of submersible barges, each one holding a V2. A U-boat would tow three barges at 12 knots for 30 days and when within range of the target (the east coast of the USA), the containers would be partially flooded and the rockets fired from just below the surface. This was supposed to be a serious project but the prospect of a U-boat, in full view on the surface, towing three barges for a month across the Atlantic is beyond credibility. Furthermore, the V2s, in the condensation-ridden atmosphere of the containers would have been useless for firing after 30 days. The team at Peenemünde had already discovered that it was virtually impossible to obtain a successful launch from any V2 beyond three or four days of its manufacture. Peenemünde eventually instituted the '*heiss Semmel*' or 'hot dumplings' scheme, whereby each V2 used operationally was launched within three days of manufacture. This was the only way to guarantee some degree of success, especially during the Holland offensive, when the pre-launch check procedures were considerably reduced owing to fear of Allied air attack.

To anyone associated with the V2, from Hitler to the most junior technician, it was obvious that the 1,650 lb high-explosive warhead of the V2 limited its effectiveness as a military weapon. Even the launching of huge numbers of V2s was unlikely to seriously affect the Allied war effort and give Germany an unassailable military advantage. Historians of the Second World War all describe the V2 project as a considerable technical achievement yet having very little worth in a military sense. Figures are presented relating to the cost of a V2 and a manned bomber, comparing the size of warhead on one hand and the bomb-load on the other. The conclusions reached are that as a weapon the V2 was an economic failure and the only reason the German leaders, especially Hitler, believed it had any future was that they were carried away by its romantic appeal. This would have been especially true after watching an actual launch, which had great spectator appeal.

There is no doubt that it was a considerable technical achievement, comparable with, for example, the American atomic-bomb project, but a comparison with manned bombers is absurd. It implies an inept reasoning by those directing Germany's war effort and those who had also designed and developed the V2. Dornberger, von Braun and others made no secret of the plans to increase the range of the V2 to 3,500 miles. This would have included areas of Russia, such as Siberia, to where most of the war production had been relocated, and way beyond the eastern seaboard of the USA.

Was the 3,500 mile range A9/A10 combination also to be fitted with a 1 ton high-explosive warhead? Dornberger, of course, never referred to warheads in this context but if this rocket was to have such a warhead it becomes even more absurd than the V2 economics argument. This same point is made in the 1958 USAF report on the ballistic missile, that it is not economically viable to build large rockets and equip them with conventional warheads, and all the US knowledge at that time was based on what it had obtained (and was still obtaining), from the Peenemünde team, by then, US citizens! In addition, nuclear weapons are enthusiastically referred to in German project documentation of the 1940s, and yet any discussion concerning a nuclear weapon must have included the means for delivering the weapon. Nevertheless, it is still assumed that this obvious point, linking rockets with nuclear weapons, was impossible to grasp and understand in Germany.

No, it all hinged on the payload or warhead, but first it is worthwhile considering Hitler's thoughts relating to his three last antagonists and for whom the rockets were intended.

From Hitler's recorded table-talk between 1941 and 1944, Russia was seen purely as a territory to be used as a breathing-space and a food provider for the Third Reich; its people were expendable. Great Britain and her empire, however, came in for some respect. The success with which a few thousand administrators and soldiers controlled the destiny of 300 million Indians impressed him to such an extent that it was a recurring theme of his conversations. With the invasion of Russia on 22 June 1941, Hitler apparently believed that what the British had achieved over a few hundred years the Germans could do in a much shorter time by ruthless methods. The USA also occupied a significant part of his conversations, especially the pre-eminence of their mass-production techniques and concern for quantity rather than quality. Hitler believed that Great Britain and the USA had very little in common, and that left alone they would probably end up at war each other over trade.

Before the war some German and American firms, especially in the chemical and electrical industries, had arrived at secret unofficial trade agreements, usually initiated by the Americans, in which they undertook not to poach on each other's territory. Hitler was well aware of the vast natural resources and production capabilities of the USA and the importance of being self-sufficient in strategic raw materials. Hence, before the war there was no 'special relationship' between the USA and Great Britain. In fact America had produced and updated war contingency plans against Great Britain since 1919; it was assumed, with the destruction of German seapower after the First World War, that America (codename Blue) had only two possible enemies: Japan (Orange) and Great Britain (Red). The question facing the American planners was how would Britain use her great naval strength if a crisis arose?

The causes of any friction would probably be the USA's large merchant fleet, its financial supremacy and its gradual encroachment into trade markets originally dominated by Britain and Japan. The suspicions of the USA reached a high point after the collapse of the Geneva Naval Conference in 1927, at which the American naval planners learned that the main British battle fleet was 96,000 tons heavier than their own. They were also concerned about the apparent *entente cordiale* which existed between Japan and Britain, emphasized by the much publicized visits by members of the Japanese Royal Family to Britain and the probability that secret trade agreements and undertakings were being arranged between the two governments.

Even after the outbreak of war in 1939, the contingency plans were kept up to date. Among the possibilities considered was that Germany (Black) and Britain would come to an agreement over South America in the event of a peace agreement being reached, and with rapidly deteriorating relations with Japan there was a very real possibility that America would stand alone. This potential rift was exploited by Hitler with some degree of success as he tried to keep America out of the war. However, in the end it was Germany which declared war on America on 11 December 1941, four days after Pearl Harbour.

These, then, were targets for the new weapons but what would the new weapon look like? If the warhead or payload was not to be high explosive, what was required and where would it come from? Finally, if the rocket offensive was to be a mixture of conventional high explosives and new weapons, what means would be needed to service and launch these two different weapons? Answers to these questions were needed quickly.

CHAPTER FIVE

The Miracle Weapon

An intriguing question is why should the V2 have been described as a vengeance or miracle weapon. After all, even the destructive effect of 5,000 V2s launched simultaneously would be less than that of a bomb-load from a single raid of 1,000 bombers, and these raids were becoming a regular feature of the war over Germany.

The real miracle weapon would have to have either a nuclear or a chemical payload. As described later, a conventional nuclear warhead could not be provided in the time available. What would be possible was a payload containing either radioactive material from a reactor or one of the two biological weapons, Tabun and Sarin, which were already available in large quantities.

Since 1939 Lieutenant-General Hermann Ochsner had been in charge of the highly secret Army organization responsible for the development and use of chemical weapons. The two most important items in this biological armoury were the nerve gases Tabun and Sarin. These caused death by paralysing the nervous system, through their absorption in microscopic quantities into the lungs or skin.

Unlike the British version, Anthrax, which could take two or three days, Tabun and Sarin took only seconds and no antidote was known to the Allies. Tabun had been mass produced in 1940 after successful trials and Sarin quickly followed. Both these chemicals could be mass produced without seriously affecting the war effort and hence by 1944 there was a stockpile of 15,000 tons. The advantages of using such chemicals were the cheapness and availability, as opposed to the disadvantages such as safety aspects during transportation and at site, together with the problem of dispersion. Both Tabun and Sarin remained active for an unknown period of time, so if the wind shifted to the wrong direction, the chemicals could end up back in Germany. There was also the question of an antidote; the Allies may have had such a substance without Germany being aware of it.

For radioactive material, however, if the correct isotopes were used it could be arranged for the radioactivity to decay to harmless levels within days or weeks of its use. This characteristic made radioactive material the most suitable both in terms of transportation, handling and its operational use. Any accidents leading to a leakage would result in only a temporary problem. To deliver such a payload the conventional high-explosive warhead on the V2 would have to be abandoned on safety grounds. This was for two very important reasons. First was the problem of accidental premature detonation of the warhead, which would lead to the material being widely dispersed over friendly territory, or worse still over

Germany. The problem of premature air-bursts of the V2 had not been completely solved. The second was the problem of a misfire at launch; even though the warhead would not be finally armed at this stage there was a very good chance that it would detonate as the fuel tanks exploded. As this type of weapon would only be launched from special sites, the whole facility, including personnel, would be affected for some time. As a bonus the weight saved by omitting the warhead could be used to ensure that the range of the V2 was not seriously reduced.

Figs 1 and 2 show a comparison between the 'standard' V2 and the 'modified' version with the addition of a payload compartment. Both these drawings have been produced by the author from originals in the Public Records Office in London. The originals form part of a collection of some 2,500 miscellaneous V2 drawings 'taken into custody by the Allied agencies engaged in collecting German documents at the end of the war'. In the first instance they were lodged with the Projectile Development Establishment (PDE) at Aberporth. PDE had been moved in 1940 for security reasons from Fort Halstead in Kent, to the newly built firing-range on the Welsh coast. Changes in organization then meant that part of the staff moved to the newly created Guided Projectile Establishment (now RPE) at Wescott in Buckinghamshire. The first Director of PDE was Dr (later Sir) Alwyn Crow. His contribution to the Allied intelligence effort against the V2 is discussed later.

Details have been added to the figures to clarify the main design changes and features. Many of the drawings in the collection are stamped on the reverse with 'Luftschiftbau Zeppelin GmbH, Friedrichshafen aB'. This indicates that many of the 60,000 modifications eventually produced for the V2 were sub-contracted to at least one other company, presumably because Peenemünde did not have the available manpower.

Fig. 1 shows a comparison between a standard operational V2 and a modified V2 (with the payload compartment). The three most obvious differences between the standard and modified V2 are:

(i)   The additional payload compartment located between the motor and fuel-tank bays;
(ii)   The resultant reduction in size of the fuel tanks;
(iii) The omission of the high-explosive warhead and its replacement by ballast weights.

The original German drawing only illustrated the modified V2 and was entitled 'Experimental Structure'.

Fig. 2 shows details of the additional payload compartment; a picture sequence has been added to illustrate how the assembly of the modified V2 would have been carried out. The original title of this second drawing was *Korsett*. The new payload compartment had the following features:

(i)   It formed a very stiff and, rigid structure owing to the longitudinal and lateral 'top-hat' stringer and skin construction. These items were made

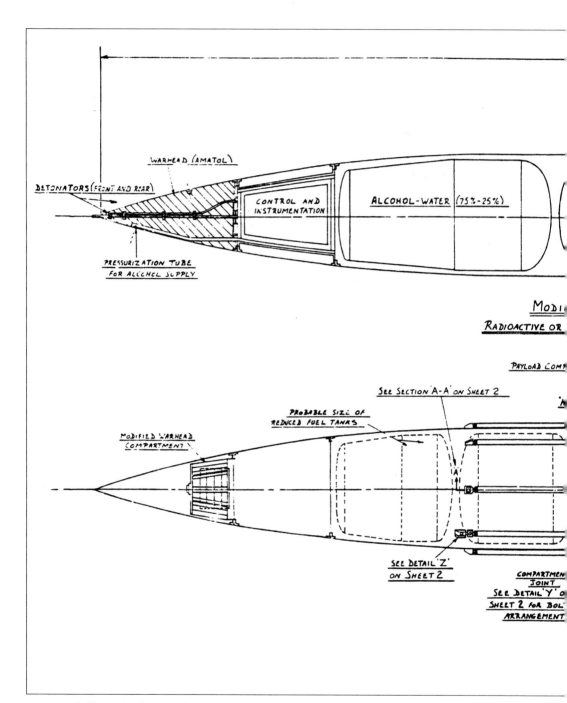

1. Composite drawing showing a standard V2 based on German drawing 7000B Ausf D, Sheet 1, Aggregat Baurethe BN Ausf D, (Assembly of type BN model D), and modified V2 based on German drawing E2460B Ausf A,B,C, Special Structure for Models A,B and C.

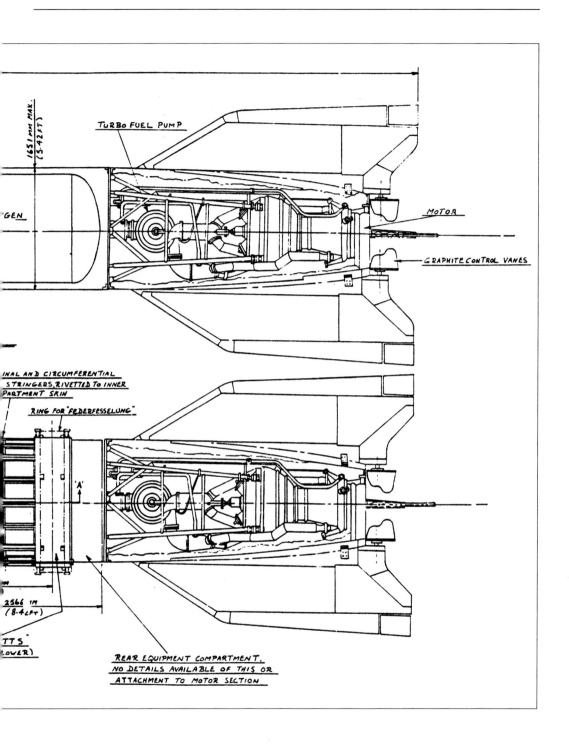

TURBO FUEL PUMP

1651 MM MAX.
(5·42 FT)

GEN

MOTOR

GRAPHITE CONTROL VANES

INAL AND CIRCUMFERENTIAL
STRINGERS, RIVETTED TO INNER
PARTMENT SKIN

RING FOR "FEDERFESSELUNG"

'A'

2566 ım
(8·4 ᴌFT)

TTS'
ᴌOWER)

REAR EQUIPMENT COMPARTMENT.
NO DETAILS AVAILABLE OF THIS OR
ATTACHMENT TO MOTOR SECTION

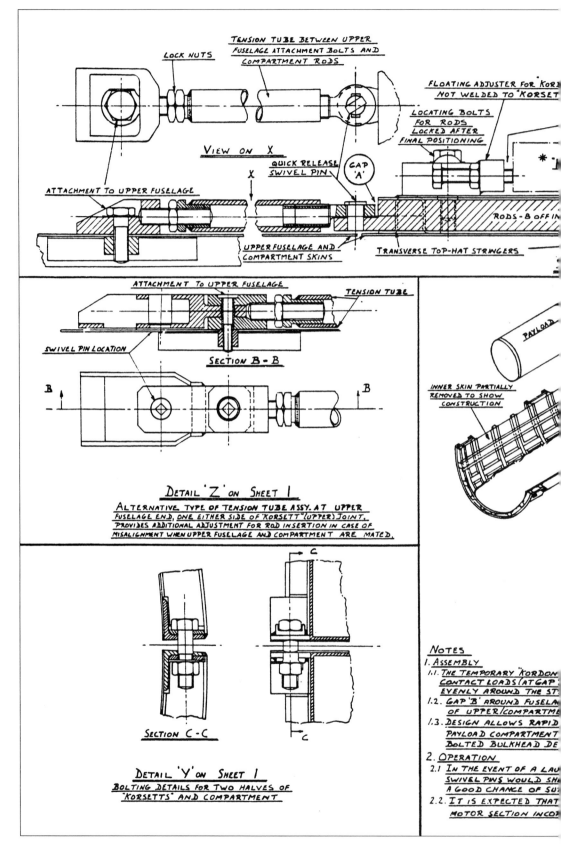

LOCK NUTS

TENSION TUBE BETWEEN UPPER FUSELAGE ATTACHMENT BOLTS AND COMPARTMENT RODS

FLOATING ADJUSTER FOR KORE NOT WELDED TO KORSET

LOCATING BOLTS FOR RODS LOCKED AFTER FINAL POSITIONING

VIEW ON X

QUICK RELEASE SWIVEL PIN

GAP 'A'

X

ATTACHMENT TO UPPER FUSELAGE

UPPER FUSELAGE AND COMPARTMENT SKINS

TRANSVERSE TOP-HAT STRINGERS

RODS - B OFF IN

ATTACHMENT TO UPPER FUSELAGE

TENSION TUBE

SWIVEL PIN LOCATION

SECTION B - B

B

B

DETAIL 'Z' ON SHEET 1

ALTERNATIVE TYPE OF TENSION TUBE ASSY. AT UPPER FUSELAGE END, ONE EITHER SIDE OF KORSETT (UPPER) JOINT. PROVIDES ADDITIONAL ADJUSTMENT FOR ROD INSERTION IN CASE OF MISALIGNMENT WHEN UPPER FUSELAGE AND COMPARTMENT ARE MATED.

PAYLOAD

INNER SKIN PARTIALLY REMOVED TO SHOW CONSTRUCTION

C

SECTION C-C

C

DETAIL 'Y' ON SHEET 1

BOLTING DETAILS FOR TWO HALVES OF KORSETTS AND COMPARTMENT

NOTES
1. ASSEMBLY
   1.1. THE TEMPORARY KORDON CONTACT LOADS (AT GAP EVENLY AROUND THE ST
   1.2. GAP 'B' AROUND FUSELA OF UPPER/COMPARTME
   1.3. DESIGN ALLOWS RAPID PAYLOAD COMPARTMENT BOLTED BULKHEAD DE
2. OPERATION
   2.1 IN THE EVENT OF A LAU SWIVEL PINS WOULD SH A GOOD CHANCE OF SU
   2.2. IT IS EXPECTED THAT MOTOR SECTION INCO

2. Composite drawing showing details of modified V2 payload compartment based on German drawing E2450B Korsett and notional modified V2 assembly sequence.

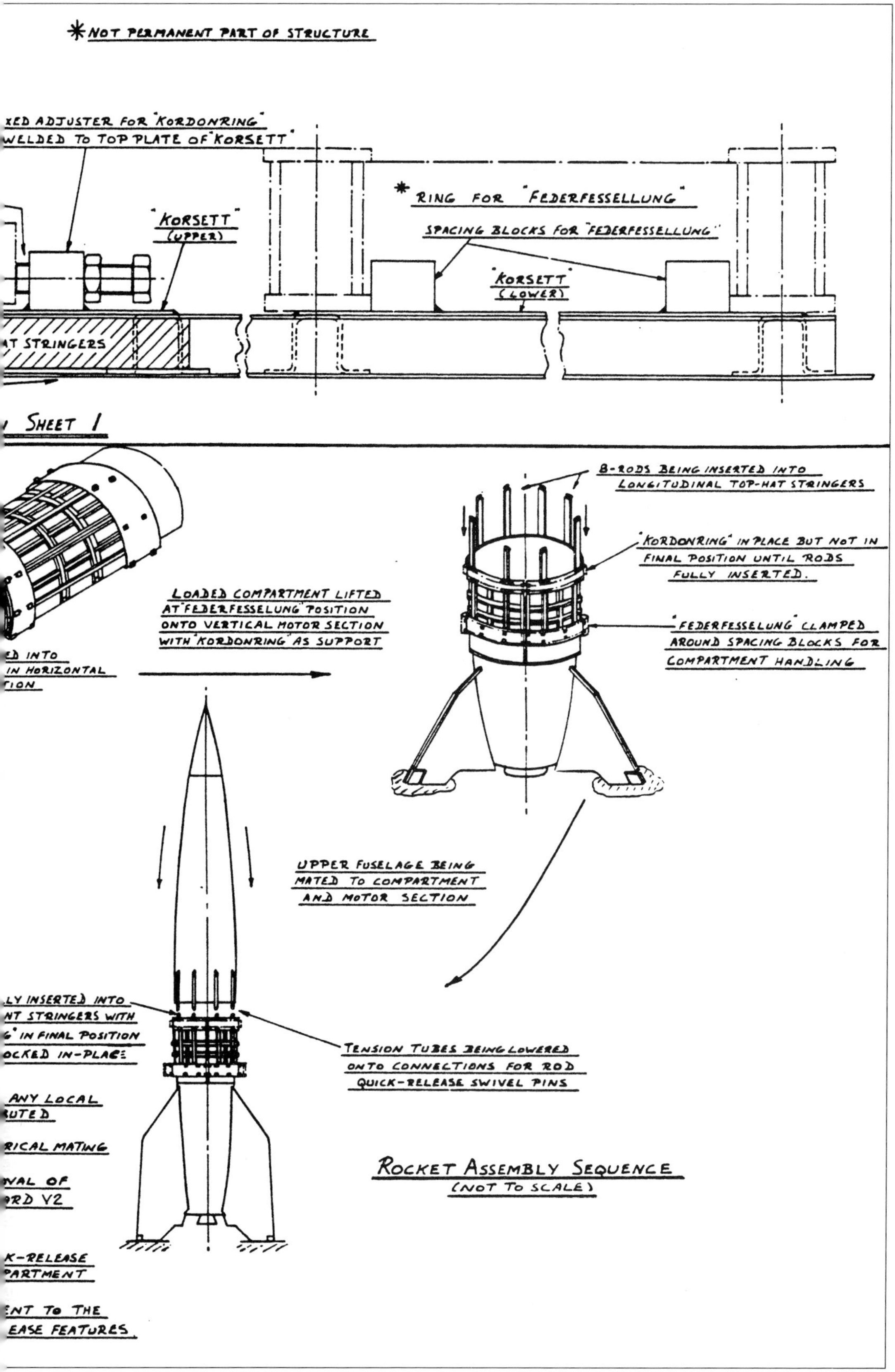

* NOT PERMANENT PART OF STRUCTURE
XED ADJUSTER FOR "KORDONRING"
WELDED TO TOP PLATE OF "KORSETT"
"KORSETT" (UPPER)
* RING FOR "FEDERFESSELLUNG"
SPACING BLOCKS FOR "FEDERFESSELLUNG"
"KORSETT" (LOWER)
AT STRINGERS
SHEET 1
B-RODS BEING INSERTED INTO LONGITUDINAL TOP-HAT STRINGERS
"KORDONRING" IN PLACE BUT NOT IN FINAL POSITION UNTIL RODS FULLY INSERTED.
LOADED COMPARTMENT LIFTED AT "FEDERFESSELUNG" POSITION ONTO VERTICAL MOTOR SECTION WITH "KORDONRING" AS SUPPORT
"FEDERFESSELUNG" CLAMPED AROUND SPACING BLOCKS FOR COMPARTMENT HANDLING
D INTO
IN HORIZONTAL
TION
UPPER FUSELAGE BEING MATED TO COMPARTMENT AND MOTOR SECTION
LY INSERTED INTO
NT STRINGERS WITH
G" IN FINAL POSITION
OCKED IN-PLACE
TENSION TUBES BEING LOWERED ONTO CONNECTIONS FOR ROD QUICK-RELEASE SWIVEL PINS
ANY LOCAL
UTED
RICAL MATING
NAL OF
RD V2
K-RELEASE
PARTMENT
ENT TO THE
EASE FEATURES

ROCKET ASSEMBLY SEQUENCE
(NOT TO SCALE)

from mild steel (as was the original structure) and hence the whole compartment assembly was extremely strong;

(ii)   The method of attaching the new payload compartment to the rest of the V2 was completely different from that used on the original. The standard V2 was broken down into four sections for construction purposes: rocket-motor bay; fuel-tank bay; control and instrumentation bay; warhead. All four sections were bolted together at bulkheads with as many as 32 bolts around the circumference at each joint; the outer skin was replaced after the various bays were connected together. This process would take a considerable period of time but it is standard practice with aircraft and missile design, as normally there is no reason to dismantle the fuselage after assembly. The new section, however, is attached to the fuselage using the eight external rods shown. These rods are fitted with screwed sections for adjustment and also with quick-release couplings. As the sequence shows, the V2 was assembled vertically, which is normal practice for large rockets; the eight rods would already have been inserted into the 'top-hat' sections of the new compartment.

The upper fuselage was then slowly lowered until contact was made with the quick-release couplings. The *Kordonring* ensured that as the heavy upper fuselage was lowered, it did not apply excessive local loading to the compartment, especially the outer skin, as the two items met. The *Kordonring*, a solid aluminium alloy ring, was clamped at the top end of the *Korsett* by a series of screwed clamps welded to the *Korsett*, which was bolted to the outside of the compartment;

(iii) The new compartment was built in two halves, which were bolted together along the longitudinal centre line. The payload was inserted and the two halves bolted together before assembly to the rocket;

(iv)   There are no details available of how the lower end of the compartment was attached to the motor bay; this would have been included on the missing drawings. However, the designs of the lower and top ends would probably have been similar;

(v)   Apart from ensuring that the new payload compartment could be assembled to the rest of the rocket in a matter of minutes rather than hours, the quick-release couplings also provided another very important feature: in the event of launch failure (i.e. the rocket not leaving the launch table), the V2 would fall back on to the concrete pad, followed by an explosion as the fuel ignited. If this happened the pins in the eight quick-release couplings would shear at each end and the compartment would separate itself from the rocket, most likely rolling clear and surviving intact, complete with the contents of the payload container;

(vi)   The location of the new compartment at the rear of the V2, rather than utilizing the redundant warhead space, was also an important feature. This would ensure that on impact at the target, the payload material was likely to be dispersed over a wide area, rather than being buried 30 ft in the ground, with the nose of the rocket.

When the V2 was used for research purposes, both from Peenemünde during the war and at White Sands, New Mexico, after the war, the redundant warhead compartment in the nose was always used to accommodate the instrumentation and recording equipment; as it was as far away as possible from the vibrations produced by the rocket motor. This was the main reason that in the standard V2 the control and guidance bay was immediately behind the warhead.

To summarize, the design of the modified V2 allowed rapid assembly of the new payload compartment to the rocket; the location of this compartment ensured maximum dispersion of the contents at the target, and if the rocket failed at launch there was a very good chance that the compartment and its contents would survive intact.

The fuel capacity would be approximately halved. However, the removal of the 1,650 lb warhead, and the probability that the contents of the payload container weighed less than the fuel, would help to compensate for the reduced fuel capacity by increasing the range of the rocket. The total oxygen/alcohol fuel weight in the standard V2 was 19,750 lb and the normal launch weight was 28,500 lb.

One of the basic factors affecting the range of a rocket is based on the ratio:

$$\frac{\text{fuel weight}}{\text{total weight}}$$

The symbol α is used to describe the ratio. Based on the above weight figures, this gives a value for α of 0.69, which corresponds to the maximum range of 200 miles for the standard V2.

If these figures are amended for the modified V2, this gives the following approximate results. The weight of fuel is 10,000 lb; the total launch weight now becomes 23,500 lb, based on the original 28,500 lb, less the weight of the warhead (1,650 lb), the weight of lost fuel (9,750 lb), plus, for example, about two-thirds of the 9,750 lb, if it is assumed that the fuel is replaced by a payload material which weighs two-thirds of the weight of the fuel (6,400 lb). This results in a new total launch weight of:

$$28,500 - (1,650 + 9,750) + 6,400 = 28,500 - 5,000 = 23,500 \text{ lb}$$
$$\text{This gives a value for } \alpha \text{ of } \frac{10,000}{23,500} = 0.43$$

If the original 200 mile range is now factored by the original alpha divided by the new alpha, this gives:

$$\frac{0.43}{0.69} \times 200 = 125 \text{ miles}$$

There is another factor which significantly affects the range of a rocket: the specific impulse of the fuel; this is greatly dependent on the heat released during combustion. The V2 used liquid oxygen, as an oxidant, and a mixture of alcohol

(75%) and water (25%) for what would be called the fuel (both the oxygen and alcohol mixtures are described for simplicity as the fuel).

The V2's fuel produced a specific impulse of 235 and hence contributed to the original range of 200 miles. If this specific impulse was increased, by only 15%, to 270, the range of the V2 would increase from 200 to 340 miles, and similarly the range of the modified V2 would increase from 125 to 213 miles. The range of the V2 would therefore be regained.

There are problems associated with increasing the specific impulse of a rocket fuel and these include increased combustion-chamber temperatures and pressures. As we have already seen, the V2's combustion-chamber design only just worked with the existing fuel and any significant increase in temperature resulted in failure of the motor.

However, by 1942 a considerable amount of work had already been carried out on rocket fuels, both liquid and solid. There were ten in general use by this time for the large variety of rockets and motors being developed by Henschel, Rheinmetall-Borsig, Walter, BMW, Messerschmitt and at Peenemünde itself. These were: A Stoff (liquid oxygen); B Stoff (gasolene); C Stoff (hydrazine hydrate and methyl alcohol); M Stoff (methanol); R Stoff (zyladene tryethalmine (Tonka 250)); SZ Stoff (nitric acid); T Stoff (hydrogen peroxide (HTP)); Z Stoff (calcium permanganate); Visol (vinylisolbutalether); Vasard 61 (solid fuel). These chemicals were used in a combination of oxidant (usually oxygen, nitric acid or HTP) and fuel (alcohol, gasolene, hydrazine). This list gives some idea of the extent to which the rocket work had progressed by 1942 and research was continuing.

The concern to provide improved fuels is shown by fig. 3, which was a contract issued by the Army Weapons Testing and Development Section at Peenemünde to the Forschungsanstalt der Deutschen Reichspost (Research Institute of the German Post Office). As shown later the German Post Office carried out a variety of research work which had no connection with the postal service, including nuclear research. The contract is dated 15 October 1942 and is given the second highest priority rating, SS (Sonderstufe), the same rating as the V2 at that time. The contract is in two parts and states:

(i)   Progress fundamental investigations into the power increases obtainable through the mixing of liquid fuels to give their highest possible energy levels for rocket propulsion;

(ii) Investigate the possibility of the use of the chain-reaction from atomic break-down for rocket propulsion.

At the bottom of the contract is the codicil issued in 1941 on Hitler's orders that no new weapons projects were to be started unless they could be completed within a specified short-term period. This was one of the consequences of the early military successes of 1939–40 and which also resulted in the V2 being removed from the priority ratings in 1940–1.

This contract, probably only one of a number issued to the competent organizations, ties in exactly with the modified V2 and its reduced range.

3. Rocket fuel research contract issued from Peenemünde to the research institute of the German Post Office, dated 15 October 1942. These were instructions to investigate the possibilities of producing improved rocket fuels including the use of the nuclear reaction.

Although it has been shown that the approximate range of the modified V2 was 125 miles, this was on the borderline of what was acceptable for the V4 miracle weapon. Unless an improved fuel could be developed the full potential of the weapon would not be realized. The reference to the possibility of using nuclear power is very interesting and shows that even as early as 1942, the potential of nuclear power was understood and was being considered for a variety of uses. The issue of the contract from Peenemünde itself is also interesting, as Dornberger and others made no reference to this contract or the concern to involve nuclear power as directly as this, and it must be remembered that this would be only one of many similar contracts awarded by Peenemünde.

CHAPTER SIX

The French Rocket Sites

To provide all the facilities necessary for the operational use of the standard high-explosive V2 and the modified V2 (V4) meant that a comprehensive system of sites was required in northern France. It would need to be capable of providing storage, servicing and launch facilities.

A problem presents itself when the archive material describing this site system is compared with what was actually built in France. There is a variety of correspondence (orders, letters, etc.) between Hitler, Speer, Goering, Dornberger and the Todt Organisation (responsible for construction) from 1942 through to 1944, giving a broad outline of construction dates for some of the large 'complex' sites described in Chapter 9.

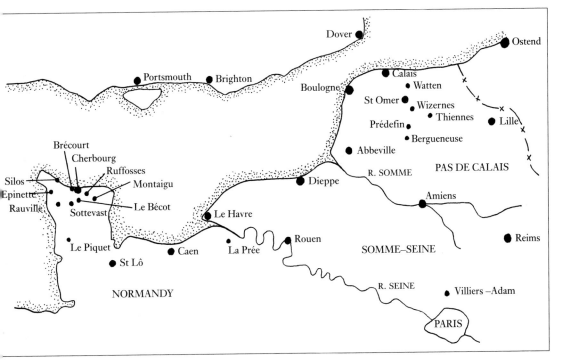

4. Site map of northern France.

This archive material only gives an indication that Hitler, Goering and Speer were aware of the overall programme for the large sites, even to the extent of knowing where they were to be built, but there are no details of what was the single largest project, in terms of manpower and resources, in the Third Reich. The area covered in northern France was huge, stretching from the Pas de Calais to Cherbourg and up to 100 miles inland – an area of over 30,000 square miles. Dornberger, one of the main 'architects' of the system, made almost no reference to this huge construction project built to launch 'his' rockets, and both his and von Braun's silence initially seems very strange. This is particularly so considering the amount of effort and material that went into their project.

Dornberger did make statements in reports and at presentations that the V2 could be launched from any piece of flat ground, but that was only part of the story. It is almost like saying that the American moon-shot could have been launched from any flat piece of concrete, which again is true but it would be unlikely to guarantee a successful mission.

What did undoubtably influence their silence was the question of why such a wide variety of complex sites was built and the fact that, like Nordhausen, one was built using forced labour in atrocious conditions.

In 1940–1 only the team at Peenemünde knew anything about rockets and what facilities would be required in terms of storage, maintenance and launching. Furthermore, only one small group of scientists knew what was required for a nuclear weapon, including the handling, storage and deployment of the material at the rocket site. This group, whose members were not always on amicable terms with each other, understood very well the implications of using nuclear weapons.

Lew Kowarski, who worked with Frédéric Joliot-Curie and von Halban in France during the war and who took out the world's first patent on a nuclear reactor, said of this group when he was interviewed by Professor Ermenc in 1970: 'One thing I do not believe in the least and never did, is that they had moral scruples'(Ermenc, J.J., *Atom Bomb Scientists, Memoirs, 1939–1945*). This group included Schumann, Esau, Gerlach and Ohnesorge on the government side and Heisenberg, Harteck, Houtermans, Bothe, Dopel, Bopp, Hahn, Weizsacker, Diebner and Wirtz as the main figures engaged in nuclear research.

For the planners, the first objective was to decide on the location of the sites, and this was obviously linked with the potential targets. Germany's enemies at the time were Great Britain, the USA and Russia. However, Russia was not considered in 1941 and 1942 as a serious military threat and therefore the targets were Great Britain and the USA. To target the latter, larger versions of the V2 would be needed and therefore any appropriate site had to be capable of handling a rocket at least 80 to 100 ft in height. The rockets would only be manufactured in Germany, and so the journey by rail from Nordhausen, for example, would be about 400 miles to the Pas de Calais or 600 miles to Cherbourg. The rockets could not be fired as soon as they arrived on site; after such a long journey they would require servicing and checking and, for the larger versions, assembly. These storage and servicing facilities would have to be of a high standard, as the rockets were complicated weapons. They would also have to be able to provide an acceptable level of security, as all the sites would be in France, previously a hostile country. With regard to servicing, this included supplies of fuel, and the two fuel items had different requirements. Alcohol could not be produced on site as this was a complicated chemical process; however, in spite of its low flashpoint of 13°C, it was not difficult to store on site. Liquid oxygen was another matter. It had to be stored at a temperature of −180°C to −200°C; it also had a high evaporation rate and storage vessels and piping had to be made from 9% nickel steel in order to obtain the necessary low-temperature properties. Nickel was in short supply – apart from stockpiles, the only other source available was from Petsamo in Finland, and nickel was already an essential ingredient for armour plate, shells and munitions. To avoid a complex transportation and storage system, it would be advantageous for each launching site over a certain size to have its own oxygen-production plant. The equipment required was relatively simple as oxygen and nitrogen are obtained from the air using a system of compressors, coolers, filters, valves, etc. But the greatest challenge was the provision of facilities for the storage and/or production of the nuclear material. In the first instance it would have to be produced in Germany, as the technology was so new and it was required quickly. The main problems were the safety aspects of transporting such a dangerous cargo by rail over hundreds of miles and the fact that the radioactivity of all isotopes decays over a period of time, so that the material loses some of its potency (although this would be a minor effect over a period of days or weeks).

Since the sites would be operational for years, especially the large complexes, it would be desirable if nuclear production could be carried out within the facility. Certainly Brécourt, Sottevast, Watten and Wizernes were built with all the necessary security and protection for a reactor to be built inside the buildings.

Sites which were also capable of launching rockets provided the greatest challenge as there would be three basic types of rocket: the standard V2 with a conventional warhead; the modified V2 with a nuclear payload; and the larger variants up to a maximum height of around 100 ft with only a nuclear capability. The launch frequency would vary depending on the type of warhead/payload, target and size of rocket. These factors would also determine the amount of handling equipment required, from arrival on site to the transfer to the launch area, and the type of launch-control equipment. At the launching sites the warhead/payload would not be attached to the rockets until shortly before launch. Separate adjacent storage arrangements would therefore be required at most sites. In certain circumstances, at one site there might be reasons for providing all the requirements for storage, servicing, fuel production, nuclear production, storage and launch for all the rocket variants.

It was also important that the precise location of any launch site was known in terms of latitude and longitude. This would enable an accurate trajectory to be calculated for the rocket so that it impacted in the target area. Dornberger's claim that mobile launchers could tour the French countryside, firing rockets from sites chosen at random, was pure fantasy designed to 'sell' the rocket to the non-experts. Only the advent of modern portable computers has enabled rapid calculations to be made and rockets to be launched in this manner.

This is how the problems presented themselves to the planners between 1940 and 1941, and there was virtually no previous experience to draw on. Only the test facilities at Peenemünde could give any indication of what was required, and this was little enough to go on. There is no doubt that faced with such problems the team tried to cater for all possibilities; the result was a wide variety of sites. The results of this policy can be seen in northern France, and although the only sites completely finished were some of the simple ones, construction was so well advanced on others that the intention is clear. None, of course, became operational.

The categories of simple and complex sites are based not only on the size of the site but also the type of rocket for which each site was intended. The following lists are based on work carried out by the author in France:

SIMPLE SITES FOR THE STANDARD V2

These were capable of dealing with the standard, conventional warhead V2:

Villiers-Adam, storage and servicing (possibly launching);
Bergueneuse, storage;
Thiennes; oxygen production and launching;
Rauville, typical launching site.

COMPLEX SITES FOR PRIMARILY THE V4 AND LONG-RANGE VERSIONS OF THE V2

These sites are believed to be unique examples and were capable of dealing with both standard and modified V2s (V4) and/or the larger A9/A10 developments:

Brécourt, storage, servicing, oxygen production and launching of both standard and modified V2s;
Silos, storage, servicing and launching of modified V2s;
Sottevast, storage, servicing, oxygen production and launching of standard and modified V2s and larger developments;
Couville, storage, servicing, oxygen production and launching of standard and modified V2s;
Watten, storage, servicing, oxygen production and launching of standard and modified V2s and larger developments;
Wizernes, storage, servicing, oxygen production and launching of standard and modified V2s and larger developments.

CHAPTER SEVEN

The Simple Sites

VILLIERS-ADAM

The Villiers-Adam site is situated on the edge of the Forêt de l'Isle-Adam, about a mile from the village and twelve miles north of Paris. There is a railway spur line which passes within a mile of the site, off the main Pontoise–Paris line, and there are two ex-Luftwaffe airfields at Bernes-sur-Oise and Cormeilles-en-Vexin, both within a 7 mile radius. The area is well known for its limestone caves, and one of these was chosen as the location for the V2 site. Very little excavation work would have been necessary to convert the site, as the only external buildings needed are those for servicing the V2s before their despatch to the launching sites.

As shown in fig. 5, there is no evidence of a site railway between the caves and these buildings, but from the buildings a double section of narrow gauge track runs for 100 yards, before changing to single track, to a concrete pad on the other side of the main road. Rail was used for site movement of the V2 as it was the most vibration-free mode of transport.

If it had been discovered by Allied intelligence the site would have provided a difficult target to attack from the air; apart from being close to Paris and behind all the Channel airfields, the Luftwaffe had two bases nearby. The evidence that it did remain undetected throughout the war is shown by the lack of any bomb damage to the site. The service buildings were not designed to withstand blast and there are no signs of air-raid shelters for the technical staff. As the service buildings were half a mile from the caves it is clear that the possibility of air raids was not considered as a serious threat. Between the caves and buildings is a large mound of earth, probably composed of excavations from the caves, covering an area of 5 acres. This mound, which is covered in trees, would provide some camouflage for the site.

As the caves would only have been used for storage the main interest is in the service buildings. These buildings are in perfect condition, except for the loss of the doors, and were designed to provide a comprehensive servicing facility for the V2. The V2 was a complicated weapon, especially in 1942, and to aid a successful launch after the long journey from Germany and then storage, a comprehensive check-out proceedure was planned. The structure of the standard V2 followed aircraft practice in that the body of the rocket was bolted together at a series of bulkheads to enable it to be fabricated in four main sections.

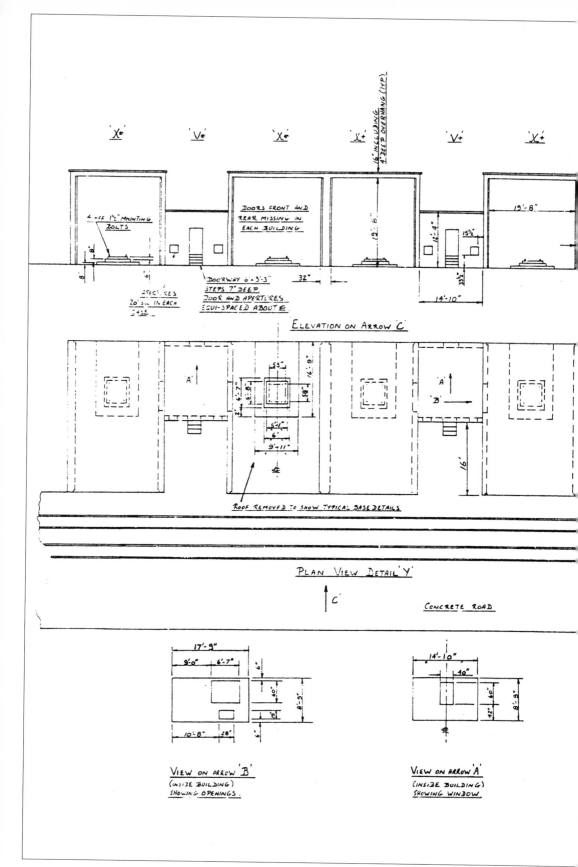

5. *The Villiers–Adam simple storage and servicing site for standard V2s. Buildings marked 'X' are for the rocket sub-assemblies and those marked 'V' are for the test equipment.*

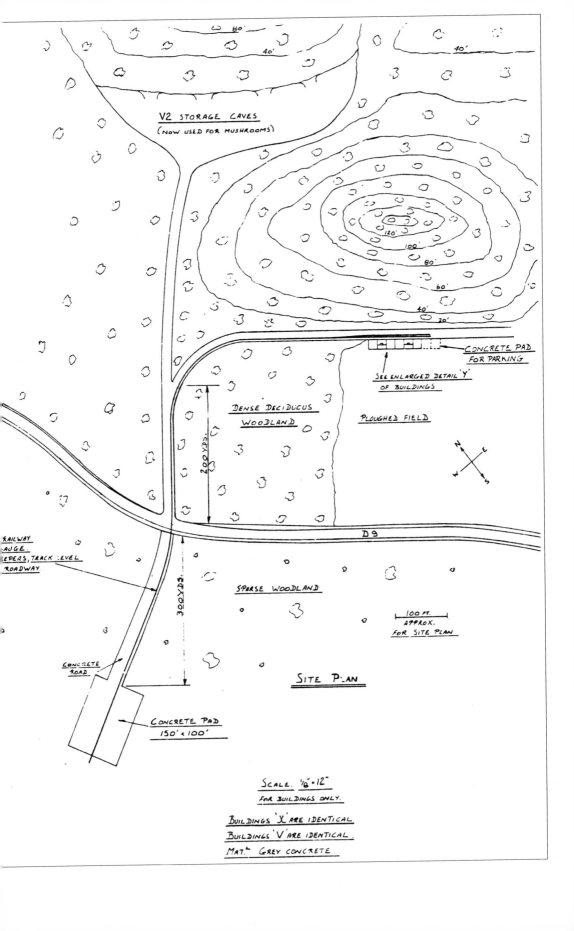

V2 STORAGE CAVES
(NOW USED FOR MUSHROOMS)

80'

40'

40'

120'

100'

80'

60'

40'

20'

CONCRETE PAD
FOR PARKING

SEE ENLARGED DETAIL 'Y'
OF BUILDINGS

DENSE DECIDUCUS
WOODLAND

PLOUGHED FIELD

200 YDS.

N E W S

RAILWAY
GAUGE
SLEEPERS, TRACK LEVEL
ROADWAY

D 9

SPARSE WOODLAND

300 YDS.

100 FT.
APPROX.
FOR SITE PLAN

CONCRETE
ROAD

SITE PLAN

CONCRETE PAD
150' x 100'

SCALE. 1/8" = 12"
FOR BUILDINGS ONLY.

BUILDINGS 'X' ARE IDENTICAL
BUILDINGS 'V' ARE IDENTICAL.
MAT.L GREY CONCRETE

The one nearest the nose was the warhead/nose section; this was 5 ft 11 in long and weighed 2,150 lb complete with a 1,650 lb Amatol high-explosive filling. This section would be kept at the same site as the main rocket but stored separately, and would travel independently as much as possible. No servicing of the warhead was required apart from the attachment of the nose-mounted detonator immediately before launch. The instrument and control bay was 4 ft 8 in long and weighed 975 lb, including a structure weight of 325 lb. The overall weight of this section varied slightly according to the type of equipment installed. The centre section, containing the alloy liquid oxygen and alcohol tanks, was 20 ft 3 in long and, with its tanks empty, weighed 1,795 lb, of which 1,185 lb comprised the supporting structure and outer skin. The motor compartment contained the HTP turbine, HTP and catalyst tanks, fuel pumps, other assorted storage cylinders, valves, etc., and the main rocket motor. It was 14 ft 8 in long and weighed 4,000 lb in total. This can be broken down: 1,595 lb for the structure, which included the cylindrical rear body section (this fitted over the motor like a sleeve and the four fins were permanently attached to it); 890 lb for the HTP turbine; 1,035 lb for the rocket motor with its pipework and valves; 480 lb for the four graphite internal control vanes and their associated control gear.

Before transportation to Villiers-Adam, it can be assumed that no integrated functional checks were carried out at the construction site. Each piece of equipment, such as valves, servos, gyros, etc., would have been inspected and tested before being installed in the V2, but the main concern at final assembly was that each rocket was built according to specification and that all the serial numbers and inspection history for each rocket was correct and recorded. This documentation would then accompany each rocket on its journey to France, eventually to be returned to Germany after launch.

To give an approximation of the service procedure, while still in the storage caves the rocket would be separated into the three main sections: motor bay; fuel tanks; instrumentation and control. The three sections would then be transferred to the service buildings. These buildings were arranged to be able to service two rockets simultaneously, and the various sections would be lifted vertically into the tallest of the buildings, as required. Tests would be carried out to determine flow rates through the fuel pipes, valves and orifices; the values would be compared with results supplied from Peenemünde, based on minimum values to give the correct thrust at launch. The system was pressurized, using nitrogen to simulate the pumps normal flow rate of 285 lb of fuel per second. This would also allow checks to be made of the connections, valves, etc., for leaks. An operational check would also be carried out on all valves, relays and switches. The motor system used over 20 valves of various types (solenoid, pressure-reducing, non-return, safety, vent and distribution) and they all required checking. The method of operation was either electrical or pneumatic, and the faulty operation of these valves had caused most of the launch failures which had occurred at Peenemünde. Each operational rocket was programmed to start inclining from the vertical 4 seconds after lift-off. Up to this time any reduction in thrust would result in the rocket toppling back onto the launch pad, producing a huge explosion as the fuel ignited, followed by the 1,650 lbs of Amatol in the warhead. The problem was the high level of vibration as the main thrust of the motor built up, and to guard against the accidental operation of valves and relays during this period they were given a high operating resistance, open or closed. This required careful adjustment if the valve or relay was not to remain open or closed when the signal was given. A leak and operational check would also be made of the nitrogen cylinders used to pressurize the HTP and catalyst tanks at 350 lb/in^2. This nitrogen was also supplied to the oxygen and alcohol tanks via a reducing valve, at 20 lb/in^2, in order to prime the fuel pumps and, later in the flight, to pressurize the alcohol tank.

During all these checks the motor bay would be mounted vertically on a handling trestle, which was attached to the $4 \times 1\frac{1}{2}$ in bolts sunk into the concrete of the plinth. Apart from ease of handling, the main reason for carrying out the testing vertically was that on the launch pad, when the main oxygen and alcohol valves were opened, fuel was allowed to flow by gravity through to the combustion chamber where it was ignited by a pyrotechnic torch or similar. Not until an observer was satisfied that this fuel had ignited were the turbine-driven fuel pumps started via the external power supply. Assuming that these tests have been satisfactorily completed and any replacement parts added, the motor bay would be removed from the plinth and placed on a rigid frame in one corner of the same building.

The fuel-tank compartment would also be tested vertically, and the height of the service buildings would only just have accommodated the 20 ft 4 in height of

Villiers-Adam: the buildings were intended for V2 testing before the transfer of the rocket to the simple sites.

the tank bays. The only checks carried out on the fuel tanks would be for leakage. Using dry nitrogen, both tanks would be pressurized to 25% above the normal maximum working-pressure (20 lb/in²) for a period of up to two hours. Although during normal use the tanks only contained fuel for approximately 30 minutes, between tanking-up and the all-burnt stage in flight, no fuel leaks could be tolerated. The main reason for this was volatility of the alcohol, which has a vapour-ignition temperature of only 13°C and the chances of an explosion would be increased by the smallest oxygen leak. In the event of a problem occurring on the launch pad during the last few seconds of the countdown, the rocket would be left standing fully fuelled while the problem was solved. During this time the rocket was a potential bomb and although the oxygen tank was vented to prevent an excessive build-up of pressure, if it was a warm day and the sun was shining on the heavily lagged outer skin of the tank with its contents at –200°C, a protracted delay could cause a considerable loss of oxygen, characterized by the plume of white vapour from the vent.

The control and instrumentation bays would simultaneously be undergoing tests. Although the height required for these tests was much less than that for the fuel and motor bays, both sets of buildings had the same overall dimensions for flexibility. The control and instrumentation of the V2 was designed to provide control over the three basic factors affecting its trajectory: height, direction and velocity. Being a ballistic missile, like an artillery shell, it had no real flight controls, but to reach its target it required accurate control over each initial stage of its trajectory, including inclination and the final height that it reached.

To obtain its maximum range the rocket had to adopt an angle of about 45° shortly after launch and this required control over pitch attitude (the angle which the longitudinal axis of the rocket makes from the horizontal). To maintain the correct direction, control was required based on the difference between a reference axis, usually north, and an accurate compass bearing of the target. The V2 used an autopilot system similar to that of the V1 and originally designed for aircraft. These systems had been developed to a high degree of reliability for aircraft use, but because there was always a pilot on hand to make manual corrections there was little incentive to eliminate errors which were due to poor design and manufacturing tolerances. When the same standards of autopilot design were applied to the V2, the high initial levels of vibration from the motor and very high rates of acceleration compared to aircraft, contributed to the fact that the V2 rarely impacted within 1½ miles of the target when launched from Peenemünde or Blitzna, or 10 miles when launched in the field against the UK and other European targets.

When the testers were trying to solve the problem of premature air-burst by visual observation of the last few seconds of flight, the cameras were very often placed in the centre of the predicted target area, as this was found to be the most unlikely impact place.

To provide two basic controls over the trajectory, the autopilot used a two-degree-of-freedom vertical gyro for pitch attitude and therefore height control. This gyro had a gimbal whose displacement about each axis was a measure of its own angular deviation from the local vertical axis, and a rotor axis which was maintained parallel to gravity by a gravity-sensing device. This provided a continuous vertical reference against which any trajectory requirement, such as that specified for the V2 of a gradual inclination from the vertical after lift-off and terminating in an approximate angle of 45° after 52 seconds, could be arranged by a simple clockwork timing-device. This gyro was also arranged to provide an indication of roll attitude of the rocket through the outer gimbal axis. To provide a horizontal alignment of the target on the compass bearing, a two-degree-of-freedom directional gyro was used.

This gyro indicated the motion of the rocket longitudinally (azimuth) from an original compass bearing. This bearing on the target was established before launch by orientation of the gyro spin axis to a reference, usually north, using an accurate surveyor's theodolite and rotating the launch platform to line up the axes; for this, an accurate plot of the latitude and longtitude of the target is an essential requirement. In this instance the outer gimbal of the directional gyro was used to sense changes to the left or right.

Electrical impulses from these two gyros were fed via a system of servo motors to four external tabs on the fins and four graphite rudders in the rocket-motor-exhaust gases. The graphite rudders provided the main control forces, while the external tabs were used to ensure that an unstable aerodynamic oscillation did not build up during the trajectory.

To determine the speed and height at which the desired range would be attained, necessitated control of velocity and hence burning time of the rocket motor. Early V2s used a radio transmitter and receiver, by which signals from the ground were sent to the rocket and then back to one of the very accurate Wurzburg radar sets; using the Doppler effect the velocity of the rocket could be determined from a direct comparison with this returning frequency. When the velocity reached a figure taken from a trajectory plot corresponding to the required range, a radio signal shut off the fuel-pump turbine, stopping the motor, and the unpowered rocket then continued on a true ballistic trajectory.

This system had obvious drawbacks, of which the most serious was its reliance on ground control. An elaborate system of electronic filters was built into the equipment to prevent spurious signals, especially from the enemy, affecting the flight path.

Later V2s (approximately 80% of all those fired operationally) used a gyro system in the form of a pendulous integrating gyroscope accelerometer. This was another example of completely new technology being used for the V2. This type of gyroscopic device utilizes an intentional imbalance in the gyro rotor. Any horizontal acceleration along the input axis, in this case the rocket-pitch axis, causes motion around the precession axis, as a result of the unbalanced mass.

The gyro, mounted in gimbals, is part of a servo loop in which motion around the precession axis is detected by a pick-off and this is fed to a gimbal torquer to produce motion between the gimbal and its case. The torquer, positioned along the gyro axis, produces a rotational motion of the gimbal in which the gyro sits which is equivalent to the integral of the rocket's horizontal acceleration (velocity). Hence at any point on the trajectory the rocket's velocity can be obtained from its longitudinal acceleration. When this velocity is the same as that required for the range, the turbine is stopped, as before. (note: a torquer is a device to put a particular gyro axis back into the correct position, by applying a torque, if it has changed owing to both manufacturing errors and the fact that the earth is not a stationery object, but spinning and tilting.)

Although this made the V2 independent from ground signals, problems did occur with errors in the gyroscopic devices, caused mainly by poor manufacturing tolerances. An example of the accuracy required in velocity measurement is illustrated by a modern intercontinental ballistic missile (ICBM); with a range of 5,000 miles, travelling at 20,000 ft per second, a velocity error of only 1 ft per second would cause the missile to miss its target by more than a mile.

These three sets of gyro devices (vertical, directional and integrating) all attempt to maintain their position fixed in space. In practice, owing to various problems, this hypothetical fixed motion in space cannot be maintained and the gyros deviate from their initial established position. The rate of deviation is called drift rate and depends on natural effects and limitations on the manufacturing accuracy of the gyros. The natural effects can be alleviated but no amount of testing can remove them. These effects result from the fact that the earth is spinning and any long-range missile must adopt a curved trajectory if it is to hit the target. This effect would be accentuated if the rocket started from the North Pole and was aimed at New York. Over a flight lasting one hour the earth would have rotated 15° and the position of New York would have shifted 900 miles in a clockwise direction. The missile, on a straight trajectory, would hit Chicago instead of New York.

The drift rates due to manufacturing limitations can be checked, as they depend on the physical characteristics of the gyros. These drift errors are caused basically by friction in the bearings and inaccurate balancing of the mass of the gyro rotor. Another area in which tests are required is the caging mechanism, by which the spin axis of the gyro rotor is locked prior to launch and uncaged a few seconds before launch. This caging is incorporated to reduce drift errors of the reference axis, and for vertical gyros the process by which the gyro is initially aligned to gravity is called the erection time.

On some operational rockets, instrumentation was fitted for transmitting information on such matters as skin temperature, pressures at various positions and structural movements (using strain gauges). A transmitting device was sometimes fitted to give a precise indication of the impact point.

The electrical checks would have taken several hours. The drift rates were checked for the individual gyros against the manufacturer's figures, and the rates are usually expressed in degrees per minute. Both the vertical and directional gyros use a mechanical caging mechanism which locks the spin axis to the reference of the particular gyro. This caging mechanism is released, uncaging the gyros a few seconds before launch, thereby ensuring that virtually no drift has taken place before flight.

The operation of the caging motor and gear train must be checked. The vertical repeatability of the vertical gyro is used to check the overall friction, balance and accuracy built into the gyro mechanism. After establishing a vertical reference, the gimbal elements are then displaced and allowed to return to the vertical, under the control of the vertical reference mechanism.

Any error in failing to reach the vertical is measured in terms of the half-cone angle, which is half the spread between the extreme settling positions. Apart from these tests, each complete gimbal device has routine checks carried out on the pick-off, torquer and motor; these checks cover impedance, output voltage, voltage gradient, torquing rate, starting and running power, and run-up time. For the accelerometers the checks cover linearity, threshold acceleration, zero stability, zero uncertainty and cross-axis error. Any measuring devices or transmitting equipment which are fitted to the particular rocket under test are also checked, as is the signal reception. These checks would not be the only ones carried out, but this gives some indication of the complicated and highly specialized nature of the work which was necessary for a successful launch and flight.

Once the three sections had been assembled the overall height would have been 39 ft 8 in. The site would have been equipped with at least one portable, all-weather, metal-framed erection tower, similar to the more substantial ones used at Peenemünde. With the three sections bolted together, the rocket would be lowered on to the railway wagon into a horizontal cradle. Assuming a rocket had successfully passed the various checks it would be loaded on to a lorry for transportation to the launch site.

As illustrated on fig. 5, the site was equipped with a launch pad, which was served by a single track of the narrow gauge railway, crossing the main road, at least half a mile from the service buildings. Because of the distance of this launch pad from the French coast (at least 80 miles), the possible targets in the UK would be strictly limited – probably only the south coast towns, and therefore launches would not regularly be made from this site.

During the checks there was the possibility of a fault being discovered which would result in the rocket becoming a complete write-off, if it was subject to another lengthy journey to the launch site. Typically this fault might be a slight fuel-tank leak, which could not be corrected *in situ*, but which would be unacceptable, if allowed to worsen. In this case the choices were to scrap the rocket immediately, putting the usable pieces back into storage, or to launch it from Villiers-Adam. If a decision was made to launch from the site, the warhead would be removed from its section of storage and attached to the main rocket, shortly before launch. Provision would have to be made for the supply of oxygen and alcohol, as the infrequency of such launches meant that ready supplies were limited.

In 1980 the only major items missing from the site were the railtracks from the caves to the main road, the handling equipment, test gear and of course the rockets. The service buildings had no obvious signs of light fittings and so either portable lighting was used or work was only carried out in daylight.

The facilities could not have dealt with a very quick turnaround of rockets and this shows that the original plans did not allow for the production of large numbers of V2s; Villiers-Adam was part of the 1942 construction programme and it seems unlikely that there are more than two or three similar sites in France. The rockets from sites such as Villiers-Adam could have been transferred straight to launch sites such as Thiennes or Rauville. Neither of these sites had facilities for servicing and at Rauville the only equipment permanently provided was the armoured launch–control vehicle.

BERGUENEUSE

Bergueneuse is a small village a few miles south of Boulogne and about 15 miles from the coast. The site is on the outskirts of the village and there are the remains of quarry workings in the area, some of which may have been used for the site. There is no sign of bomb damage either to the site or to the village.

The storage site at Bergueneuse was intended to provide temporary secure storage for the rockets as they were moved between service sites (such as Villiers–Adam) and the launch sites. This might be necessary if, for various reasons, the launch site was temporarily out of action: the site might have been bombed; a rocket misfire at launch would require the site to be cleared of all debris and checks made to ensure that it was safe to be used again; a bottleneck might have formed at the launching sites; there might have been sites planned, or even built, similar to Villiers–Adam, but without storage facilities.

It should be remembered that for the operational use of the standard V2 it would be assumed that the flow of rockets would proceed at a predetermined steady rate from Germany via service sites to the launch sites. The planners would recognize that there were bound to be factors which could not be

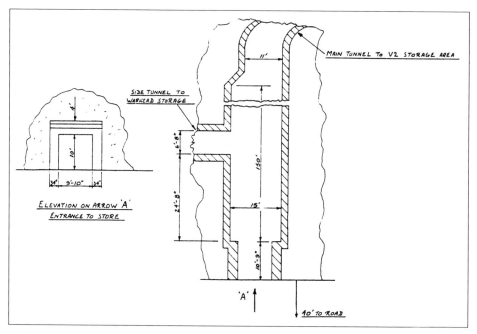

6. Bergueneuse intermediate storage site for standard V2s, intended to supply Thiennes and Rauville type sites after transfer from Villiers–Adam. Construction unfinished.

Bergueneuse: intermediate storage for the standard V2 before its transfer to a simple launching site.

anticipated and which would upset the normal smooth running of the system. This is especially true as there was no precedent. The storage had to be secure for both the rocket and its warhead, because the V2 would probably be almost ready for launch at the point at which a delay might occur.

The site construction does not appear to have been finished; the main tunnel ends abruptly in a rock face and from the curvature of this tunnel it appears that another entrance or exit was intended some yards further on. A layout of the site is shown in fig. 6 and this shows that it was built into a hillside. The entrance is 9 ft 10 in wide, which provided about 10 in clearance for the widest section of the V2 (the rear section with fins fitted); the fuselage was positioned on the vehicle so that the fins were aligned at 45° during transport. The main tunnel opens out to a width of 15 ft; 10 ft 9 in from the entrance this width extends in a straight line into the hillside for 150 ft, at which point the width is reduced to 11 ft. Immediately afterwards the tunnel curves to the right at approximately 45° and extends another 300 ft, before the excavation ends in a rough, unfinished state, indicating that construction stopped before the tunnel was finished.

Both the sides of the tunnel and the flat roof are of reinforced concrete, and the height is approximately 18 ft. There is a 6 ft 8 in wide side tunnel on the left, at right angles to the main section and 45 ft from the entrance. This side tunnel extends for 30 ft before it also widens out to 15 ft. After a further 60 ft the way is blocked by two massive steel doors, completely blocking the tunnel.

Although there are no signs of how the rockets were to be moved inside the tunnels, close to the entrance there are several sections of narrow gauge railway which were probably used during construction and intended also for internal use. As the removal of the warhead would have involved a considerable safety risk the side tunnel was clearly intended for warhead storage, on occasions when it appeared that the storage period was going to exceed some nominal deadline. Away from the remainder of the stored rockets, potential damage could be kept to a minimum should premature detonation occur.

THIENNES

The site at Thiennes is a good example of innovative thinking. Providing its own liquid-oxygen production and alcohol-storage facilities, yet compact and well hidden in a secure area, its true purpose would have been difficult to determine; it

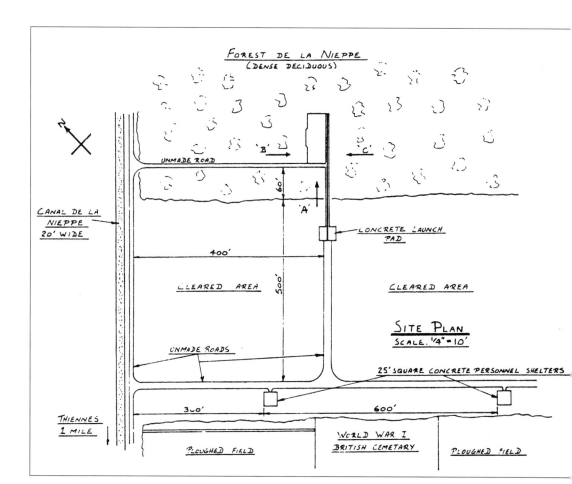

7. Thiennes launching site for standard V2s. Site has liquid oxygen production and storage capability and alcohol storage but no rocket storage facilities.

seems likely that the area contains one or two similar sites, not yet discovered. The village is situated midway between Boulogne and Lille in the Pas de Calais. It is on the edge of a large area of woodland, covering approximately 20 square miles, and lies close to the villages of La Motte and Merville. The area is completely encircled by the Canal de la Nieppe, which is still usable and which joins one of the main canal networks leading into the Low Countries and Germany. The area is also encircled by a railway line, the main line from Hazebrouk to Belgium; off this is a now disused and partially dismantled loop which used to connect La Motte and Merville to the main line at Thiennes. This loop passes through the Forêt de la Nieppe and would have been used for rocket traffic.

There are many remains of concrete personnel shelters guarding all the roads in the area. Among the trees around La Motte there are still signs of bomb craters, and one or two of these quite substantial shelters (30 x 30 ft) have been damaged.

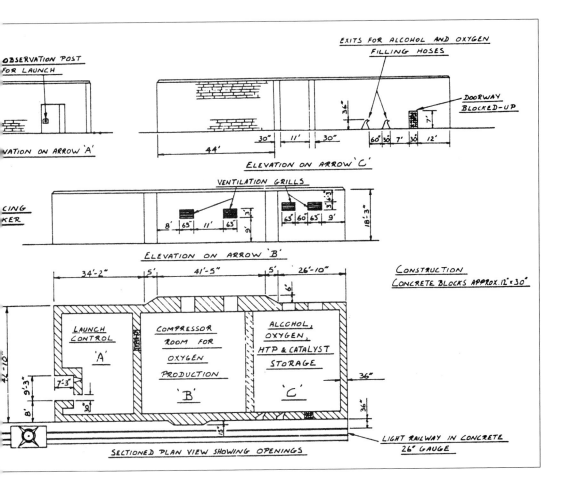

The actual Thiennes site is situated in a clearing which marks the edge of the forest, about one mile from the village and only a few yards from the canal. Despite a 40 year interval the growth of new trees is only 10–20 years old and this makes the site look more recent. On the edge of the clearing are two concrete personnel shelters, each with 3–4 ft thick walls and each capable of accommodating 20–30 men.

Along the south-east wall is a concrete foundation into which is set a stretch of railway. The gauge of this line is 26 in, compared to the 36 in gauge at Villiers-Adam, and indicates the different usage at the two sites, Villiers-Adam would have needed a system that could withstand regular and fairly heavy use, while at Thiennes the rails would have been used to move a rocket only a few yards to the launch pad; judging by the size of this site, only a small number of launchings would have been made per week.

The rails finish just beyond the end of the building, and the most likely explanation is that where they were not set in concrete, they were removed after the war to alleviate the immediate shortage of steel in France. It is noticeable that the concrete used on the sites generally was of a very good quality. At Thiennes, though it is over 40 years since it was laid and there has been no maintenance, there is still little sign of defects.

The main building is similar to the much larger site at Watten, a few miles away. It is approximately a quarter of the size of Watten, with a correspondingly

Thiennes simple site: the front of the main building has a recessed viewing port for observing the launch from the pad, 150 ft away. Narrow gauge rails to the pad run alongside the right-hand wall for the fuel tanks to be filled at the far end of the building.

scaled-down operating capability. The building was intended to provide three main services to the standard V2 organization. First, it was to accommodate the equipment and personnel required for the immediate pre-launch countdown checks; the absence of any storage arrangements or permanent all-weather cover meant that each rocket would arrive virtually ready for launch. Second, it was to manufacture enough oxygen and store enough alcohol, HTP and catalyst to enable the launch of 20 to 30 V2s over a period of about three weeks; this implies that the site was intended for relatively few launches, with intervals while the oxygen was replenished. Third, it was to act as a permanent launch facility and so contain the necessary equipment for the launching, recording, observing, immediate post-launch tracking, communications and security; the main advantage of this site was its self-sufficiency. It is extremely unlikely that there would have been any launch delays due to fuel shortages, or to transportation problems from the main production centres.

The main building, shown in fig. 7, is 400 ft from the canal and 60 ft from the edge of the forest; the mature trees would have provided effective camouflage. There are no signs of bomb damage to the building or bomb craters in the area around Thiennes itself. It can be assumed therefore that Thiennes was never visited by Allied bombers.

The overall size of the building is 112 ft x 43 ft x 18 ft high; it is constructed of precast concrete blocks measuring 30 in x 12 in and generally looks in very good condition. This impression is reinforced by the almost complete large wooden shutters over the inlet ducts for the oxygen production plant, along the north side of the building. The entrance is a narrow doorway, recessed 7 ft from the 9 ft wide entrance at the southern end. The wall containing the doorway is fitted with a steel-framed observation point which overlooks the launch pad a few yards away. The main advantage of this layout is that if an explosion were to occur at launch the blast probably would not to penetrate the building. Unfortunately not all of the interior can be inspected, as the doorway through to the second room is bricked up; so, too, is another entrance on the adjacent wall.

The first room is 28 ft wide and was intended to house the control and instrumentation equipment used for the countdown checks and the actual launch. The second room, fitted with the wooden shutters, contained the compressors, coolers, filters, vessels, etc. for producing liquid oxygen from air supplied through the ducts in the north wall. From the size of the compressor room it is estimated that it could house equipment capable of producing 2 tons of liquid oxygen per day, operating round the clock. The V2 required a total of 4.9 tons at the launch if the maximum range was to be achieved. Because of the large amount of fuel lost through evaporation from the $-200°C$ storage temperature, it would take approximately three days' continuous operation to produce sufficient for one launch. In this case it is unlikely that a continuous-launch programme was envisaged for the site; it is more likely that oxygen would have been produced non-stop for a number of days, and this would go straight into storage, until sufficient had been produced for the launch of perhaps ten V2s.

The room at the end of the building contained the storage tanks for the oxygen, alcohol, HTP, catalyst and nitrogen (a by-product of oxygen production). As the oxygen was produced on site, the remaining fuel requirements were for the storage of around 40 tons of alcohol (which required no special arrangements other than precautions against fire), 2 tons of HTP (which needed to be kept in aluminium containers, as it reacted violently with most other materials including steel and concrete) and 300 lb of calcium permanganate catalyst.

On the outside wall of the end room, adjacent to the rail track, are two staggered, funnel-shaped openings, pointing downwards. These were intended for the two hoses which supplied the oxygen and alcohol to the fuel tanks of the rocket before it was moved to the launching pad. Care was taken with the openings to ensure that there was not a straight line access path through to the interior in the event of an accident during this fuelling operation. During the fuelling, the rocket would be mounted vertically on a flat wagon directly opposite these openings, hoses would be connected to the filling points and the tanks filled.

Like all other V2 sites in France, Thiennes never became operational. Nevertheless, it is more than likely that once these sites were completed, test runs were carried out, using dummy rockets. At one of the sites, white-painted dummy rockets were discovered by Allied troops advancing into northern France after the D-Day landings.

The V2 arrives from a storage site, such as Bergueneuse or direct from a Villiers-Adam type of site, in which case the road/rail journey is about 90 miles. The location of the Villiers-Adam type of site did mean that it provided a relatively safe environment for leisurely carrying out the test proceedures but it did mean that to reach the launching site a day's journey was involved and this meant a long countdown check at site.

The warhead arrives, possibly on a separate vehicle and is parked under the trees, some distance from the main building. From reports of launches carried out at Peenemünde, before the emphasis changed to achieving the fastest possible launch when the rockets were eventually used against the UK, Paris, etc., from launching sites in Holland, the normal length of countdown checklist when the rockets had been through their workshops was from one to one and a half hours. This time did not include the fitting and initial arming of the warhead and hence the actual operational countdown procedure would have been:

–3 hours	warhead removed from transport and attached to the main body of the rocket, still in the horizontal position; arming devices added; rocket inspected for any obvious damage;
–2 hours	rocket elevated to vertical position and placed on to flat railway wagon;
–1½ hours	clamps removed from fin trim tabs; batteries fitted for auxiliary power supplies; fuel tanks pressurized at 30 lb/sq in to check for leaks and the complete fuel system purged with dry nitrogen (obtained as a by-product of oxygen production);
–1 hour	rocket moved along rails until opposite hose positions in wall and fuel tanks filled in the following order: alcohol 8,750 lb, oxygen 11,000 lb, HTP 370 lb, calcium permanganate catalyst 30 lb; while it is in the rocket, the venting system allows 5–10 lbs of oxygen to evaporate per minute, depending on the

ambient temperature; rocket moved to launching pad and stabilizing legs added to wagon, and four graphite internal guide vanes fitted (in path of motor exhaust and provided rocket's directional control);

−30 minutes   external power supplies connected via umbilical cables to control and instrumentation bay; trajectory checked using accurate compass bearings of launching site and target; gyros set to the required vertical and horizontal reference axes using two collimator readings at 90° to each other and some yards from the rocket; initial system checks carried out on guidance, control, fuel, and motor circuits; warhead armed; detonator in nose has already been fitted; by now the launching area has been cleared and all personnel not involved with the launch withdraw to the two concrete shelters;

−10 minutes   final run through of all the system switches and valves in their firing sequence; pressures and temperatures checked;

−3 minutes   all gyros start running;

−2 minutes   rocket checks finished; oxygen vent valve closed; gyros uncaged and no longer tied to reference axes;

−60 seconds   black powder igniter lit under motor; main alcohol and oxygen valves opened allowing 20 lb of fuel per second by gravity into combustion chamber;

−20 seconds   visual observer confirms that fuel has ignited; HTP system initiated and turbine starts rotating to power fuel pumps and associated systems;

−10 seconds   turbine now running at maximum revs; external power supplies switched off; internal batteries switched on; initial thrust stage starts;

−5 seconds   thrust now at 8 tons, and all systems working;

0 seconds   main thrust stage of 25 tons starts; final check of all systems working;

+8 seconds   external power supply jettisoned; all systems now running on internal power; thrust rises to 25 tons;

+10 seconds   lift-off; trajectory timing sequence starts; vertical axis still at 90°;

+14 seconds   rocket starts inclining from vertical;

+18 seconds   maximum inclination of approximately 45° reached;

+24 seconds   speed of sound, Mach 1;

+35 seconds   Mach 2 reached;

+54 seconds   HTP turbine stopped at height of 20 miles and Mach 5.5; rocket now continues on ballistic trajectory.

Immediately the rocket leaves the local air-space the site is cleared of equipment and returned to its camouflaged state.

All clerical work associated with the launch is carried out, files are kept of the checks carried out, any results, readings and details of any problems are recorded; these are used to analyse the results of the flight, when, or if, the results are known.

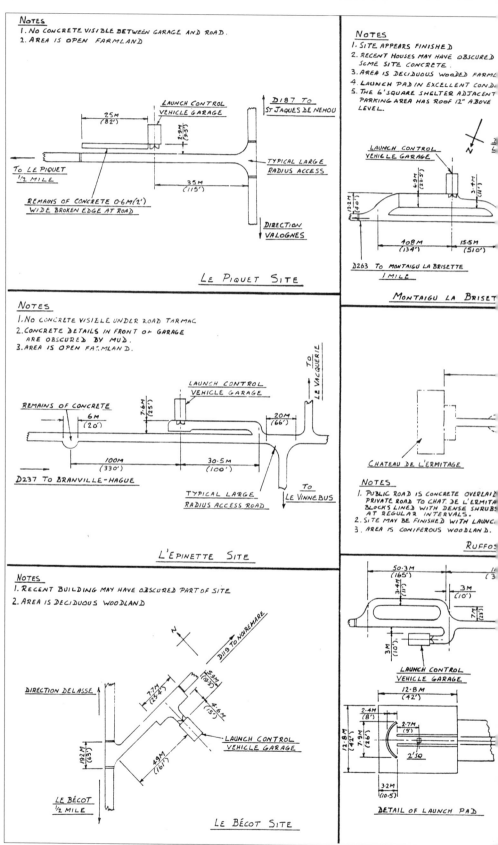

NOTES
1. No concrete visible between garage and road.
2. Area is open farmland

LAUNCH CONTROL
VEHICLE GARAGE

25M (82')

2.9M (9.5')

D187 TO
ST JAQUES DE NEHOU

To LE PIQUET
½ MILE

TYPICAL LARGE
RADIUS ACCESS

35M (115')

REMAINS OF CONCRETE 0.6M (2')
WIDE BROKEN EDGE AT ROAD

DIRECTION
VALOGNES

LE PIQUET SITE

NOTES
1. Site appears finished
2. Recent houses may have obscured some site concrete.
3. Area is deciduous wooded farml...
4. Launch pad in excellent cond...
5. The 6' square shelter adjacent parking area has roof 12" above level.

LAUNCH CONTROL
VEHICLE GARAGE

6.9M (22.5')

3.4M (11')

12.2M (40')

408M (134')

15.5M (510')

D263 TO MONTAIGU LA BRISETTE
1 MILE

MONTAIGU LA BRISET...

NOTES
1. No concrete visible under road tarmac
2. Concrete details in front of garage are obscured by mud.
3. Area is open farmland.

To
LE VACQUERIE

LAUNCH CONTROL
VEHICLE GARAGE

REMAINS OF CONCRETE

6M (20')

7.6M (25')

20M (66')

100M (330')

30.5M (100')

D237 TO BRANVILLE-HAGUE

TYPICAL LARGE
RADIUS ACCESS ROAD

To
LE VINNEBUS

L'EPINETTE SITE

CHATEAU DE L'ERMITAGE

NOTES
1. Public road is concrete overlaid private road to Chat. de l'Ermita... blocks lined with dense shrubs at regular intervals.
2. Site may be finished with launc...
3. Area is coniferous woodland.

RUFFO...

NOTES
1. Recent building may have obscured part of site
2. Area is deciduous woodland

D119 TO NOUREMARE

DIRECTION DELASSE

7.7M (23.5')

5.9M (19.3')

4.6M (15')

19.2M (63')

49M (161')

LAUNCH CONTROL
VEHICLE GARAGE

LE BÉCOT
½ MILE

LE BÉCOT SITE

50.3M (165')

3.4M (11')

3M (10')

7.7M (25')

3M (10')

LAUNCH CONTROL
VEHICLE GARAGE

12.8M (42')

2.4M (8')

2.7M (9')

2'50

12.8M (42')

7.9M (26')

3.2M (10.5')

DETAIL OF LAUNCH PAD

8. *Rauville type of simple site for standard V2s. The only construction is a garage for the launch control vehicle. La Prée is south-west of Rouen, and the remainder are within 30 miles of Cherbourg. Of the eig... so far discovered, only two are complete with launching pad.*

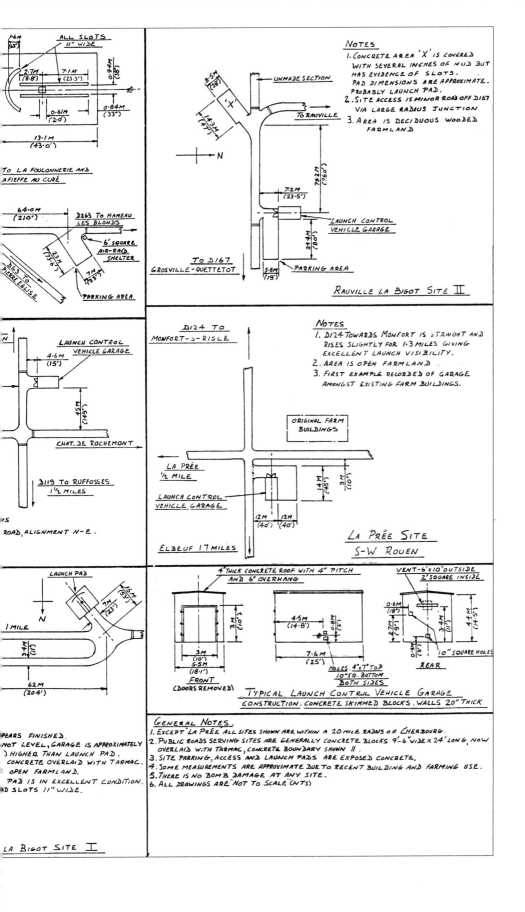

RAUVILLE

The Rauville site illustrates the minimum requirements for launching the standard V2, and fig. 8 shows the eight sites of this type which have been discovered so far. The most intact examples are Rauville I (on the D222) and Montaigu (on the D263), both of which are on the Cherbourg Peninsula. Indeed, of these eight only La Prée is not on this peninsula; it is situated south-west of Rouen. With this type of site, apart from an innocent-looking 'garage' building there is nothing above ground to give any indication of what was intended. There are no large storage buildings, railtracks, or massive concrete emplacements; the only signs of activity are one small building and some improvements to existing roads. It is not surprising therefore that Allied intelligence was mystified by these sites; eventually they were listed as V1 launching sites.

Despite often-repeated statements from Peenemünde that large complex sites were not required to launch the V2, and that all that was needed were mobile teams able to choose at random the most convenient piece of flat ground, the fact was such ideas were for postwar consumption only. Eventually, it was hoped, the truth would become lost in the mists of time.

Although the standard V2 did only need a flat piece of ground to act as a launching pad, it also required some additional features. The flat piece of ground had to be concrete, or something very similar, and it had to be as flat as possible; at launch, for at least 10 seconds as the thrust slowly built up to the 25 ton maximum, the ground underneath the motor exhaust was being subjected to an ever-increasing blast from gases at 2,000°C; this eventually reached a speed of 7,000 ft per second. This blasting effect would very quickly erode any surface that did not have the consistency of concrete, with the result that the supporting legs of the launching table, although fitted with a deflector, would lose their stability, thereby throwing the rocket out of alignment before it had left the ground. There was also the question of knowing in advance the precise location of the launching site so that an accurate trajectory calculation could be carried out before the launch.

The launch of a V2 from a 'field' site required a considerable number of vehicles to support the operation. The illustration on page 11 shows what was needed just to provide the fuel and external power supplies. In addition a launch control vehicle was required and this was an extremely specialized piece of equipment. Based on the Hanomag design for the 3 ton *Mittlerer Shutzenpanzerwagen*, with its six overlapping wheels and two driving half-track wheels, it was one of over 20 specialist vehicles built on this chassis; it was originally intended as an armoured troop carrier for the Army.

It would be parked only a few yards from the actual launching pad and therefore it had to be armoured to protect the occupants. Furthermore, the vehicle contained delicate instrumentation, which meant that it could not travel long distances without causing damage to the equipment; consequently it had to be permanently located at the launching site. All the sites such as Rauville used public roads, rebuilt with a layer of concrete (except Ruffosses, where the fuel tanker parking and launching pad are on the private road leading to the Château de l'Hermitage). The only building required was for the launch control vehicle.

All the examples shown were constructed between 1942 and 1943, and they probably formed part of a group of about 50 such sites. This will be discussed further in Chapter 8.

From looking at the eight sites a picture can be gained of the construction sequence. On those sites where construction had only just started, very few improvements were made to the existing roads, but the garage for the launch control vehicle was always in place and complete. This building was intended for the launch control vehicle (shown on page 64).

There appears to have been no systematic attempt to use natural camouflage for the garage or to use existing buildings. In most cases they are situated a few yards from the road, and are fairly exposed. Their usefulness since the war as a store for agricultural equipment has meant that they have survived remarkably well and there are no signs of bomb damage to any of those shown here. The illustration on page 62 shows the Montaigu garage, taken from the D263.

The site at Rauville II is about a mile from the village of Rauville-la-Bigot; it is in a cul-de-sac and is much less exposed than Rauville I. The village itself is a large settlement on the D900, 15 miles west of Valognes. It has excellent transport links: about 2 miles north of Rauville the railway crosses the D900 en route to Cherbourg.

The transport arrangements for this type of launching site meant that adequate hard parking areas had to be provided for a variety of equipment: the 50 ft *Meilerwagen* and its V2, the towing vehicle; the tankers supplying the alcohol, liquid oxygen and HTP; a pumping vehicle; electric power generator; and the armoured launch vehicle.

At only two of the sites shown was the construction, with launching pad, completed. These are Rauville I and Montaigu, and the pad at Rauville I is shown on page 62. It is made of concrete, approximately 43 ft x 42 ft, into which are cast 11 in wide troughs. Two of these are parallel to the line of fire and one forms an arc behind this line; the arrangement as a whole gives the impression of a gigantic arrowhead. The troughs would have originally been supplied with steel covers and would have prevented damage to cables which were connected to the rocket before launch. The actual launching position is indicated by the 2 ft-square hole into which the centre of the launch table would have fitted. Both the launching pads face north-west and the arc which contained the umbilical cables, jettisoned seconds before lift-off, allowed for a 20° to 30° range of variation in the launch direction.

At Rauville I the first parking area is 165 ft long and 11 ft wide. It is here that the three tankers and the pump would have parked.

Almost opposite the exit to this parking area, on the opposite side of the road, is a short driveway to the garage, which is undamaged except that its doors are missing. These probably would have been made of steel, judging from the size of the hinge supports.

During the pre-launch checks and countdown the armoured control vehicle would be parked only yards from the launching pad, and to ensure that it operated effectively the distance it travelled would have been kept to a minimum. Even so, the instrumentation would need to be recalibrated at regular intervals.

Rauville I simple site launching pad: the slots were intended for cables, etc., and the launch was from the centre of the square recess.

Montaigu la Brisette simple site on the Cherbourg Peninsula: the launch vehicle garage.

Le Bécot simple site on the Cherbourg Peninsula: the launch vehicle garage.

La Prée simple site, near Rouen, 120 miles from the Cherbourg sites: the launch vehicle garage.

V2 launch control vehicle: this type of armoured half-track was to be stationed at each of the Rauville type of simple sites in the garage provided. (Imperial War Museum)

The garage has no windows. The walls are made of concrete blocks 20 in thick and the roof is 4 in thick, so it was not intended to withstand any form of air attack. On the rear wall, near the top, is a large opening, 2 ft square on the inside and changing to a rectangle, 6 ft x 10 in deep, on the outside. This points downwards. In addition there are several smaller rectangular holes in the other three walls.

During the pre-launch checks the vehicle required its own electrical power and therefore contained additional batteries, which had to be kept fully charged by the vehicle's own charging system. The rear wall vent would allow the vehicle to charge its batteries from inside the garage with the doors closed, and the exhaust was removed via a flexible connection to the outside.

The entrance to the second parking area is 376 ft from the exit of the first and is on the opposite side of the road. The second parking area is further from the road, 51 ft, and, at 204 ft, it is longer than the first. As it is adjacent to the launching pad it was clearly intended for the rocket. The entrance and exit to this section are considerably wider than the first parking area, to ensure that the 50 ft

This disused rail loop on the Cherbourg Peninsula between Sottevast and La Haye du Puits runs adjacent to several V2 sites.

Meilerwagen and its towing vehicle could be manoeuvred. There is enough parking space here to accommodate three rockets if necessary, but it is unlikely that they would remain this close to the launching pad during the actual launch. Instead they would have been moved temporarily back up the hill.

The launching of three V2s per day from this type of site would represent a good day's work. If this rate was achieved at 50 sites, this would give a weekly total of 1,050 launches. This was unlikely to be realized in practice owing to the various problems that could arise, but it does indicate that a production programme of 2,000 standard V2s per month could have been launched from this type of site alone, if the rockets had been available.

To sum up, the sites at Villiers-Adam, Bergueneuse, Thiennes and those of the Rauville type were built for the storage, servicing and launching of the standard V2, fitted with a high-explosive warhead. All these simple sites were under construction at the same time as the complex sites. This is significant as it indicates that the intention was to have both types of weapons and their respective sites ready for use at approximately the same time.

CHAPTER EIGHT

The Allied Intelligence War

As early as November 1939, the Oslo Report, which had landed unsolicited on the desk of the British Embassador in Oslo, gave brief details of several secret German military projects and the locations of the establishments where the work was being carried out. Peenemünde was identified as the centre for top-secret work on long-range rockets and pilotless aircraft; mention was also made of work on two types of radar.

For several reasons, the report was filed and no real attempt made to take it any further. For the next three years the file slowly grew, filled mainly with unconfirmed reports from agents in the occupied countries.

The first photographs of Peenemünde were taken by accident on 15 May 1942. A Photo Reconnaissance Unit (PRU) Spitfire on its way back from Kiel with some unexposed film overflew the island of Usedom and, noticing the new airfield and general signs of frantic activity, took a few shots of the area. Back at RAF Medmenham, (home of the Central Interpretation Unit, which later became the Allied Central Interpretation Unit (ACIU)) the prints were studied and the construction work noted. The report was then filed away and no further action taken.

From 1942 onwards, the rapid expansion at Peenemünde, especially of personnel (over 20,000), put a strain on the security arrangements. In addition the shortage of highly qualified and skilled staff meant that the rule that only German nationals should be employed had to be relaxed; engineers and scientists, without their dependants, were brought in from the occupied countries, and security lapses were inevitable. A prisoner-of-war camp was also built for specially selected and screened prisoners, to assist in the more mundane and manual tasks around the site.

By the end of 1942, there was a regular flow of reports from agents into the London headquarters of MI6. Peenemünde was frequently mentioned. Since the first successful V2 launch on 3 October 1942, launches were taking place at regular intervals, the trajectory taking it 200 miles down the Baltic coast, and this could not easily be kept secret. Neither could the sonic 'boom', as the V2 passed through the sound barrier on its way back to earth. By January 1943 the number of reports from agents, and the evidence from photo-reconnaissance, had reached such proportions that General Nye, Vice-Chief of the General Staff, arranged for the circulation of an up-to-date report on German rocket and secret weapon development. Cabinet Ministers were shown this paper, and on 12 April the Prime Minister, Winston Churchill, was apprised of the investigations being carried out. It was clear that the full extent of the threat needed to be determined, and based on the recommendations of the chiefs of staff to appoint a co-ordinator, the following week Churchill assigned his son-in-law, Duncan Sandys, to the post.

Sandys, an Army colonel with some knowledge of artillery and ballistics, had injured his feet in a motoring accident. His military career over, he had returned to parliament as an MP and Churchill had appointed him to a post at the Ministry of Supply. This was responsible for the research, development and production of weapons, and Sandys was therefore ideally placed to be put in charge of the new investigation. From the very start, however, personality problems developed, and these very nearly ensured that the German rocket threat was never taken seriously.

From his political wilderness of the 1930s, Churchill had brought with him friends and confidants who had supported him. When he had been made Prime Minister, he had rewarded them with posts in his new government. Some of these people resented the personal confidences now shared with his 35-year-old son-in-law. When Sandys started putting together a report his foes were presented with an ideal opportunity to discredit him.

Secret agents are rarely technically trained to make objective reports and the size of the rockets often varied according to the agent's imagination. Another problem was that rocket development in the UK, as in the USA and elsewhere, had not progressed beyond small, solid-fuel, unguided anti-aircraft rockets. Consequently, when Sandys' first reports of launchings from Peenemünde mentioned 100 ft rockets, weighing 60 tons, the scepticism increased.

Nevertheless, one of Sandys' first tasks was to pay a visit to RAF Medmenham to see for himself the photographic evidence. On 9 May 1943 he spent the day looking at the photographic records of Peenemünde and the surrounding area and on his return to London, he requested further detailed coverage of the site. In June Peenemünde was visited four times by PRU Spitfires and Mosquitoes and each time, the photographs produced pieces of the jigsaw that was beginning to take shape.

At the Air Ministry branch of MI6 the task of collating and assessing the various agents' reports was entrusted to a young scientist, Dr R.V. Jones. This turned out to be a wise choice. Dr Jones had already established his reputation in 1940 for his work on the use by the Luftwaffe of radio beams. His insistence, against overwhelming scientific opinion, that the use of radio beams over the long distances between Germany and England was possible as a means of guiding bombers to the target, had resulted in the resignation of Sir Henry Tizard, Chief Scientific Adviser to the Air Ministry, who had been the main opponent to Jones' theory.

Sandys' first generally circulated report was produced on 14 May 1943 and from a combination of agents' reports, information from Dr Jones and the

Peenemünde photographs, he concluded that a large rocket actually existed. After the results of the latest Peenemünde photographs had been collated, a more detailed report on 28 June provided even stronger evidence of the rocket's existence; on the latest prints several rocket-like objects were clearly visible. Added to this evidence were reports from the bugged conversations of several captured high-ranking German officers who had referred to experiments with large rockets.

Now that Sandys believed the rocket threat was real, he requested that PRU flights should be carried out over the whole of northern France, within a 200 mile range of London, Photographs of any large new buildings, especially if they were served by rail, were to receive detailed attention from the ACIU experts at Medmenham. Almost immediately, a report came through to Sandys about a suspicious new concrete structure near Watten, a few miles inland from Calais.

The report of 28 June was discussed by Churchill and the Defence Committee (Operations) the next day. Among those present at this meeting were Sandys, Jones, Lord Cherwell (Churchill's chief scientific adviser) and Dr A.D. Crow, Director General of Projectiles at the Ministry of Supply.

Cherwell played an important part in trying to discredit the rocket theory. Born in 1886 at Baden-Baden, Germany, he was brought up at Sidmouth in Devon and educated at Berlin University and the Sorbonne. His work on the thermal effects in the new science of nuclear reactions attracted worldwide recognition. In 1914 he became Director of the RAE Physical Laboratory, Farnborough, and in 1919 he was made Professor of Experimental Philosophy at Oxford. As Professor Lindemann he made the Clarendon Laboratory the centre of low temperature research in the UK. He became a close friend of Churchill during his wilderness years, and Lindemann obviously enjoyed the political fringe and the aristocratic circles in which Churchill moved. Churchill was also impressed by Lindemann's ability to explain complicated scientific ideas in simple terms and relate them to everyday facts of life. Lindemann benefited from Churchill's appointment as Prime Minister, becoming his Chief Scientific Adviser in 1940; he was created a baron in 1941 and was Paymaster General from 1942 to 1945 – a job of considerable power and influence.

From his own knowledge of rockets he regarded Sandys' attempts to prove the existence of revolutionary German weapons with the utmost scepticism. Even with rocket-like objects clearly in view at Peenemünde, Cherwell, supported by Crow, estimated that solid-fuel rockets weighing 60–100 tons would require huge launching installations in northern France, resembling the type used for a giant mortar. Nothing like this had been found so far, despite the enormous coverage by the PRU. The rocket-like objects were judged by Cherwell and Crow to be a massive hoax, and although Jones was able to provide evidence that Peenemünde now had the highest priority rating, it was assumed that the main purpose of the establishment was for the development of some type of radio-controlled bomb and research on jet aircraft.

Despite this 'expert' opinion, the meeting agreed to several actions. These were: an attack on Peenemünde by Bomber Command should be made as soon as possible; an extremely detailed photographic survey should be made of northern

France, covering a radius of 130 miles from London; the investigations should include not only rockets, but also remote-piloted and jet-propelled aircraft. On 17 August 1943, 597 aircraft of Bomber Command attacked Peenemünde. Forty failed to return, and on 27 August, 185 B-17 Flying Fortresses of the US 8th Air Force carried out a precision daylight raid on the large concrete construction project at Watten.

These raids were really only shots in the dark as there was no firm evidence as to the true purpose of Watten, and no connection had been established between Peenemünde and Watten. Nevertheless, the timing of the raids was significant for both the rocket work at Peenemünde and the progress at Watten.

By September 1943 the War Cabinet Defence Committee Operations (DCO) was labouring under the advice of two conflicting camps.

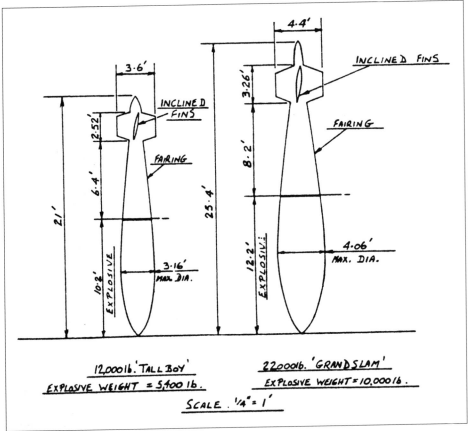

16. Details of Tallboy and Grand Slam (Earthquake) bombs as dropped on some of the complex V2 sites, including Watten. One of the bombs was carried by a specially modified Lancaster and to obtain the most destructive effect, the bombs were intended to impact on the target at the maximum possible speed. In the case of the Earthquake it was used on hardened targets, at supersonic speed.

One side was supported by the vast file of agents' and prisoners' reports, together with the photographs and their interpretation from the ACIU, and the opinion of Sandys and Jones. On the other side was the extremely influential technical knowledge of Cherwell and Crow, who maintained that a rocket of 60–100 tons would have to be at least 100 ft long and launched like a giant mortar, in which case the 45 ft objects photographed at Peenemünde could not possibly be genuine rockets.

In response, Sandys arranged an investigation to determine if it was possible to power a rocket by any means other than solid fuel. Experiments were being carried out in the USA on small liquid-fuelled rockets, and a Shell engineer, Isaac Lubbock, was ordered to return to the UK and report on trials using liquid oxygen and petrol as a fuel. At a meeting of the DCO on 25 October Lubbock was asked to give details of his first-hand knowledge of the American experiments with liquid rocket fuels. The discussion included the fact that for a large rocket, very high fuel-flow rates would be required; this would require a power unit capable of generating several thousand horsepower and yet be able to fit inside the relatively small diameter of the Peenemünde rockets. Cherwell estimated from the Peenemünde photographs that the diameter of the power unit would need to be no larger than 20 in, which was patently absurd. (The actual diameter of the blades of the V2's HTP fuel-pump turbine was 18.5 in and it developed over 4,000 hp.) Crow, backing up Cherwell as ever, suggested that the Peenemünde rockets were in fact barrage balloons!

Ultimately it was extremely fortunate for the Allies that such advice did not prevail. To have abandoned the investigation at that time would have been disastrous.

Despite this opposition the evidence that the Germans were planning some sort of missile attack on the UK was becoming irrefutable. Its exact form could not be determined and therefore all suspicious new concrete structures in northern France were to be bombed. By November 1943 a multiplicity of installations was appearing in northern France within a 130–200 mile radius of London. This included a site for the 'super-gun' or V3, at Mimoyecques near Cap Gris Nez. However, investigation was still being hampered by the belief that the rocket, weighing at least 60 tons and powered by cordite, must require at least two propulsion stages; therefore the launching installations would be massive with numerous rail links. Jones had also been trying to follow the movements, via agents and intercepted radio traffic, of the Luftnachrichten Versuchs Regiment, which specialized in radio and radar tracking. It was eventually established that the 14th Company of this regiment had moved to radar stations along the coast from Peenemünde, giving further credence to the rocket.

By October 1943 Churchill was apparently becoming tired of the scientific bickering that was still going on. He convened a meeting on 28 October to which Cabinet ministers, chiefs of staff, Cherwell, Sandys and his fuel experts were summoned, to determine finally the truth about the threat from long-range weapons. Cherwell again tried to convince everyone that the rocket threat was a myth, a 'mare's nest'. He still believed that it was impossible to design a device capable of pumping the huge amount of fuel required per second for a large liquid-fuelled rocket.

Lubbock and other engineers had re-examined the problem a few days earlier, in the light of the release of some details of Frank Whittle's work on gas turbines. The point was made at the meeting that the Germans might have perfected some type of gas turbine-driven pump.

Once the meeting accepted that such a device was possible, the main foundation of Cherwell's argument vanished and he abruptly left the meeting after refusing Churchill's offer to lead a committee to advise the War Cabinet on the progress of the missile threat. In his place Sir Stafford Cripps accepted the post and a few days later, after studying the available evidence, he advised Churchill that the threat of an attack by long-range missiles definitely existed.

As early as 29 September the German propaganda machine had been promising revenge for the mass bombing of its cities. Speer had publicly stated that retribution by a secret weapon would be carried out for these attacks. Together with various similar statements from other German leaders, the threat could not be ignored.

The ACIU experts at Medmenham were now engaged in a frantic search of northern France and after information from an agent about a new type of construction, eight examples were photographed. They were in fact the first of the V1 launching sites, although of course this was not known at the time. The main intelligence effort now shifted to this pilotless aeroplane, and though German activity in France seemed to have been stepped up, there were still no definite sightings of a rocket, other than the first Peenemünde photographs.

'Ski' launching sites (so called because the VI storage buildings resembled giant skis on their sides) were springing up at a frantic rate over most of northern France. By 10 November over 26 had been identified and other sites under construction were thought to be connected with the pilotless weapon. On 28 November another PRU flight over Peenemünde revealed a tiny, winged object at the base of one of the structures, which until then was thought to be part of a sewage system; it was now clear from its similarity with objects seen at the new sites in France that this structure was the launching ramp for what was to be known as the V1.

By December 1943 the number of confirmed V1 launching sites had increased to 96, while others were also thought to be connected with the V1. Bombing of these launching sites, supply sites and other structures continued on a regular basis and in fact some of the sites bombed were intended for rockets. By mid-July 1944 an average of 100 V1 launches per day were being made against the UK, and at that stage there appeared to be nothing left to discover about the V1. Instead, the main concern was to find and destroy the launching and storage sites as quickly as possible.

The emphasis of the intelligence effort now returned to the V2 as reports were still accumulating on the rocket threat. The situation changed dramatically at the end of September 1944 when a complete V2 was reconstructed at Farnborough from the remains of two rockets and parts from another. The remains of the first came from a V2 which had been launched from Peenemünde on 14 June to test the guidance system for the Wasserfall rocket. It suffered a control failure and landed 200 miles away in Sweden. The remains were obtained after clandestine negotiations with the Swedish government, which was wary of offending the Germans. The remains of the second were recovered by the Polish resistance from marshes next to the River Bug. These remains and pieces from several others were hidden until they could be flown to the UK by a Dakota on 26 July. These various parts enabled Farnborough to produce one almost complete V2, which provided answers to all the important questions concerning the V2's size, weight of warhead and method of propulsion, which had still not been completely resolved at the regular Defence Committee meetings.

In 1944 the rapid advance of the Allied armies in France and the capture of the French V1 sites resulted in a temporary halt to V1 launchings. This caused the intelligence advisers to the V1 Crossbow Committee to state that it was extremely unlikely that a rocket attack would develop. A week later on 8 September the first V2 launched from Holland landed on London.

Since 1943, with Himmler's growing interest in the rocket programme, a power struggle had been taking place to control the complete rocket project, especially the operational launches. Himmler and the SS, represented by Dr Kammler (now General Kammler), began to take control. General Fromm had been in charge of the rocket project, but after an assassination attempt on Hitler on 20 July 1944 he was implicated and arrested. Himmler now took over his position. Generals Heinemann and Metz, who originally were going to take control of the operational V2, disappeared from the scene.

With the whole of northern France under Allied control, including all the German rocket sites, the last stage in the V2 campaign moved to Holland, with General Kammler and SS launch teams now controlling all launches of the standard V2 from very simple sites in Holland. Between 8 September 1944 and 27 March 1945, Kammler and his three launch teams fired 1,346 V2s at UK targets, of which 1,115 were launched successfully. (There is still some dispute about how many V2s were actually launched from Holland.) The large proportion of failures, one in five, was partly due to the lack of permanent facilities at the launch sites, which usually consisted of a section of roadway. In addition, the urgency to launch the rockets as soon as possible reduced the effectiveness of the pre-launch checks, and the rockets, when they finally arrived in Holland, were in a poor state after a devious journey from Nordhausen. Despite the large number of launches from a relatively small area of Holland, the three launch batteries involved were hardly ever restricted in their activities by Allied air attack.

The intelligence effort against the rockets had from the very start adopted the wrong approach and it is amazing that any of the V2 sites in France were bombed at all. When the rocket campaign started in earnest, there must have been many in London who still believed it was a 'mare's nest'. This attitude, combined with the difficulty in locating the simple sites where launches were taking place, resulted in almost an unobstructed launch effort by General Kammler.

There were also problems with obtaining reliable information from Dutch resistance sources, as these had been almost completely infiltrated by the Germans. Indeed, the Germans labelled the Dutch Special Operations Executive (SOE) '*Der Englandspiel*'. As a result, agents sent from the UK were quickly arrested by the *Sicherheitspolizei* (German counter intelligence). The case of Huub Lauwers, who was arrested by the Germans and tricked into sending false messages to England, led to the capture of over 60 SOE agents and spelt disaster for many RAF crews taking part. Why the coded security check, omitted by Lauwers in his messages, was not picked up in London is unknown; the information is still classified.

The V2 offensive ended on 28 March 1945, when the launching batteries were withdrawn to Germany. They were finally surrendered to the American 9th Army on 9 May. Kammler disappeared but he was reported to have rejoined SS ground forces fighting the Russians in Romania and to have been shot by his adjutant to avoid capture.

In Appendix A are copies of Allied intelligence documents describing the offensive against the 'conventional' V2 in Holland. One last word on the Allied intelligence and photographic interpretation of the rocket and, in particular, the sites in France.

As has already been mentioned, many V2 sites including all those of the Rauville type were thought to be intended for the V1 flying bomb and were listed as such on AICU plan no. R/41, plotted on 30 August 1944, and which originated from the intelligence/interpretation headquarters at Medmenham House.

This plan of northern France and its accompanying list shows the location of some 204 sites, all stated to be V1 sites. The plan and list formed the basis of the bombing campaign against the V1, as it was the V1 which was thought to be the major threat; apart from the obvious ones like Watten, any V2 sites which were bombed were targeted by chance.

As this plan and its list have been used over the years as a standard reference on the V1 and V2 this has produced considerable misunderstanding about the rocket programme (and also the V1). It is true that the interpretation staff at Medmenham House were working under difficult conditions; as Cherwell and Crow, the two most influential rocket experts close to the Prime Minister, were convinced that the rocket was a myth, this attitude was bound to filter down.

From the grandiose plans first drawn up in the 1930s it was an ignominious end for the V2. But this was not the end of the story for Hitler's miracle weapon; it was only the end for a weapon that was never intended to play more than a supporting role to its more deadly companion.

CHAPTER NINE

The Complex Sites

BRÉCOURT

Brécourt is situated 3 miles west of Cherbourg and is half a mile inland. The site is in a small wooded ravine, backing on to a hillside. In the 1920s, the French Navy, like those of other modern countries, was converting its coal-fired warships to oil-burning. Cherbourg was then, and is still, a large naval base and it needed to be able to store a considerable amount of heavy oil for the ships. This storage had to be in a secure environment, protected from air attack, and also convenient for the base.

In 1926 tunnels were cut into the hillside at Brécourt and construction started on eight huge underground oil reservoirs (the last two were never finished). As can be seen from fig. 9, they are approximately 240 ft long, 50 ft wide and 46 ft deep, and are made of concrete with steel liners. The whole underground system was connected by tunnels for personnel and equipment.

The site is still under the control of the French Navy, although oil is now stored in tanks above ground, inside the actual naval base, and there is a high security fence around the area. With the permission of Admiral Canonne, the naval commander at Cherbourg, I was shown around the site, including reservoir 3 and the adjacent tunnels.

The Germans arrived in Cherbourg shortly after the French capitulation in June 1940 and although Brécourt had already been superseded as an oil-storage depot, the possibilities of other uses for the underground workings must have been obvious. It is not surprising, therefore, that when suitable sites for the V weapons were being investigated, Brécourt was chosen on the basis that most of the excavation had already been done. Originally the site was intended only for rockets, but this was later amended to include the V1.

Internally, the original oil-storage depot was converted as follows. Reservoirs 1–6 remained unchanged, while reservoirs 7 and 8 were modified to provide workshops (7) and offices (8) for the personnel. The entrances into the hillside for reservoirs 1–3 were augmented by additional doors – the original French doors were left in place and 30 ft from each entrance a recess was constructed for a massive steel and concrete sliding door, 12 ft thick. Now only the recesses remain. It is likely that the remaining reservoir entrances were also intended to have similar doors.

The various connecting tunnels and other underground rooms were intended for the storage of rockets, fuel, oxygen production and other necessary facilities.

Brécourt complex site: the unfinished vent to direct rocket exhaust upwards at 45°.

Supplies of rockets, equipment and other materials were to be brought in via a spur off the main line from Cherbourg; this ran along the coast a few hundred yards away, and the remains of it can still be seen on the site. Each of the original reservoir entrances, together with some of the underground workings, were served by a 24 in narrow gauge railway, most of which is still in place. The actual rocket-launching facility, as shown in fig. 9, was not completed, but enough was finished to indicate what the finished site would have looked like.

From photographs taken in 1945 and 1946, and from inspection, it is clear that there is an additional storey (H) missing from the main building. There are the remains of vertical, steel reinforcement bars, evident in the earlier photographs, and there are two large rectangular openings, obviously intended for stairwells. This additional storey was most likely intended for equipment associated with the launch.

A description of the facility is as follows. The V2 would emerge from the workshops and service area at (A), where it would be given an initial pre-launch check. As can be seen from the small plan (bottom right of fig. 9), the rocket exit is connected to the original reservoir 7, via a tunnel, which is now blocked off. There would be a temporary weatherproof cover over (A) and as the rocket emerged horizontally, equipment would have been provided to rotate the V2 into a vertical position for launch at (B).

From the dimensions of the area from (A) through to (B), it is virtually certain that rockets of only the size of the V2 were intended to be launched. The launching pad, (B), where the rocket would also be fuelled and all the pre-launch

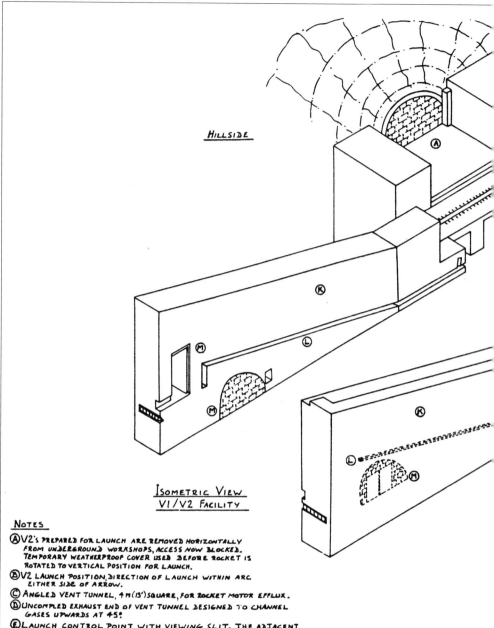

HILLSIDE

Ⓐ

Ⓚ

Ⓜ

Ⓛ

Ⓜ

Ⓚ

Ⓛ

Ⓜ

ISOMETRIC VIEW
VI/V2 FACILITY

NOT BUILT

NOTES

Ⓐ V2's PREPARED FOR LAUNCH ARE REMOVED HORIZONTALLY FROM UNDERGROUND WORKSHOPS, ACCESS NOW BLOCKED. TEMPORARY WEATHERPROOF COVER USED BEFORE ROCKET IS ROTATED TO VERTICAL POSITION FOR LAUNCH.

Ⓑ V2 LAUNCH POSITION, DIRECTION OF LAUNCH WITHIN ARC EITHER SIDE OF ARROW.

Ⓒ ANGLED VENT TUNNEL, 4M (13') SQUARE, FOR ROCKET MOTOR EFFLUX.

Ⓓ UNCOMPLETED EXHAUST END OF VENT TUNNEL DESIGNED TO CHANNEL GASES UPWARDS AT 45°.

Ⓔ LAUNCH CONTROL POINT WITH VIEWING SLIT. THE ADJACENT DOORWAY HAS BEEN BLOCKED BUT DOOR ON OPPOSITE SIDE OF VENT TUNNEL IS STEEL, 2" THICK.

Ⓕ ACCESS FOR ROCKET FUEL SUPPLIES AND TEST EQUIPMENT. ALSO USED FOR VI TRANSFER TO LAUNCHING RAMP. CONNECTED TO SAME TUNNEL SYSTEM AS Ⓐ.

Ⓖ TO ENSURE V2 MOTOR GASES EXHAUST ALONG VENT TUNNEL Ⓒ THE FRONT AND SIDE Ⓐ OF THE LAUNCH PAD WOULD REQUIRE ENCLOSING BY A MOVABLE SHIELD, HENCE SLOTS FOR STEEL ROLLER SHUTTER.

Ⓗ CONTEMPORARY PHOTOGRAPHS AND REMAINS OF VERTICAL REINFORCING BARS INDICATE THAT ANOTHER LEVEL WAS TO BE ADDED TO THE EXISTING BUILDING.

Ⓙ ACCESS STAIRWELLS FOR PROJECTED UPPER LEVEL.

Ⓚ BLAST WALLS FOR VI LAUNCHING RAMP. THE ENDS OF THE RAMP ARE 4M WIDE 8M HIGH AND 7M APART, TOTAL RAMP LENGH 50M.

Ⓛ SLOTS IN BLAST WALLS TO SUPPORT VI LAUNCHING RAMP STRUCTURE.

Ⓜ ENTRANCES TO INTERIOR OF BLAST WALLS.

SITE IS WITHIN 5 MILES OF CENTRE OF CHERBOURG.

9. *Brécourt complex V2 storage, servicing and launching site for modified V2s, which was also capable of launching standard V2s and possibly larger rocket developments. Modified later to*

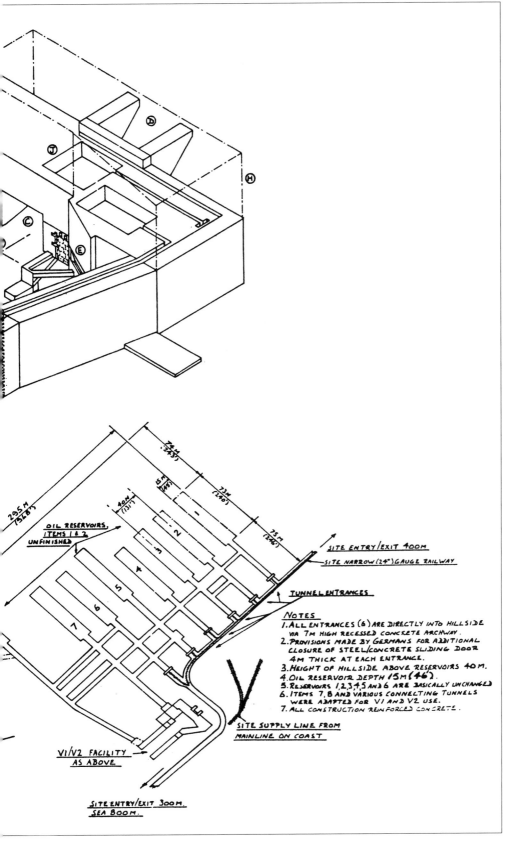

OIL RESERVOIRS,
ITEMS 1 & 2
UNFINISHED

SITE ENTRY/EXIT 400M

SITE NARROW (24") GAUGE RAILWAY

TUNNEL ENTRANCES

NOTES
1. ALL ENTRANCES (6) ARE DIRECTLY INTO HILLSIDE
VIA 7M HIGH RECESSED CONCRETE ARCHWAY.
2. PROVISIONS MADE BY GERMANS FOR ADDITIONAL
CLOSURE OF STEEL/CONCRETE SLIDING DOOR
4M THICK AT EACH ENTRANCE.
3. HEIGHT OF HILLSIDE ABOVE RESERVOIRS 40M.
4. OIL RESERVOIR DEPTH 15M (46').
5. RESERVOIRS 1,2,3,4,5 AND 6 ARE BASICALLY UNCHANGED
6. ITEMS 7, 8 AND VARIOUS CONNECTING TUNNELS
WERE ADAPTED FOR VI AND V2 USE.
7. ALL CONSTRUCTION REINFORCED CONCRETE.

SITE SUPPLY LINE FROM
MAINLINE ON COAST

VI/V2 FACILITY
AS ABOVE

SITE ENTRY/EXIT 300M.
SEA BOOM.

provide similar facilities for V1. Original underground facility was French Navy oil storage depot.

Brécourt: the end of the V1 launching ramp looking towards the V2 launch area and vent tunnel.

checks carried out, is enclosed on three sides by the building. The feature from (C) through to (D) is extremely innovative. The V2 exhaust gases had a velocity of 7,000 ft per second and a temperature of 2,000°C at maximum thrust. Although a deflector could be fitted, the very high temperature and velocity of this gas, together with the presence of solid particles in the combustion gases, has a very abrasive effect; this causes problems to adjacent equipment.

At Brécourt a novel solution was adopted. A sloping exhaust-vent tunnel was provided, (C), with an exit, (D) (which was uncompleted). The problem of the exhaust efflux from rocket motors increases with the size of the rocket. Twenty-five years after the conversion of Brécourt, a similar solution was adopted for the Blue Streak/Europa launching pad (the UK's last real involvement with space exploration and satellites), at Woomera, South Australia. There the launching pad was positioned on the edge of a 50 ft precipice and a curved tunnel was built from the pad, exiting near the bottom of the cliff wall. The exhaust gases shot out horizontally along the floor of the valley. This conveniently removed the exhaust problem, but unfortunately for the wildlife at least one unsuspecting kangaroo experienced the hot gases firsthand.

The V2 would have been fuelled at (F), as the site had its own underground oxygen production and fuel storage. The launch control is located at (E), only a few feet from the launching pad, and a viewing port is provided. One essential piece of equipment that is missing is some means of sealing off the building opposite (C), to ensure that the exhaust gases were channelled along the vent tunnel.

Brécourt: the view from the top of the structure looking at the hillside underground workings (originally oil storage).

The slots at (G) were probably intended for a flexible steel curtain; the long slot on the opposite side would have been able to accommodate a device like a steel roller shutter which came right across in front of the launching pad. By this means, the complete area in front of the rocket would have been blanked off.

Access to the V2 launch building is still possible and underground there is extensive space, which is now flooded. There was certainly ample scope for the preparation and storage of radioactive material, both in the original tunnels and the later German additions. There would also have been ample room for the secure preparation of the type of nuclear reactor referred to later, if it was intended to produce radioactive isotopes on site.

Shown above and on page 80 are various features of the facility. The first photograph is a view taken from the top of the V1 blast walls, looking back towards the hillside, with the reservoir entrances on the left. On the ground, to the right, can be seen the remains of the spur line from the coastal main line. The second picture, taken further to the left, shows the entrance to the exhaust tunnel vent (centre) and the rocket exit from storage, etc. (left). The third photograph gives a complete view of the rocket exit from the tunnel complex. The concrete beams across the roof are a recent safety measure to prevent anyone at the top

Brécourt: the rocket launching area and the entrance to the exhaust vent tunnel.

Brécourt: the rocket exit (now blocked) from the modified oil-storage underground workings.

Brécourt: the end of the blast walls added to accommodate the V1 launching ramp.

falling into the open bay. Originally there would have been a temporary weatherproof cover over the exit bay, which would be removed as the rocket was rotated into the vertical position, before being installed on the launching pad.

The blast walls (K) were added when the site was modified to handle V1s. The V1 would be launched between the blast walls, with the ramp structure attached to the slots at (L). Apparently a second V2/V1 launch facility was planned. This would have been connected by a tunnel to reservoir 8, but it was never started.

The site never became operational and it is unfortunate that virtually the only hardware remaining is a 2 in-thick steel door, adjacent to the launching pad (pictured on page 80). There are some plans of the site in the German archives but these do not give any indication of the equipment that was to be fitted.

SILOS

Compared to the massive visual impact of Watten and the ingenuity of other complex sites, the silos near Cherbourg appear much too unobtrusive and inoffensive to be part of a weapons system with such horrendous destructive capabilities. Yet despite the lack of obvious concrete structures, the site provides perhaps the most important piece in the jigsaw.

The postwar German archives at Koblenz and Freiburg have nothing in their records about the silos. If the real vengeance weapon had been a standard V2 with a high-explosive warhead, then an argument, albeit a very weak one, could have

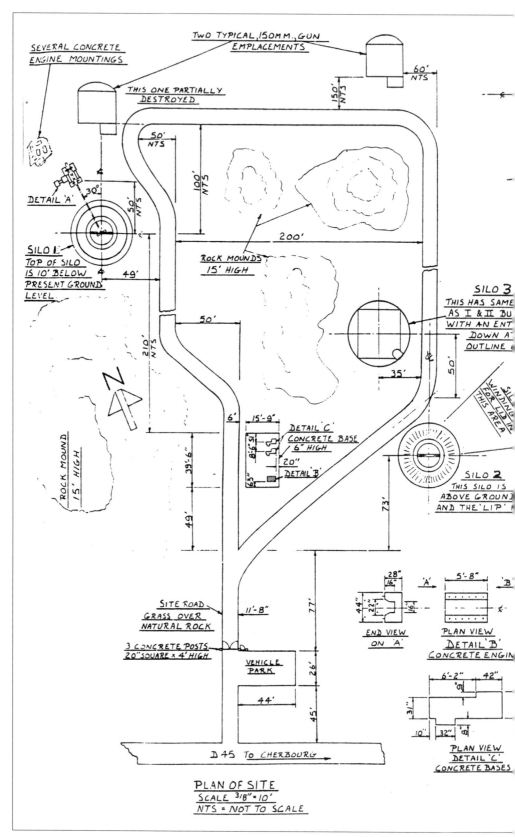

SEVERAL CONCRETE
ENGINE MOUNTINGS

TWO TYPICAL 150MM GUN
EMPLACEMENTS

THIS ONE PARTIALLY
DESTROYED

60'
NTS

150'
NTS

50'
NTS

100'
NTS

DETAIL 'A'

30°

50'
NTS

SILO 1
TOP OF SILO
IS 10' BELOW
PRESENT GROUND
LEVEL

49'

ROCK MOUNDS
15' HIGH

200'

SILO 3
THIS HAS SAME
AS I & II BU
WITH AN ENT
DOWN A
OUTLINE

50'

SILO
WINDING
FOR LIP IN
THIS AREA

50'

35'

SILO 2
THIS SILO IS
ABOVE GROUN
AND THE 'LIP'

210'
NTS

N

ROCK MOUND
15' HIGH

39'6"

6'

15'-9"

DETAIL 'C'
CONCRETE BASE
6" HIGH

5'-9"

20"
DETAIL 'B'

63"

49'

73'

77'

28"
16"

4"
22"

'A'

16"

END VIEW
ON 'A'

5'-8"

'B'

PLAN VIEW
DETAIL 'B'
CONCRETE ENGIN

SITE ROAD
GRASS OVER
NATURAL ROCK

11'-8"

3 CONCRETE POSTS
20" SQUARE x 4' HIGH

VEHICLE
PARK

26'

6'-2"

42"

3"

10"   32"

PLAN VIEW
DETAIL 'C'
CONCRETE BASES

44'

45'

D 45 TO CHERBOURG

PLAN OF SITE
SCALE 3/8" = 10'
NTS = NOT TO SCALE

10. Silos for launching modified V2s. One silo is complete except for the lid; the second silo is
80 per cent complete; the third silo is roofed over and used for administration, equipment, etc.

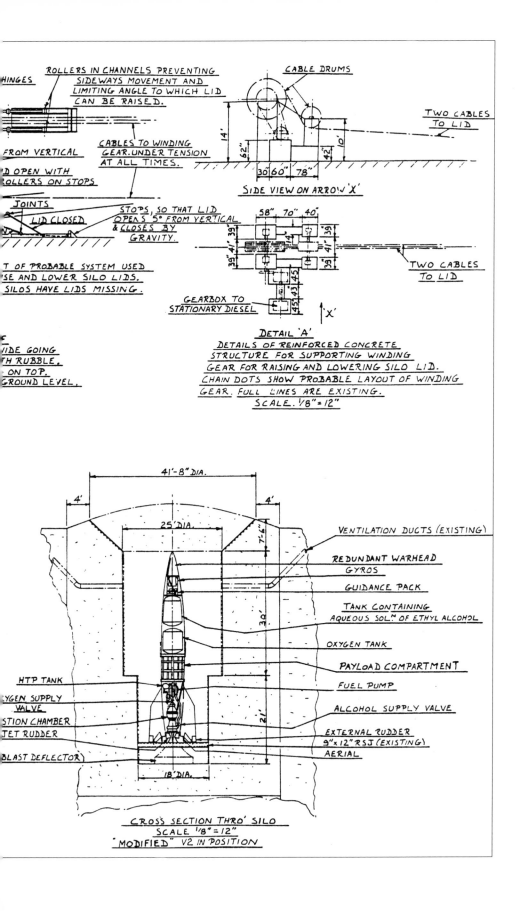

HINGES

ROLLERS IN CHANNELS PREVENTING SIDEWAYS MOVEMENT AND LIMITING ANGLE TO WHICH LID CAN BE RAISED.

CABLE DRUMS

TWO CABLES TO LID

FROM VERTICAL

CABLES TO WINDING GEAR. UNDER TENSION AT ALL TIMES.

D OPEN WITH ROLLERS ON STOPS

14'

62"

42"

10'

30" 60" 78"

SIDE VIEW ON ARROW 'X'

JOINTS

LID CLOSED

STOPS, SO THAT LID OPENS 5° FROM VERTICAL & CLOSES BY GRAVITY.

58" 70" 40"

39' 41' 39'

39' 41' 39'

TWO CABLES TO LID

T OF PROBABLE SYSTEM USED SE AND LOWER SILO LIDS. SILOS HAVE LIDS MISSING.

GEARBOX TO STATIONARY DIESEL

45 43 45

'X'

DETAIL 'A'
DETAILS OF REINFORCED CONCRETE STRUCTURE FOR SUPPORTING WINDING GEAR FOR RAISING AND LOWERING SILO LID. CHAIN DOTS SHOW PROBABLE LAYOUT OF WINDING GEAR. FULL LINES ARE EXISTING.
SCALE. 1/8" = 12"

IDE GOING TH RUBBLE, ON TOP. GROUND LEVEL,

41'-8" DIA.

4'

25' DIA.

7'-6"

4'

VENTILATION DUCTS (EXISTING)

REDUNDANT WARHEAD

GYROS

GUIDANCE PACK

30'

TANK CONTAINING AQUEOUS SOL.ⁿ OF ETHYL ALCOHOL

OXYGEN TANK

PAYLOAD COMPARTMENT

HTP TANK

FUEL PUMP

YGEN SUPPLY VALVE

ALCOHOL SUPPLY VALVE

STION CHAMBER

EXTERNAL RUDDER

JET RUDDER

9" x 12" RSJ (EXISTING)

BLAST DEFLECTOR)

AERIAL

21'

18' DIA.

CROSS SECTION THRO' SILO
SCALE 1/8" = 12"
"MODIFIED" V2 IN POSITION

been put forward that the complex sites, with their huge concrete structures, just might have been built to provide the ultimate in protection for the weapon and still have the capability of carrying out a considerable launching programme. The silos also provided a virtually bombproof facility, but there the similarity ends.

There are three silos on the site, two for rockets and one as a control centre, as shown in fig. 10. They are 51 ft deep and 25 ft in diameter. Each silo held only one V2, and once fired, the rocket would take hours, possibly all day, to replace. It has already been shown from the descriptions of the simple sites, especially the Rauville type, that for the V2 the minimum requirement was a concrete pad, of which the latitude and longitude were accurately known, and somewhere to park all the vehicles. Why, therefore, go to the immense effort of building two concrete silos, each capable of holding only one rocket, unless that rocket was something very special?

The silos are situated on the coast, 7 miles west of Cherbourg and only 4 miles from Brécourt. From local information it seems that construction was started in 1942 and the site was never completed.

This part of the Cherbourg Peninsula is sparsely populated, and in 1942, because of the German occupation, the whole area could be isolated quite easily from the rest of France. Cherbourg itself was designated a fortress under the command of General von Schlieben, and two infantry divisions (243rd and 709th) and one motorized division (91st) were based there. Totalling some 50,000 troops, they had the task of maintaining security on the peninsula. This provided security for the large number of sites that were built close to Cherbourg.

The precise location of the site is 100 yd from the sea, on the edge of 200 ft-high cliffs. The ground is solid granite, and this rock foundation removed the necessity for the usual concrete site roads; it also improved the structural integrity of the silos themselves. The D45 from Cherbourg to Cap de la Hague passes within yards of one of the silos and as there is no natural camouflage this would suggest that a satisfactory security system existed.

Only 45 ft from the road is the vehicle park. Measuring 44 ft x 26 ft it was just large enough to accommodate two V2s on trailers, side by side. At the left corner of the parking area is the entrance to the site. Until recently access was easy, but there is now a high security fence and the area is under the control of the Cherbourg naval authorities.

On entering the site, the road divides after 77 ft, forming a loop; the right-hand branch passes silo 2 on the right, and then on the left silo 3, which is roofed over. The left-hand loop carries straight on, passing a concrete foundation, 39 ft x 16 ft, on the right. This foundation has the remains of three mountings for stationary generators, which provided power to the site during construction. Approximately 210 ft further on the left the road passes silo 1, 20 ft below the road level and hidden by gorse bushes. The road then bends to the right, to complete the loop.

There are two V2 silos. One is complete (1) and on the other (2) the lip is unfinished. There is a third silo, in between, but although it has the same diameter as the others, it has a solid concrete roof with a single 7 ft wide entrance,

Silos: silo 2, unfinished.

which inclines downwards into the interior and is now blocked up. This would have been intended for the rocket test and launch equipment, as well as secure quarters for the site personnel. All three silos are made of reinforced concrete and have an outer diameter of 48 ft 8 in. The two V2 silos have a maximum inner diameter of 25 ft and an internal height just sufficient for a V2. The top of silo 2 is 8 ft above the ground; silo 1 stands 20 ft below road level and silo 3 is at ground level. The two V2 silos have chamfered top edges at 45° to accommodate the dome-shaped lid, whose thickness is estimated to have varied from 7 ft to 12 ft at the centre.

There is no sign of the lids, but there is still a structure, built 50 ft from silo 1, for mounting the machinery for raising and lowering the lid, like a giant clam. This is a rather vulnerable solution to the lid problem, as all the lid machinery was above ground and exposed to air attack. It contrasts with the modern ICBM silos, whose lids are in two halves and are actuated from inside the silo.

There are no signs of any foundations of buildings above ground and so all the personnel must have been accommodated inside silo 3, leaving almost nothing above ground to indicate the site's purpose. There is also no evidence of bomb damage or craters at the site or the surrounding area and therefore it appears that the site never received any attention from Allied bombers. This is a little surprising as in 1943 Churchill's Bodyline Committee was investigating Hitler's secret weapon threat. Cherwell and Crow had reluctantly put forward the idea that if it did exist, it would have to be launched like a giant mortar. In March

1943, therefore, the PRU effort was ordered to cover the whole of northern France, in an attempt to discover anything of recent construction that resembled a 100 ft-long tube, inclined or buried in the ground and served by a railway spur. This futile search continued on until November 1943 when the first V1 sites were identified, and emphasis then switched to the V1. However, it is surprising that the silos were not mistakenly identified as Cherwell and Crow's giant mortars.

On the very edge of the cliffs, overlooking the sea, are two 150 mm gun emplacements, one of which has been damaged by a large-calibre shell. It is unlikely that these guns were intended to protect the site against seaborne attack. The most probable reasons for their presence were to form part of the Cherbourg defences, which are fairly numerous along the coast, and to disguise the true purpose of the site.

The Germans were well aware of the activities of the lone Spitfires and Mosquitoes that regularly flew over at heights varying from sea level to 25,000 ft, and with enough radar warning they were sometimes shot down. But this photo-reconnaissance had to be endured, and where possible it became a game of bluff and double bluff. There were dozens of gun batteries along the Channel coast and they certainly did not warrant individual attention from Allied bombers. Therefore two or three 25 ft-diameter excavations a few yards behind a typical battery would not arouse much interest from the intelligence officers back at RAF Medmenham. In this case, the bluff seems to have worked.

Unlike other complex sites the silos were not supplied with a direct rail link. The nearest railway was the coast line which ended near Brécourt and this supports the theory that this site was not intended to be used for regular launchings. The rockets, fuel and equipment had to be carried by road and the D45 is certainly not suitable for regular traffic of long, cumbersome loads.

With a rocket arriving by road and the limited access to the silos, it certainly would not be an easy task to lift a V2 into a silo; indeed it might well take all day. One of the problems would be the inexperience of the personnel; in spite of the use of dummy rockets to practice the operation, the infrequent launches from the site would mean that personnel would lose their expertise very quickly, leading to delays with reloading.

Judging by the structure adjacent to silo 1, the device for raising and lowering the silo lid would have comprised a 10–15 ft-diameter cable drum, with a stationary engine providing power. Although it was vulnerable it would have provided a fairly rapid means of operating the lid. The diameter of the silos narrows to 18 ft at a height from the floor of 21 ft. This would allow a platform to be installed for working on the payload compartment of the modified V2, and, with an extension, work could also be done on the fuel tanks, control and instrumentation bay as well as the redundant warhead compartment, where there were weights to be added.

Silo 3 would have been used by the site personnel for fuel storage and for the test equipment. Covered over with soil, it would eventually have been undetectable from the air, while the V2 silos would be only slightly less so, when their lids were camouflaged.

The importance of these silos in the German weapons programme cannot be over-emphasized, as they were the first examples of rocket silos. Later, there were the ICBM silos of America, Russia, France and China, which, in turn, were superseded by the mobile submarine deterrents of Polaris, Trident and their equivalent.

In 1958 (still pre-Polaris) the importance of silos as part of the American nuclear-deterrent system was emphasized in a USAF report on the ballistic missile. The problem of providing protection at an airbase for a manned-aircraft nuclear deterrent was considered to be impractical in terms of costs. As a result the only type of facility considered suitable to provide protection against the enemy's nuclear or conventional weapons was a hardened silo (embedded in concrete). By 1958 techniques had been developed for determining the effectiveness of silos against enemy attack.

These methods produced data relating to the effectiveness of the silo system, including the probabilities of: the enemy destroying any one missile; the survival of any one missile; the enemy knowing the location of the silo(s); a rocket being launched before the arrival of the enemy missile; the lethal radius of the enemy missile and the Circular Error Probability (CEP); the radius of the circle into which half the enemy's missiles arriving at the target might be expected to impact.

Among the assumptions made in this USAF study are some which are relevant to the Cherbourg silo site. For instance, for the V2 to be destroyed it must be assumed that: the enemy must know the location of the silo at the time he launches his attack; the V2 must not be launched before the arrival of the enemy missile; the enemy weapons must impact within a lethal radius of the silo. The report also indicates that, with a hardness value for the silo of 75 lb per square inch, and assuming the enemy missiles were 2,000 lb and 10,000 lb bombs, the lethal radius of these bombs would be 37 ft and 64 ft respectively. If several such sites had been built in France, the chances of them being knocked out by conventional bombs would have been almost zero.

The figure which was of more interest to the USAF in 1958 was the percentage of its missiles surviving an attack. A typical calculation for a system of several silo sites, each with five missiles per site, showed that around 86% of the US force would survive the attack. What has only recently been realized is that as weapons improved, this would be reflected in an improved accuracy, and with higher-yield warheads the silo would be completely redundant. For instance, the US Minuteman I ICBM of 1959 had a warhead of 1.3 megatons and a CEP of 1 mile, whereas the submarine-based Trident I of 1977 had a multiple warhead (unknown yield) with a CEP of 0.10 miles. The change from static hardened sites to mobile submarine launchers also resulted in a change in the rockets. In the early days of the silo ICBM's liquid fuel was preferred, partially as a result of wartime German work, but there were problems with long-term storage of some of the chemicals used and the time taken to refuel the rocket. In particular liquid oxygen was difficult to store at $-200°C$. The team at Peenemünde was working on this problem and with the Wasserfall, which was almost a half-scale V2, it was hoping to keep it fully fuelled, ready for launch for up to three months. This is very much what was required for the modified V2 in its silo.

As the reaction times of the modern ICBMs improved there was a slow change to solid fuel, which meant better storage and an almost instantaneous launch. The advent of submarine launchers meant that the problems with liquid fuels inside a submarine were not acceptable and solid fuel took over completely.

Returning to the Cherbourg silos, it is clear from the internal dimensions that they were intended for the modified V2 with the payload compartment, probably filled with radioactive material brought from Brécourt. This argument is reinforced by the fact that the ledge inside the silo is the same height as the payload compartment, as well as the low launch rate and the complete lack of any information from Peenemünde or in the archives.

In the world of the nuclear deterrent the silo would have been a considerable kudos point when the Peenemünde team was negotiating its terms for working in the USA. In the USA, Russia, France and China (they were even contemplated in the UK), it was the silo that was built to hold the new long-range nuclear rockets, not massive installations like those at Watten and Wizernes; they would have been too vulnerable to the new, accurate ICBMs, with their megaton warheads. Even now silo-based missiles still form a major part of each country's deterrent system.

COUVILLE AND SOTTEVAST

Sottevast and Couville are discussed together because of their many similarities and their proximity to each other (they are 5 miles apart). These two sites illustrate another facet of the wide range of innovation used when planning and building the complex sites. Those involved were starting with a blank sheet of paper and they had to provide operation facilities for rockets of up to 100 ft in length. In addition, protection had to be provided against bombing and this meant that the rockets had to be handled underground, but be brought to the surface for launching.

Couville is a small village, half a mile from the station on the main Paris–Cherbourg line. The actual site is 1½ miles from the village and 2½ miles from the railway, so communications were not the most obvious reason for choosing the location. The railway at Couville is on an embankment, making access even more difficult. As a result, a loop line was planned to serve the site, starting half a mile north of Couville and rejoining the track a mile further along. This was never finished. Apparently a siding containing 35 tracks was also started within the loop and this gives some idea of the site's importance.

To provide sand for the concrete a quarry was opened adjacent to the station, and a narrow gauge track was laid along the D22 to the site. The combination of poor site access and what must have been a fairly relaxed building programme meant that construction was not very far advanced when the first Allied bombing raid took place on 11 November 1943.

It was a quirk of fate that the initial stages of the work resulted in two long parallel walls, 28 ft apart, which from the air must have resembled a V1 launching ramp. It must have caused Allied intelligence some confusion as it had no rail connections. The 'ramp' was not in alignment with London or any other British city and there were no other buildings of note which might have suggested that it was a V1 site. However, it was obviously a large construction project and as such it was included in the list of targets. The bombing raid was the end as far as construction was concerned. The site offices and buildings were destroyed, together with 60% of the material and 30% of the partially completed work. After this, construction was abandoned but it was decided to create the illusion that it was still important. A large AA flak battery was installed by the Luftwaffe and casual work continued. The ruse attracted Allied bombing raids for several weeks before the site was finally abandoned in 1944.

As can be seen in fig. 11, the main part remaining is two low walls 28 ft apart, 515 ft long, 4 ft 7 in wide and 8 ft high, and these were intended to be the supporting walls for the main building. How much of the walls are underground cannot be determined but, as at Sottevast, there would be enough headroom for a V2 standing vertical.

At the north-west corner of the walls the site is overgrown with a dense jungle of gorse, brambles and young trees, making access impossible, but there is enough room for another short leg of an 'L' (as item 2 at Sottevast).

The photograph shows the above-ground remains of the walls. The far south-east end of the right-hand wall has been damaged by the bombing.

At the other end of the site, on the edge of the overgrown area, are the remains of a thin-skinned concrete building, probably part of the offices destroyed in the first raid.

While the plans for Couville were never realized, less than 5 miles away is a 'sister' site that fared a lot better. Sottevast is 9 miles north-west of Valognes, in a wooded valley pierced by the railway, the D50 and a tributary of the river Douve. The site itself is about half a mile from the village. Construction started slightly earlier than at Couville and it is much closer to completion. This is because it was realized that with Allied bombing going on it was impossible to complete two sites, and hence only the more advanced of the two was continued. Sottevast also had the advantage of having existing sidings and a nearby quarry.

Construction started in early 1943. There had been little bombing and an air-raid siren had been placed on the top of a concrete shelter. There were only one or two filled-in craters and minor damage to the end of the long 'leg' (item 1 on fig. 10).

Approaching from the south-east, the main building is like a giant 'L' laid on its side; the legs are 600 ft and 190 ft long, enclosing a concrete parking area of 263 ft x 127 ft. There is no access above ground; the rockets came from the sidings at Sottevast via the site narrow gauge railway and entered the main building via a vertical shaft at the end of the shorter leg. The entrance shaft is 40 ft x 37 ft, now roofed over with concrete beams, and makes an opening on the other side of the leg. The short leg varies in height from 14 ft on the inside of the 'L' to 20 ft on the outside and is 16 ft wide.

Inside the 21 ft-wide entrance of the shaft, the concrete on both sides disappears into the ground, and according to a local farmer the shaft was originally '30–40 m' deep.

On the inside of the opening, pointing back down the leg, are two rectangular slots, 32 in x 21 in, 5 ft 6 in apart and extending approximately 30 ft into the leg. These slots must have been intended for part of the lifting gear for either a door

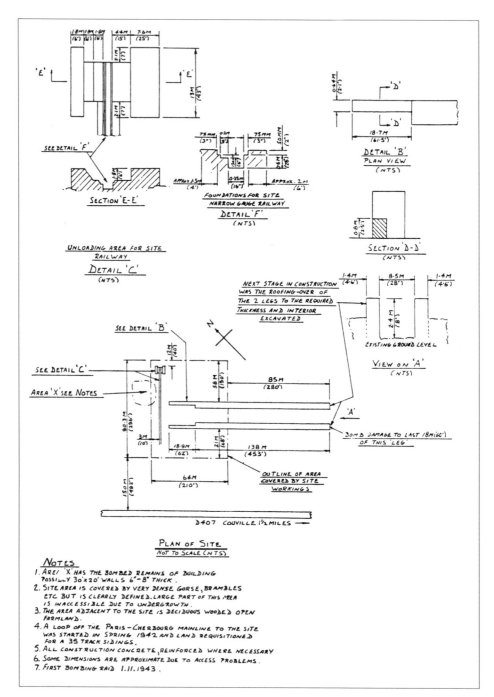

11. Couville and Sottevast modified V2 storage and servicing site with possible launch capability. All facilities were well protected and suitable for nuclear material. Sottevast is 70 per cent complete, Couville is 30 per cent.

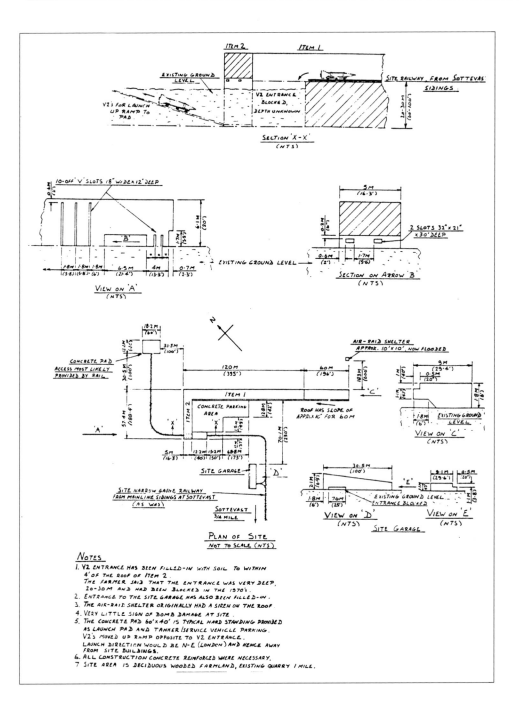

NOTES

1. V2 ENTRANCE HAS BEEN FILLED-IN WITH SOIL TO WITHIN 4' OF THE ROOF OF ITEM 2.
   THE FARMER SAID THAT THE ENTRANCE WAS VERY DEEP, 20-30M AND HAD BEEN BLOCKED IN THE 1970's.
2. ENTRANCE TO THE SITE GARAGE HAS ALSO BEEN FILLED-IN.
3. THE AIR-RAID SHELTER ORIGINALLY HAD A SIREN ON THE ROOF.
4. VERY LITTLE SIGN OF BOMB DAMAGE AT SITE.
5. THE CONCRETE PAD 60'x40' IS TYPICAL HARD STANDING PROVIDED AS LAUNCH PAD AND TANKER / SERVICE VEHICLE PARKING.
   V2's MOVED UP RAMP OPPOSITE TO V2 ENTRANCE.
   LAUNCH DIRECTION WOULD BE N-E (LONDON) AND HENCE AWAY FROM SITE BUILDINGS.
6. ALL CONSTRUCTION CONCRETE REINFORCED WHERE NECESSARY.
7. SITE AREA IS DECIDUOUS WOODED FARMLAND, EXISTING QUARRY 1 MILE.

Couville complex site: one of the main supporting walls for the roof (missing).

Couville: the concrete foundations for the site narrow gauge railway.

(remains of which are hidden under the soil) and/or the rockets as they were lowered into the bunker.

Other constructional details of the short leg are steel reinforcing bars which protrude above the rocket entrance shaft, indicating that an extension or cover was meant to be added over the entrance, and on the opposite side there are eight vertical V-shaped recesses 18 in wide and 24 in deep, arranged at regular intervals, 5 ft 8 in apart. These also disappear into the soil. The recesses were probably intended for beams which would have supported a lightweight structure attached to this outer wall, providing a weatherproof cover over this opening.

The long section of the leg is 600 ft x 29 ft. Its height above ground varies from 4 ft to 6 ft, and the last 196 ft of the leg slightly slope downwards (10°). Its purpose is unknown. However, at Couville, too, there is a slight slope to the last 100 ft of the two walls. The concrete for this longer leg also disappears into the ground but it appears that the roof, supported by the ground, was constructed first and that the supporting walls were to be added later, and there is a 6 ft-wide recess on one side where this wall would be added. On the roof of this section are several scrap pieces of the site's narrow gauge railway.

On the inside of the 'L' is a large irregular concrete parking area, which overall measures 263 ft x 91 ft. Just outside the area enclosed by the 'L' is another smaller structure, parallel to the short leg. This concrete building, which is partially buried, is 100 ft x 31.3 ft and its height varies from 3.5 ft to 6.9 ft above the ground.

The entrance, 30 ft wide, is at the south end and it is now blocked with soil. On the roof are more pieces of the site narrow gauge railway. This building appears to have been the site garage and locomotive shed.

Sottevast, like Couville, was intended to provide a secure storage and servicing facility for the modified V2 and its larger developments. The rockets would have arrived by rail from Germany and been unloaded at the Sottevast sidings. These sidings still exist and are unusually large for a village of this size. A milk-processing plant has since been built on the edge and this has obscured the original unloading area.

Using the narrow gauge railway, the rockets would have been moved horizontally to the bunker entrance where they would have been lowered vertically into the shaft. The machinery for doing this is now missing.

Judging by the widths of both legs, all rocket movements would have been carried out vertically, as normal, and underground there may have been enough space for only one line of rockets. However, it is likely that the underground area was wider than the roof.

There is a plain concrete pad, 60 ft x 40 ft and 100 ft beyond the north end of the 'L'. The absence of any foundation bolts or other means of attachment indicates that it was not intended for AA guns or a building. Most likely it was intended as a launching pad, despite the lack of cable troughs, as it is situated so that the launch direction is away from the site buildings and parking areas.

A possible means of reaching this pad would have been by ramp, through the opening opposite the entrance shaft, as shown on fig. 11. It is also possible that launches were intended to be carried out from the entrance shaft itself, in which case the rocket would have been raised to near ground level by a lift. This would

Sottevast complex site:the inner parking area of two legs; the rocket entrance is blocked with concrete beams.

Sottevast: the roof of the unfinished leg awaiting the addition of a supporting wall.

explain the purpose of the opening on the opposite side of the leg, where the notional ramp is shown, as this opening would act as an exhaust path for the rocket efflux. (The American Titan I ICBM of 1959 was silo based but raised to the surface immediately before launch, when all the pre-flight checks had been carried out, so this mode of operation would not be that unusual.)

There is no way of determining the actual storage capacity at Sottevast, other than the fact that the combined legs give a total length of 750 ft. This would provide a vertical storage capacity of around 65 V2s, but if the area under ground is wider than the roofs, then this could provide considerably more space. Although Couville is much less complete than Sottevast, the two sites would have been able to provide a considerable storage and servicing facility for the modified V2s and their developments.

WATTEN

Watten is the largest and certainly the most impressive of the complex sites and must have been one of the major elements in the rocket programme. It is the only site which has been in any way preserved since the end of the war and it is now maintained as a national monument by the French. In many respects this has been a good thing but unfortunately, as will be explained later, the 1993 guidebook contains many changes and contradictions from those printed in 1980 and there is the danger that the true purpose and history of the site will be permanently changed for the benefit of the visitors.

The location chosen for what was to be the last word in rocket bases was the Forêt d'Eperlecques, which lies 3 miles from the town of Watten and a few miles inland from Calais. Watten is on a junction of the main canal network from France and Belgium through to Germany and is also on the main line from France to Germany. St Omer, 6 miles away, was a Luftwaffe base; it was part of Luftflotte 2 under Field Marshal Kesselring and provided Me109s, 110s and Junkers 87s during the Battle of Britain. It remained a first-line base until the evacuation of France.

There are several gravel and sand quarries in the area, together with cement works, and these supplied the huge amount of materials required for Watten. In one respect in particular Watten is different from other sites. It was built using forced labour (prisoners from the countries occupied by the Germans provided the labour in a regime that was only slightly less harsh than that at Nordhausen).

Because of its size and importance it appeared in several wartime reports and it is referred to by Dornberger and other authors, who obviously never visited the site, as being a derelict heap of broken concrete. It is true that it has been badly damaged by bombing, but some of this was caused after the site came into Allied hands; the destructive power of the 22,000 lb Grand Slam bombs was tested against its structure. From a distance, the size of the main building is deceptive, and it is only close up that its real size becomes apparent: 300 ft long, 138 ft wide and 80 ft high. At a conservative estimate the walls alone (which are a maximum of 23 ft thick) would have required 200,000 tons of concrete and 20,000 tons of steel.

The site was inspected during Christmas 1942 by the War Department, civil engineers from the Todt Organisation (OT) and representatives from

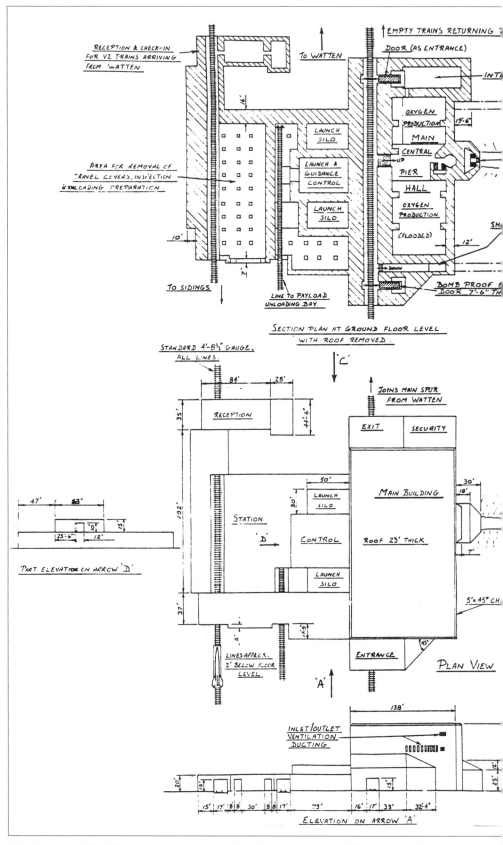

RECEPTION & CHECK-IN FOR V2 TRAINS ARRIVING FROM WATTEN

TO WATTEN

EMPTY TRAINS RETURNING T

DOOR (AS ENTRANCE)

INT

OXYGEN PRODUCTION
MAIN
CENTRAL

LAUNCH SILO

LAUNCH & GUIDANCE CONTROL

AREA FOR REMOVAL OF TRAVEL COVERS, INSPECTION & UNLOADING PREPARATION

PIER

HALL

OXYGEN PRODUCTION

LAUNCH SILO

(FLOODED)

SH

10'

12'

TO SIDINGS

LINE TO PAYLOAD UNLOADING BAY

BOMB PROOF
DOOR 7'-6" TH

SECTION PLAN AT GROUND FLOOR LEVEL
WITH ROOF REMOVED.

C

STANDARD 4'-8½" GAUGE, ALL LINES.

84'   28'

RECEPTION

44'-6"

35'

JOINS MAIN SPUR FROM WATTEN

EXIT   SECURITY

47'   23'

50'

30'

LAUNCH SILO

MAIN BUILDING

30'   18'

15'

STATION

192'

D

CONTROL

ROOF 23' THICK

25'-6'   12'

PART ELEVATION ON ARROW 'D'

LAUNCH SILO

5' x 45° CH.

37'

LINES APPROX.
2' BELOW FLOOR LEVEL

45'

ENTRANCE

PLAN VIEW

A

INLET/OUTLET VENTILATION DUCTING

138'

20'

15' 17' 8 8 30' 8 8 17'   73'   16' 17' 33'   32'-4"

25'

ELEVATION ON ARROW 'A'

12. Watten modified V2 storage, servicing and launching site with capability for handling
largest rocket developments and with protection for nuclear material. Site is administered by

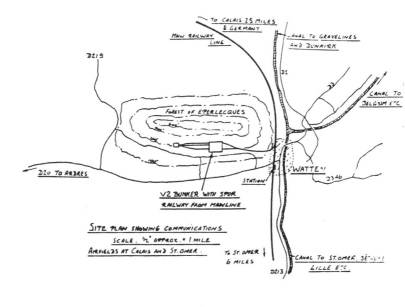

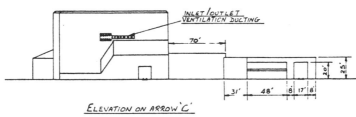

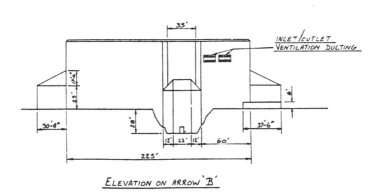

French authorities and its history has recently been 'amended', possibly because of current political entente cordiale *with Germany.*

Peenemünde. There was already a gravel quarry at the location which had been excavated to more than 100 ft. The main problem was drainage; the site tended to fill with water, as it is situated at the base of a low escarpment. The advantages were good communication links, ample power supplies and raw materials, and good security and air-cover. Furthermore, an important operational factor, as will be explained later, was its position in relation to Wizernes and Prédefin. All this outweighed the drainage concern.

Construction started in early March 1943, and the schedule required that the site should be operational by October. The only resource that was not readily available in the area was personnel and although the OT was experienced in this type of work, the size and short construction programme meant that they were unable to provide the necessary manpower from their normal labour force. The problem was put into the hands of Fritz Saukel, Hitler's organizer of civilian workers in all the Reich's occupied territories. Saukel, who was hanged at Nuremberg on 16 October 1946 for war crimes, admitted in the courtroom that of all the millions of foreign workers who were brought in to work for Germany, not more than 200,000 came voluntarily.

In the first stage 6,000 were brought to Watten from Russia, Poland, Belgium, Holland, Czechoslovakia and France. They were put into two camps, 1½ miles from the site, and the work schedules were organized into a shift system, working 24 hours a day, 7 days a week. Each shift worked 12 hours and at any one time there were always 3,000–4,000 men at work. These *Sklavenarbeiter* were controlled by armed guards of the SS, who very often had been transferred from concentration-camp duties. Needless to say, discipline was strict and as at Nordhausen, to fall ill was the equivalent of a death sentence. Those who were unable to work were transported back to the concentration camps.

During the six months that the site was under construction over 35,000 workers passed through the camps. A memorial has now been placed at the entrance to the site, but of course the buildings themselves act as a memorial.

It is not surprising that in *V2* Dornberger played down his involvement at Watten, giving the impression that neither he nor anyone else at Peenemünde, had anything to do with its design, construction or the project in general. But the fact was that no one in Germany had a better general knowledge of the operational requirements of the V2 and rockets than Dornberger, von Braun and the rest of the team.

Plans for the V2 and its developments meant that they had to provide facilities capable of handling weapons over twice the size of the V2. This produced unique construction problems. With Watten the design was conventional in that it is a rectangular main building, with ample provision for deep foundations. What was unconventional was the method used to turn those plans into reality.

The main concern was the roof. Hitler, with his ability to grasp the most important points of any technical subject, understood the most significant advantages of reinforced concrete. It was cheap, used mainly non-strategic materials and could easily be made thick enough to withstand the heaviest bombs used (or ever likely to be used in the future).

Xaver Dorsch of the OT provided the figures from tests carried out on captured bunkers and shelters. These showed that with sufficiently thick

Watten complex site: the main building, south wall looking east.

concrete, a building could be constructed which would require a bomb so large to demolish it that it would be physically impossible for an aeroplane to lift it. The magical figure was 23 ft of steel-reinforced concrete. Dorsch showed that to pierce this thickness of concrete a bomb would have to weigh 12 tons (27,000 lb) and that it would also have to strike the target at the correct angle and at the speed of sound, Mach 1. This figure of 23 ft became fixed in Hitler's mind to such an extent that any concrete structure that needed to be bombproof was always provided with a roof at least 23 ft thick. This is mentioned several times in his recorded 'table-talk'.

The accuracy of this figure was demonstrated after the site's capture when tests were carried out on the main building using the heaviest bombs available to the Allies, the 22,000 lb Grand Slam. Apart from its ability to penetrate concrete, a missile can damage the interior by causing 'scabbing', by which a cone-shaped piece of concrete is ejected from the underside of the roof, even though penetration has not taken place.

From a fairly recently released formula, issued by the American National Defence Research Council and using the dimensions and impact velocity of the Grand Slam, a figure of 12 ft is produced for its penetration depth and 22.6 ft for its scabbing depth. At Watten the ceiling of the main building has been provided with additional protection against scabbing by a mattress of steel beams, and this is now standard practice for similar structures.

Only two of the Grand Slams dropped actually hit the building and the results can still be seen. One hit, above the east entrance, struck the building at one of its strongest points, the juncture between the ceiling and the wall. The shock waves from the explosion caused a number of the steel reinforcing bars to be forced out and 'spalling' (a large piece of concrete was ejected from the impacted face). Otherwise though, no serious structural damage was caused.

The other hit, near the centre of the building, blasted a piece of concrete, weighing several tons, off the roof. From the inside it can be seen that the ceiling has started to crack and a large piece of concrete has become partially detached from the 'mattress'. This indicates that the explosive effect of the bomb was just sufficient to produce the onset of scabbing, though the extra strength of the steel 'mattress' prevents any concrete falling from the ceiling.

If it is assumed that the Germans were not aware of the Grand Slam at the time the site was planned – the bomb did not become operational until after 1943 – it is likely that the design took into account the largest bomb in the Allied armoury of 1941/2, the 12,000 lb Tallboy. This could penetrate 9.9 ft of reinforced concrete and had a scabbing depth of 18.4 ft, in which case a roof thickness of 23 ft gave ample protection.

Once 23 ft had been established as the required thickness, the problem was then how to construct such a roof 60–80 ft above the ground. The finished roof weighed 50,000 tons and this would have required specialized lifting gear and heavy scaffolding and shuttering, which would have been difficult to obtain and extremely vulnerable to bombing.

The problem was solved by Dorsch in an unusual way. The walls were built up to a height of 15 ft and then the 23 ft-thick roof was constructed on top of these

Watten: the main building, south wall looking west.

walls, with little problem of access at this height. Under the protection of this shelter, the whole roof was slowly raised, inches at a time, using hundreds of jacks. The walls were built up underneath to their full thickness, which varied from 12 ft to 23 ft.

To transport the vast amounts of cement, sand, gravel, steel, etc., and eventually the rockets, a standard gauge railway line was run from Watten, with two narrow gauge tracks running from a siding to the high ground behind the site. Quarry materials were loaded into skips at the siding, pushed to the edge of the escarpment and allowed to run down by gravity, pulling an unloaded wagon back to the top at the same time. Each shift had a fixed daily amount of work to do, such as the unloading of 5,000 bags of cement and the workers were not relieved until their set quota had been attained. From March until August 1943 construction proceeded without hindrance and enough progress had been made to be able to predict with some certainty that the target date of October would be achieved. However, on the night of 17 August, Peenemünde was bombed for the first time and on 27 August Watten suffered the same fate.

The raid, by 185 B-17 Flying Fortresses of the US 8th Air Force, had to be carried out in daylight as it required precision bombing. Hence it was timed for 6.30 p.m. This was also one of the few times when the site was almost clear of workers, as they changed afternoon shifts, and this information had been passed on by members of the resistance. Unfortunately that particular day happened to be one on which the set work quota had not been achieved and the day shift was still at work when the B-17s arrived, resulting in many casualties.

From 7 September until October there were a series of regular air raids, after which both the construction work and the bombing were halted, while both sides assessed the situation. The timing of the first Allied raid had been completely random in that no one on the Allied side really knew what Watten was for, but it was extremely fortuitous.

From the German point of view, although negligible damage had been done to the main building, the ancillary buildings had suffered badly and much of the construction equipment and material had been destroyed.

It was obvious that there would be further raids and in 1943 the ability of the Luftwaffe to stop them was almost zero, as this had not been allowed for in the original plans. But there were other things to be taken into account, including Watten's position in the overall weapon system and the progress with the V2's larger developments. Everything related to the project was late, including the ultimate warhead, and for the immediate aim of using a modified V2, Watten was not essential. Sometime late in 1943, therefore, the decision was taken to change Watten's role. Work would continue, but only so far as the main building would be used for the production of oxygen, which had been the original intent for the ground-level part of the structure.

For the Allied Crossbow Committee concerned with planning the bombing offensive against suspected rocket targets, the attacks against Watten had not been very rewarding. Several hundred aircrews and aircraft had been lost, and Watten was still standing, even though there had been numerous hits and construction had been disrupted.

While on the subject of bombing, mention must be made of project Aphrodite (she assisted Paris in the Trojan war). As little serious damage appeared to have been done to Watten, a plan was evolved to use B-17s which had passed their maximum permitted number of flying hours, as gigantic flying bombs. Redesignated BQ-7, a small number, possibly ten, were stripped of all unnecessary equipment and loaded with 22,000 lb of high explosive. The intention was that the crew should fly the aeroplane to the vicinity of the target, set the fuses and then bail out. The final dive to the target would be radio controlled from an accompanying aircraft.

Fortunately for Watten this proved to be more difficult to carry out in practice than it was to plan and the project was abandoned without any results being achieved. At least one of the bombers exploded prematurely while still over England, and this was carrying Joseph P. Kennedy, brother of the future president of the USA. As already mentioned, high explosives are very unstable materials and can be detonated accidentally whether armed or not.

The final results of the bombing can be summarized into two stages. The first stage was from 27 August to October 1943 and involved attacks by the USAF

Watten: penetration of the reception station roof by an unexploded bomb.

using conventional bombs of up to 4,000 lb. The total dropped was around 2,000 tons. The second stage was from 10 to 20 November 1944; after the site had been captured, a single Lancaster attempted to hit the main building with one Grand Slam. In the event, visibility was suitable for the release of only three or four bombs, resulting in two, possibly three, hits.

With regard to the other site buildings, the reception area received three or four hits from 1,000 lb or 2,000 lb bombs, from the first bombing stage. The damage is severe, accentuated by the fact that this part was incomplete when the bombing started and it is of relatively light construction.

The 'station', where the V2 trains from Watten went immediately after the reception, received some minor damage. The roof was penetrated, but the device, probably a 1,000 lb or 2,000 lb armour-piercing bomb, failed to explode. This damage could have been repaired in a matter of days.

The launch silo nearest to Watten received some damage but as the interior is flooded the exact extent cannot be determined. The launch control centre has also been slightly damaged, although it does not appear to have been penetrated.

The total bombing results, including the second stage Grand Slam operation, did not seriously affect the main structure and it is most likely that all the damage could have been rectified in two to three weeks. There is no doubt, however, that the site construction activities would have been seriously disrupted and a continued bombing programme would have resulted in a halt to repair work and further construction. If the probability of actually destroying a well-protected hardened target appears to be small, this demonstrates the difficulty of accurate bombing in these circumstances and it was only when the site was unprotected, as for the Grand Slam drops, that any real damage was done. Even if the site had been finished and operational, it is doubtful that it could have operated as intended, owing to the general disruption from the regular bombing.

The site layout is shown in fig. 12. At the entrance to the grounds are some wartime remains including B-17 Wright Cyclone and BMW radial engines, a German 88 mm gun and some inert bomb cases. The approach to the buildings is now made so as to reach the southern corner of the main building first, moving anti-clockwise round the site. The various stages are described in the guidebook and also via a recorded commentary from a loudspeaker system.

There are only two entrances to the main building, through what was originally occupied by the single-track standard gauge spur line from Watten. The track has been removed and the bombproof doors at either end are open. These doors, some 20 ft in from each entrance, are of steel and concrete, 7 ft 6 in thick. They ran on rails and fitted into recesses when closed, effectively sealing off the main building from the outside. Similar doors were intended at Brécourt. The electrically driven operating machinery is situated above the doors and could close the doors, which weigh 30 tons, in one minute.

The west door is now in working order and demonstrations are carried out for visitors. The east door, which is the first one passed on the tour, is blocked off and surrounded by water. Passing the east exit, with its sharply sloping anti-missile

Watten: the reception station for trains loaded with rockets arriving from Germany.

roof, leads to the edge of the first launch silo. The interior is filled with water and apparently has a depth of over 200 ft. From the size of the opening it is obvious that it could take one large rocket or two V2s side by side.

The next building is the reception and offices for the clerical staff. It suffered bomb damage before it could be completed and since 1980 it has been allowed to become overgrown. It was intended to provide accommodation for clerical staff in the totally enclosed section, a canteen and recreational area in what is now the open section, and an arrival section for the trains from Watten. The construction is fairly light reinforced concrete, and the roof of the open section is only 2 ft thick.

Proceeding anti-clockwise, the path continues along the top of the 25 ft-thick concrete reinforcing wall of the edge of the main station. This is open where the track stood, to allow smoke to escape, but the remainder is roofed over to a depth of 5 ft.

Access can now be made down to the platform (as in the photograph) and the single penetration of a bomb (which did not explode) can be seen in the roof of one of the bays.

From the top of the wall, looking back towards the main building, is the launch control centre. This is 63 ft wide, 70 ft long and 15 ft high and adjoins the main building.

Following the path round, it passes the two railway exits with their adjacent personnel entrances. Further west, in the grounds, were the locomotive sheds and sidings, which enabled the trains to be reversed into the main building. The main building is now entered at the west (operational) door and on the right is an opening with steps leading down to the lower levels. This was to enable the unloaded rockets to be passed straight down to the working and storage areas, which are now flooded. In the roof above the track are the remains of the rail for the crane which would be used for the unloading.

The passage on the right has recently been covered over with concrete and a full-size cardboard V2 has been placed against the end wall. This is to show that, supposedly, a huge exit was intended in this wall; the V2s would have been moved on to piers outside for launching. As will be explained later, this is an incorrect assumption resulting from a misinterpretation of the archives.

Carrying on towards the centre of the interior a flight of steps leads up into the main hall. This was the section intended for oxygen production. The compressors would be mounted on large plinths, with the ventilation ducts in the outside wall used to provide the air. Since the 1980s this area has also been modified; the plinths have vanished and the ceiling, with its evidence of a Grand Slam impact on the roof, can no longer be seen. Instead the area has been converted for the viewing of a short film, of dubious historical value, on the history of the V2.

In the 1980s it was possible to walk through the building and go out at the east door, but this exit is now blocked and flooded. In the 1980 guidebook it was said that the intention was to pump the interior free of water but this plan has obviously been abandoned.

When the Germans left the site in September 1944 they also removed or smashed the pumps in the basement, which were keeping the interior clear of water, and all these lower levels are now flooded. It was hinted in the early guidebooks that nuclear and laser experiments may have been carried out at these levels. On 10 September, just four days after the site had been captured by the Canadians and cleared of booby traps and unexploded bombs, a small party of Allied VIPs arrived to inspect the interior. Included in the party was Duncan Sandys, who was in charge of the rocket investigations, and Frederic Joliot-Curie, who probably knew more about the German nuclear programme at that time than anyone else working for the Allies. At that time the interior would still have been clear of water and all the levels would have been inspected. No report on the visit has ever been made public and a few weeks later an attempt was made to destroy the building with the Grand Slam bombs.

The west door is now used as both the exit and the entrance. Turning left outside, a good view may be gained of the main building. Among the points worth noting is the evidence of the bomb strikes on the roof and the remains of the personnel access to the lower levels, attached to the centre of the west wall.

I first visited Watten in 1980 and between then and my latest visit in 1993 some major changes had been made in the guidebook to the description of the site, which radically affect its history. These changes can be summarized as follows. In 1980 statements were made that the underground workings extend to 260 ft and that these are now flooded. The intention was to pump out the water as soon as possible. Reference was made to both the harsh working conditions for those in forced labour and the numbers involved. The entrance of the main building via the west door revealed a passage to the right, filled with water, but it was described as leading to the lower depths, 260 ft below. The launch of rockets was depicted as having been made from the silos shown on fig. 12. The ceiling of the main building was clearly visible. Finally, reference was made inside the main building to the Prédefin radar-tracking site. By 1993 no mention was made of underground workings, the depth underground or any intention to pump out the water. No mention was made of forced labour having been used to build the site or the conditions they endured. The launching of the rockets is now shown as having been made via the passage to the right of the west door, the theory being that there would be two 50 ft-high slots cut in the main south wall, and two piers built at right angles to this wall. Finally, no reference is made to Prédefin (the significance of this particular point will be discussed in the next chapter).

The modified launching scheme is said to be based on OT drawings, dated February–March 1943 and recently discovered in the archives. The most obvious of these changes involves the launching of the rockets and although it is clear that the drawings referred to actually exist it is very unlikely that they represent a serious design intent, for the following reasons. Two huge slots would have had to have been made in the south wall of the main building, 50 ft x 9 ft minimum, to remove the rockets vertically, and this would have destroyed the security of the building and rendered the two 7 ft 6 in sliding doors redundant. The rockets would have had to have been removed vertically as there is insufficient horizontal clearance. There are no signs of foundations for the two piers on the outside, at right angles to the south wall, even though the construction of the main building was almost complete when the bombing halted the work. Launching from the two piers, as suggested, would have taken the rockets back over the main building. In general the launch trajectory at any site is away from the site buildings, for safety reasons.

It is likely that these changes have been made for the following reasons. The fact that no mention is made of the underground workings or removal of the water is to give visitors the impression that they are not missing anything or that there areas of the site still to be revealed. Reference to slave labour and working conditions has been omitted to make the site tour more palatable, though it should be noted that the recorded commentary is only in French, English and Dutch. The change to the description of the launch facility provides the visitor with more to see. However, though based on the OT drawings from the archives at Freiburg, the results are a misinterpretation. These drawings were produced to show a possible method of launching V2s, in the event that the original purpose of the site could not be achieved. They were only schematic and were not intended to be taken as the final design solution to the problems which might arise from Allied bombing. The site is more likely to have operated along the following lines.

The train, loaded with rockets, would arrive from Germany via Watten and the initial documentation would be checked at the reception building. It would then pass through to the station, where the travel covers would be removed, all the documentation checked and each wagon and its load inspected for damage, sabotage and any other irregularities. Any non-essential material, spares, etc. would be removed into the adjacent bays.

The importance of this initial checking before the rocket train entered the main building cannot be over emphasized. It was a form of Quality Assurance (QA) quarantine and was essential, as the main building would have been regarded almost like a sterile area in a hospital; no 'foreign' material was allowed to enter. For instance, the possibility of a bomb going down with a rocket to the lower levels could have been catastrophic.

After the checks had been carried out, the train would move forward and then reverse through the west door of the main building. The engine would leave and the sliding door would be closed, sealing the cargo inside from the outside world.

The rockets (V2 size) would arrive from Germany on 'triple-flats' (as described in Appendix A, item 2); these were the special wagons solely for V2 rail transportation, and comprised three articulated wagons, which held two V2s with their noses overlapping on the middle wagon. The complete load would be covered over and camouflaged. The overall length of a triple-flat would be around 90 ft. This meant that two triple-flats, carrying a total of four V2s, could be accommodated simultaneously within the main building.

The rockets would be unloaded in turn, using the overhead crane (judging from the rails still visible in the roof). They would then be lowered via the shaft in the west corridor (now floored over) to the storage and servicing areas some distance below. This procedure would be repeated until all the wagons on that particular train had been unloaded. The engine would attach itself to the front of the empty wagons which had been shunted through the east door, and the train would return to Watten and on to Germany.

The payload compartments would either arrive from Germany in special lead-

Watten: the main building and the entrance for trains which have been cleared through reception.

lined containers or, more likely, the radioactive material would be produced on site, in the lower levels of the main building.

Whichever, it was essential in the layout of the site to have separate unloading facilities for the rockets and the material providing the destructive capabilities of the weapon. They could not enter the main site working area through the same entrance, as there were too many safety risks.

The same initial route would be taken for the payload train as for the rockets; the documentation would be inspected in the station, but after clearance the train would proceed into the unloading bay in between the station and the main building. Here the same headroom would not be required as for the rockets; hence, this building had a single storey. The cargo would be unloaded and passed down to the storage and working areas. Liquid oxygen was produced in the hall of the main building and piped to storage in the lower levels. The alcohol and other items, such as spares, would be unloaded at the same place as the payloads, for storage underground. After servicing and pre-launch checks the rocket would be raised almost to the surface at either of the silos, shown on fig. 12, via a lift system (a similar concept was used for the Minuteman I ICBM). Final checks would be carried out, with the nose of the V2 just below the surface, and the launch would take place.

The facility could easily handle rockets twice the size of the V2; in the main building unloading area there is 60 ft headroom. A 100 ft rocket would be transported from Germany in two 50 ft lengths, to avoid distorting the relatively lightweight structure and owing to limitations of the railway system.

The actual launching silos have an exit measuring 30 ft x 50 ft and although it would be possible to have two V2s ready for launch, but launched separately, from the same silo, this is unlikely. The large opening was provided to ensure that the site could launch all projected developments of the V2, including the 3,500 mile range A9/A10 booster combination.

As mentioned at the beginning of this section, Dornberger and his team made little reference to Watten; in fact it received about the same coverage in their writings as Nordhausen. Dornberger did mention that Dr Steinhoff was present at the initial inspections of the Watten site and we now know that Steinhoff was also present at at least one Nordhausen meeting, when the supply of 1,800 more workers (slave labour, that is) was discussed. Although this point has already been made it is worth repeating because Watten is such a huge facility. Consequently, the OT would have been involved at the site. Its members were civil engineers, pure and simple, and knew nothing about the equipment required to handle, service and launch rockets. A similar situation is the involvement of civil engineers in a nuclear power station. They need know nothing about the workings of the nuclear side, what equipment is needed for the reactor, safety systems and turbine generators, but they have to provide buildings and a structure which houses the nuclear 'package'. In the case of Watten, only one group knew what equipment was needed or had any knowledge of the nuclear aspect, and this group was at Peenemünde. The silence, therefore, is all the more surprising when the size of Watten is taken into account.

The urgency with which the attempt was made to complete Watten by October 1943 is also significant when viewed against the simultaneous deterioration of the German military situation, the change in priority rating for the rocket programme, the modified V2 drawings and the nuclear work.

WIZERNES

The complex site at Wizernes again provides a completely different solution to the problem of storage, servicing and launching the modified V2 and its larger versions.

Wizernes is only 9½ miles from Watten, on the opposite side of St Omer, and so, in theory, benefited, from the protection the Luftwaffe could offer from the various airfields in the vicinity.

It would also benefit from the high level of security available. Wizernes itself is a small town and is very modern, so was obviously rebuilt as the result of wartime damage. The area is known for its chalk quarries and the site, a mile or so out of the town, was built at the location of one of these quarries.

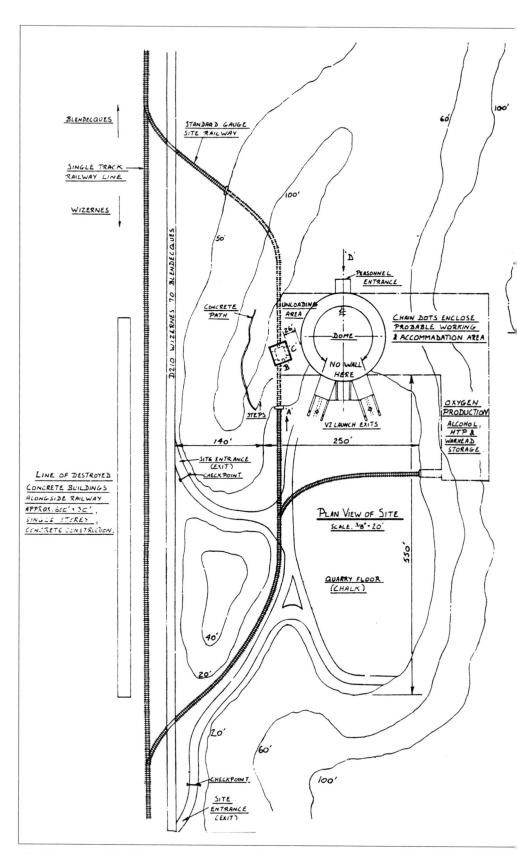

13. *Wizernes modified V2 site, providing almost identical facilities to Watten but with a different approach to construction.*

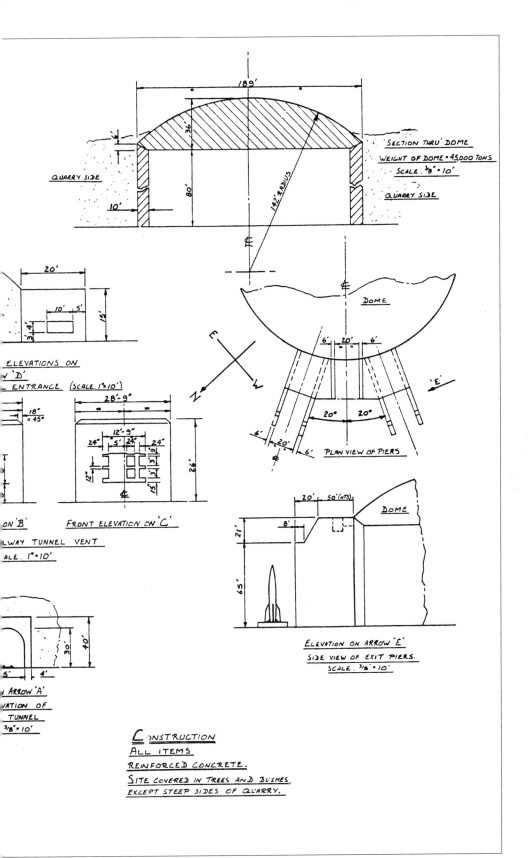

189'

36'

80'

10'

142' RADIUS

QUARRY SIDE

'SECTION THRU' DOME
WEIGHT OF DOME = 45,000 TONS
SCALE. ³/₈" = 10'

QUARRY SIDE

20'

10'   5'

15'

3' 4'

ELEVATIONS ON
'D'
ENTRANCE (SCALE. 1" = 10')

18"
45°

28'-9"

12'-9"
24"   5' 24"   24"
12"
15' 3' 3' 9'

26'

ON 'B'   FRONT ELEVATION ON 'C'
LWAY TUNNEL VENT
ALE. 1" = 10'

30'   40'

5'   4'

ARROW 'A'
VATION OF
TUNNEL
³/₈" = 10'

DOME

6'   20'   6'

20°   20°

6'   20'   6'

PLAN VIEW OF PIERS

'E'

E

N

W

20'   50'(NTS)

8'

21'

65'

DOME

ELEVATION ON ARROW 'E'
SIDE VIEW OF EXIT PIERS.
SCALE. ³/₈" = 10'

Construction
All items
Reinforced Concrete.
Site covered in trees and bushes,
except steep sides of quarry.

Construction started at Wizernes in July 1943 and the work proceeded unhindered by Allied bombing until January 1944. From November 1943 photo-reconnaissance of the site had been carried out, as with all new, large construction projects which might be associated with rocket weapons. From that time until the first bombing raid, progress at the site was recorded on a regular basis.

Wizernes was designed to satisfy the same basic specification as Watten, in that one of the main requirements was that the area where the rockets were stored and serviced had to be absolutely impregnable from air attack. As at Watten, this resulted in a minimum thickness for the roof of 23 ft of reinforced concrete; this also brought its attendant constructional problems, especially of height access and weight. However, the solution adopted at Wizernes was completely different, and was really very simple.

First the bombproof concrete roof was built, on the ground at the edge of a cliff. Then the ground underneath the roof was excavated, while at the same time a supporting wall for the roof was built and the foundations laid. Although the idea was simple, if not novel, the actual location chosen had to have a number of basic features: the ground had to be stable to prevent any possibility of the roof moving while it was resting on the ground; the soil structure had to be hard enough to support the huge mass of concrete but soft enough to facilitate the task of hollowing out the ground under the roof.

Based on dimensions taken at the site, the weights of the various sections have been estimated as follows: domed roof, 45,000 tons (including extra steel reinforcement and anti-scabbing plates attached to the ceiling); walls supporting roof, 38,000 tons; intermediate dividing walls, 20,000 tons. This gives a total weight for the structure of 103,000 tons. The area underneath the circular supporting wall for the roof is 28,000 square ft and this results in a ground pressure of

$$\frac{103,000}{28,000} \quad = \quad 3.7 \text{ tons/sq ft}$$

If this ground pressure is increased by 15% to allow for inaccuracies and unknowns in the calculations, the resulting figure is 4.26 tons/sq ft.

Ordinary soil, sand, or clay, all of which are easily worked, have allowable ground pressures (that is, provide stable support) of less than 3 tons/sq ft. The only appropriate subsoils are sandstone and chalk, with allowable ground pressures of 23 and 6 tons/sq ft respectively. There is no suitable sandstone in this area of northern France, but Wizernes is surrounded by hills of solid chalk. Some of these were already being quarried, including the one chosen, which fitted the requirements perfectly.

The walls of the quarry were steep sided, giving a working height of 100 ft without further excavation, and a rail link and main road passed within yards of the site entrance.

The choice of a dome-shaped roof over the main building provided a more efficient solution to the problem of protection than the flat roof at Watten, but of course the Watten roof had to provide protection over a larger area than Wizernes and a very large dome would have caused additional problems. The main advantage of a curved roof is that the maximum thickness is in the centre, where maximum protection is required. At this point a bomb dropping vertically would hit the roof as if it were completely flat. Moving outwards from the centre of the dome to where the thickness reduces to 20 ft, if a 22,000 lb Grand Slam were to strike the roof at this point (at an oblique angle) the resultant explosive force would be reduced to the equivalent of that of a 19,000 lb bomb. Using the same formula as at Watten, this would reduce the penetration and scabbing depths to 10 ft and 21 ft respectively. These figures are only approximate as there is virtually nothing published on the effects of large missiles striking reinforced concrete at oblique angles. However, it does indicate that a calculation of the ratio of usable floor area to weight of concrete would give a value of 0.5 for Wizernes and 0.4 for Watten.

The dome shape at Wizernes is a section through a sphere, with a maximum thickness estimated at 36 ft at the centre, a radius of 142 ft, and supported on a ring of concrete 10 ft thick (the dome was chamfered at the edges to obtain the best fit against the supporting wall). Fitted with an anti-scabbing steel mattress on the inside of the dome, the roof would have ensured protection against the heaviest bombs.

Wizernes complex site: the dome, the railway tunnel vent and remains of the launching piers.

Wizernes: the railway tunnel vent from the top of the dome.

Another important advantage that the Wizernes design had over Watten was in the launching arrangements. At Watten the rockets had to be raised to a considerable height from the lower working levels to the top of the silos, perhaps as much as 200 ft, which required a complicated piece of lifting equipment. At Wizernes, on the other hand, the rockets which were ready for launch were transferred at ground level via the two launching piers. The walls of these piers are almost complete, but as a result either of bombing or natural slippage over the years, they now lean over. Their current angle of orientation is interesting, as with no modification the launch direction for a ballistic missile would result in a trajectory to the mid-Atlantic states of the USA, including New York.

At the rear of the dome is a personnel entrance/exit, which is now bricked up. This was most likely intended as an emergency exit from the working areas under the dome; as at Watten, the main working areas would have been sealed from the outside world for most of the time.

The site was served by a standard gauge railway, linked to the main line which runs alongside the site, and also the main road from Lumbres to Blendecques, the D211. The remains of the rail link, complete with track, are still in evidence, and the line disappears into a tunnel in the hillside, to the left of the dome. Inside the tunnel the track is complete, but access is now blocked by a steel gate. Above the tunnel, visible on the skyline from some distance, is the tunnel vent, a rectangular structure, 29 sq ft across and 26 ft high. It is a substantial concrete structure, with walls 7 ft thick, and the vents are irregular slots in each of the four faces.

Access to the top of the dome is facilitated by the remains of the original steps and paths, complete with trenches, which were used by the security forces guarding the site. From the top is a panoramic view of the site layout, as shown in fig. 13.

Alongside the main road and railway line adjacent to the site is a long line (600 ft x 30 ft) of thin-skinned concrete single-storey buildings. These would have been provided for the initial checks and inspections of the train and its load as it arrived from Germany, and it is the equivalent of the station at Watten. Once the contents had been formally accepted, the train would proceed onto the quarry floor and into the tunnel, where unloading would take place in complete safety, under a roof of 100 ft of chalk.

German plans, drawn up as late as August 1944, around which time the site had been abandoned as a rocket base, show a maze of underground workings to the right of the dome, served by another rail link on the quarry floor. A third line is shown entering the workings to the right of the right-hand launching pier. The whole site, as planned, would have provided a self-contained facility for rocket storage, servicing and launching, as well as oxygen production, fuel storage and personnel accommodation, in an impregnable environment. In addition, like Watten, it would have provided a secure location for the production of radioactive material. Its proximity to Watten was intentional, for various reasons (one of which will be explained in the next section). It would have ensured that experience could be transferred easily between the two sites as they became operational.

The condition of the site in the 1980s and 1993 provides something of a mystery. British photo-reconnaissance material of the site in July 1944 showed the whole site resembling a lunar landscape, pockmarked with bomb craters; the dome was barely visible in the chaos. There is now little sign of this bombing. The only damage visible is to the reception buildings by the railway, at the tunnel entrance and a few craters on the hillside. The dome is undamaged, as is the tunnel vent, and the piers appear to have slipped as a result of natural causes, as the final connection to the dome was never completed. Also, it is clear that the railway track on the quarry floor is the original one, and it has suffered no damage. Certainly the quarry was not used after the war for its original purpose and so there would be no point in repairing or filling in bomb craters.

Since the 1960s, I have visited many V1 and V2 sites in northern France, and where bombing raids have been carried out there are, without exception, obvious signs of these raids. In many cases, craters on farmland have never been filled in despite the hazard to cattle. It is all the more surprising, therefore, when comparing the ACIU pictures of the site after the bombing with the actual situation at the site. There is a large discrepancy here which needs an explanation.

Finally, it is worthwhile comparing the two sites of Watten and Wizernes. As they are so close to each other they were obviously intended to provide the same facilities, yet there are so many differences. Watten is a massive and impressive site, and when finished would have provided a showpiece for the ultimate in rocket bases. Nevertheless, its operation would have caused many headaches, even assuming there was no bombing. Unloading in the main building was complicated and the rockets required a considerable amount of handling in a restricted space to reach the working levels, and then they had to be raised a considerable distance for launch. Wizernes does not have the visual impact of Watten, as almost everything is hidden under the chalk, but it certainly would have provided a more user-friendly site as far as operations were concerned. Everything of importance was carried out at ground level and the height of the dome meant that rockets of at least 100 ft could be handled without difficulty and complicated lifting gear was not required.

However, there is something missing from this duo of ultimate rocket bases: they were 'blind'. Here we have two sites, capable of launching the 'real' vengeance weapon – not something with a relatively insignificant effect, but carrying a payload that was devastating. Yet, once the rocket was launched into space that was the last that was heard or seen of it. Where would it land? Was no one bothered or interested to discover what eventually happened to this weapon? Of course they were, and it was unconceivable that the trajectory of the rockets was not followed for as long and as far as technology would allow. Just over 17 and 10 miles from Watten and Wizernes respectively, are the 'eyes' that would follow every launch to its ultimate destination. Those eyes were Prédefin.

CHAPTER TEN

Prédefin

Eighteen miles south of St Omer are a few houses, a couple of shops and a bar. Outside the village, 300 yd up the D93, on the left-hand side of the road, is a little group of single-storey concrete buildings. On the right-hand side are some foundations and bits of wire – nothing to attract the attention. But it was here that the eyes for Watten and Wizernes were built.

To return to Peenemünde for a moment, one of the most essential requirements of such an establishment was the ability to track all the test vehicles that were launched, and in addition to send or receive telemetry signals from these rockets as they flew down the range.

For a ballistic missile, like the V2, the trajectory in a plan view is a straight line. This straight line was, and still is for modern ICBMs, an essential part of their ability to hit the target, as any deviation from this straight line produces errors which are built into the guidance system. To obtain the most accurate plot of the trajectory, the ideal situation was to position the equipment that transmitted and received these signals immediately behind the launching pad. For early V2s, this accuracy was essential as the rocket motor had to be stopped at precisely the right time if the correct trajectory was to be obtained. As part of this facility a Würzburg-Riese (giant) radar set was installed on the mainland, 5 miles behind Test Stand 7 at Peenemünde.

The Würzburg radar was originally developed by Telefunken as an aid to anti-aircraft gunners and with its 10 ft diameter dish, it could scan through 360° and from –5° to +95° in elevation. Operating on what was for 1939 the very high frequency of 550 megacycles, it could plot the range and height of aircraft to within a few feet at ranges of up to 25 miles. When the need came to improve the range as aircraft performance improved, in 1941 the Telefunken engineers took the most obvious path.

The ability to accurately plot aircraft depends on two main variables: the frequency at which the signals are transmitted and the diameter of the dish. By increasing the Würzburg dish to 25 ft, the range improved to 50 miles in the general-scanning search mode and 37 miles in the direction-finding mode. The disadvantages of the new Giant Würzburg were its narrower beam width, and therefore reduced general surveillance capability, and owing to its size, it now required a static emplacement, unlike the smaller, mobile version. (As these factors did not seriously affect missile work, it was a Giant Würzburg that Dornberger acquired when Peenemünde was being built.) Apart from following the trajectory and transmitting the motor shut-off signal, the Würzburg received the numerous data signals that were sent from each test vehicle (temperatures, pressures, etc.) Even with a range of 50 miles the Würzburg could not follow the full trajectory of 200 miles, and so a string of Würzburg stations were built along the Baltic coastline.

When the rocket offensive was being planned in 1940 and 1941, it was obvious that a tracking centre similar to that at Peenemünde would be required, though not for every launch site, as it was not economical, or for any of those launching standard V2s with high-explosive warheads. However, for the modified V2s and the larger versions, it was almost essential that its trajectory should be followed for as long as possible. The two sites in the Pas de Calais where this was required were Watten and Wizernes. As part of the planning to reduce any duplication, the two sites were built as close together as was practicable, so that only one tracking station would be required.

One of the problems was the position of this station. Ideally it should be immediately behind the launching site, but this would be difficult with Watten and Wizernes as they range from east to west. The next most suitable location was 90° from this position and still in line with the launching sites.

Instead of providing radar cover in line with the trajectory, moved through 90°, a side elevation was provided for the two sites. As a result, on the map a straight line can be drawn through Watten, Wizernes and Prédefin, in that order. As any form of radar plotting becomes a three-dimensional trigonometry problem when the radar and vehicle being plotted are at different angles, it was a considerable advantage for each one to start off with the same bearing. For the Giant Würzburg with its narrow beam width, trying to find or pick up the radar signal of a fast-moving object with a small echo, like the V2, it was essential that the radar crew knew the exact trajectory and radar 'print' beforehand.

The actual site is in two sections, on either side of the D93. Leaving the village, on the left are the majority of the buildings, including the accommodation for site security, which is in a slight depression. Next to these buildings are the canteen, kitchen and commandant's offices. Behind are two further blocks for the technical staff. All these buildings are single storey.

During our inspection we were approached by one of the local inhabitants who had actually been employed by the Germans as a labourer on the site, and he was able to point out what the various buildings had been used for. A number of the villagers worked at the site and there appears to have been no animosity towards the Germans. One of the high points of village life seems to be the annual reunion in the local bar, of those who had been on the site during the war. Security had been low key and only a low barbed-wire fence surrounded the site.

Standing 300 yd to the right of the office is a circular concrete enclosure with walls 7 ft 10 in high x 3 ft 4 in thick and one opening, 10 ft wide, where the Giant Würzburg was installed. The Würzburg was an impressive piece of equipment; together with its control gear it weighed a total of 15 tons, but compared to the earlier, smaller version it had lost its mobility.

Around the Würzburg were three single-storey buildings, partially sunk into the ground, 60 ft x 40 ft, 25 ft x 15 ft, and 30 ft square. They provided accommodation for the operating staff for all the site, and their equipment. The total number of staff was divided up as follows: security 80–100; technical and clerical 25; and one site commandant. Although work was carried out on shifts, all personnel were housed on site.

Because of the limited range of the Würzburg, an additional long-range radar was required to take over from it when it reached its limit. On the right-hand side of the road are the remains of two structures and they supported two further pieces of equipment. The first item was a sensitive listening device to provide additional early warning of approaching aircraft. This augmented the coastal radar stations, and took the form of two large 'ears'. The second item was the long-range radar, a FuMG 402 Wassermann.

The Wassermann was developed by Siemens as a long-range early-warning and fighter ground-control radar. It required an operating crew of seven and was even more impressive than the Würzburg. It had a vertical rectangular aerial, which could vary in height, depending on the installation, from 120 ft to 186 ft, while its width could vary from 20 ft to 41 ft. Mounted at the base of a rotating pillar, it was capable of scanning through a circular 360°, but if this facility was not required the aerial was fixed. It had a range capability of over 140 miles and benefited over the Würzburg from four years of wartime radar development.

The Würzburg operated on a fixed frequency, which could easily be jammed by aluminium foil, (this was dropped by Allied aircraft in an operation codenamed Window). In contrast, Wassermann operated on a continually changing frequency in the ranges 1.9–2.5 metres, 1.2–1.9 metres and 2.4–4.0 metres. At its maximum range it could plot its target at an altitude of up to 30,000 ft, with a range accuracy of +/– 900 ft, and acquire its target at an altitude of over 40,000 ft. For an early-warning radar it was probably the best of its type available anywhere and incorporated such modern devices as IFF (Identification, Friend or Foe).

The Wassermann, like the Würzburg, also had a narrow beam width and it usually operated with one of the wide-beam surveillance radars, such as Freya, to first acquire its target.

For Prédefin, the precise trajectory was known, enabling the Wassermann to find the rocket unaided. With a V2 fired from Watten and Wizernes the Würzburg would plot the initial few seconds of flight. After 30 seconds the V2 would have reached a height of 30,000 ft and be out of range, but it was essential to have confirmation that this critical part of the trajectory was satisfactory. Consequently, the Wassermann acquired the rocket again on its downward path, a few seconds before it hit the ground.

Although Watten and Wizernes never became operational, for a number of reasons including the Allied bombing, at Prédefin there were no problems with bombing or lack of equipment, and it would have been operational far in advance of the rocket sites it was intended to support. In fact there are no particular signs of bomb damage and the villager confirmed that it had not been a problem at the site. Prédefin did become operational and would have been used to augment the normal radar detection service against Allied aircraft.

Prédefin provides one more piece in the jigsaw for the 'real' vengeance weapon. As mentioned the Rauville type of site had the minimum facilities necessary to launch a standard V2 – a parking area, garage and concrete pad. Watten and Wizernes were massive, complicated sites and the weapons they were to launch were so special that they had to have their own personal tracking station, to follow their every move on the glowing screen. Of course, Prédefin was not mentioned by Dornberger or von Braun, as the trail would have led back to Watten and Wizernes. Inevitably, questions would have been asked, as these were only supposed to be protected sites for launching the standard V2, and this certainly did not justify their having their own tracking station. Why was a facility necessary for these two sites when nothing like it was provided, or even hinted at, for all the other V2 launching sites in the Pas de Calais? The answer is obvious. No V4 or a rocket to the USA was going to be launched into a vacuum; it had to be followed for as long as possible.

One further point: in 1980 there was a display board inside the main building at Watten, showing the physical and technical link between Watten, Wizernes and Prédefin. By 1993, together with the other 'changes' to its history, this has now disappeared from Watten, and Prédefin is not mentioned.

CHAPTER ELEVEN

The Voyage of U-234

The long grey hull of U-234 edged slowly against the quayside and with one last grunt from the exhaust, all was quiet. It was Saturday 19 May 1945, and for the inquisitive dock workers and the waiting military in Portsmouth, New Hampshire, USA, it was the last of Hitler's infamous U-boats that they were likely to see in the flesh.

It was obvious that U-234 was heavily laden, and most of her 290 ft hull could be seen through the clear water of the inner harbour. Its features were distinctive: the grey paint, still smart; the black flag and *Kriegsmarine* pennant; the group of three AA guns on the conning tower. The bulges on either side of the hull gave it a slightly 'pregnant' appearance, breaking up the smooth, shark-like profile. U-234 was low in the water for a very good reason. This was no 800 ton Atlantic raider – not a member of Grand Admiral Doenitz's wolfpacks that had tried to stop the endless traffic across the Atlantic. U-234 was a 2,000 ton ocean-going type XB with a range of 15,000 miles, and only a quarter of her fuel had been used. But it was not only fuel weighing her down. In her holds were 260 tons of cargo. This cargo was meant for Japan and included one very special item which produced a long tenuous link with Peenemünde and Hitler's miracle weapon. It was a link that would put U-234 into the history books.

The war in Europe was over, the Third Reich had survived the death of its leader by seven days and on the night of 8/9 May 1945 the noises of war finally subsided. Yet thousands of miles away in the Pacific, the war was still alive. Japan, starved of vital raw materials, increasingly was resorting to desperate measures to forestall the inevitable. Kamikazes were sinking US ships, while other suicidal tactics were being used by the Army and Navy to prevent bases being set up within bombing range of Japan. The *Yamato*, pride of the Imperial Navy, the last remaining symbol of Japan's naval power and at 73,000 tons the largest battleship afloat, was sent on a suicide mission, with only enough fuel for a one-way trip. Leaving Kure naval base on 6 April 1945 the plan was to try to stop the US landings at Okinawa, but only hours after leaving Japan she was intercepted and sunk by carrier-based aircraft. This then was the atmosphere of the war as the final strategic moves were played out by Japan and the USA in the Pacific.

In September 1942 the career of U-234 started ignominiously in the submarine yards of Germania Werft, Kiel. There was no particular rush to complete this big minelayer. Certainly she was not likely to win the war by dropping a few mines in

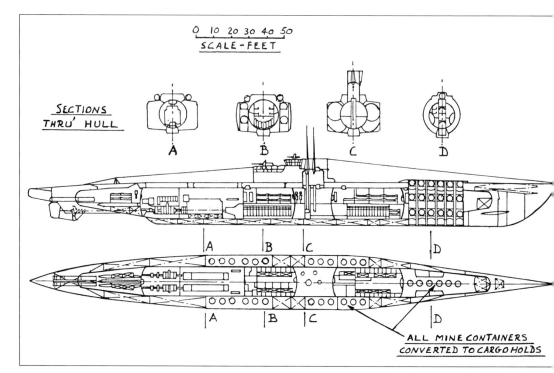

15. Details of U-boat type XB minelayer, as U-234: 2,150 tons submerged displacement, 1,760 tons surfaced displacement; 294 ft long × 30 ft beam × 13 ft draft. Radius of action, 14,500 miles at 12 knots surfaced, and 4 knots submerged. Two 21 in torpedo tubes; 66 mines; crew of 52. U-234 was the last of her type constructed.

the path of the Atlantic convoys and so work progressed slowly. The partially completed hull was still in the construction yard when, during a particularly heavy raid by the USAF, the front section of the boat was badly damaged. Eventually U-234 was repaired and given a complete new front end. Two days before Christmas 1943 she slid into the water for the first time. After sea trials she was handed over to the *Kriegsmarine* and her Captain, Johann Fehler, on 3 March 1944.

Fehler was new to submarines. His first experience of action had been as Mines and Explosives Officer on board the commerce raider *Atlantis*, and between March 1940 and November 1941 *Atlantis* sank 22 Allied merchant ships, before being sunk herself by the cruiser *Devonshire*. All the crew was rescued by U-boats and returned to Germany. This was Fehler's first taste of life underwater and by September 1943 he had qualified as a U-boat commander.

After successful acceptance trials, U-234 first joined the 4th Flotilla at Stettin and then, on 14 June 1944, the 5th Flotilla at Kiel. On 5 September she returned to the Germania yards at Kiel for an overhaul and major structural modifications. Originally built as a minelayer, 24 vertical mineshafts passed through the fuel

German submarine U-234. The commissioning ceremony on 2 March 1944 at Kiel. Captain Fehler and crew. (via author)

saddle tanks, 12 on either side of the conning tower, and the remaining mine storage consisted of 6 shafts, 60 ft back from the bows, passing right through the pressure hull, as in fig. 15.

All the fittings for the mines were now removed and two large storage areas built either side of the conning tower, with 6 watertight tubes replacing the forward mineshafts. In addition, 4 above-deck horizontal containers for torpedoes were adapted for cargo stowage.

In December 1944, almost a year to the day since she was originally launched, U-234 put to sea again for trials in her new role. Ten weeks later, back at Kiel, and with the trials completed, the new crew started loading fuel, provisions and cargo for U-234's first and last voyage. Her destination was supposed to be secret but everyone seemed to know where she were heading; having two Japanese officers supervising the loading of some of the cargo made it a bit obvious.

Among the cargo being loaded were: drugs; radar and radio equipment; technical drawings; lenses; anti-aircraft rockets and other munitions; mercury; lead; zinc; and a disassembled Me262 jet fighter. In addition, one particular item was receiving special attention from the two Japanese officers travelling with the boat: about 50 small lead containers, approximately 10 in sq.

One member of the crew, Wolfgang Hirschfeld, the telecommunications officer, clearly remembered on that cold January morning, watching the two Japanese as they sat on the foredeck, wrapping gummed paper round the lead cubes and then writing the figures U.235 on the outside in black paint. With some difficulty crew members lowered them into the forward storage tubes and when Hirschfeld asked one of the officers, Captain Tomonaga, what the symbols meant, he was told that the cargo was originally intended for U-235 and that boat was no longer going to Japan. For some reason Hirschfeld pursued the matter and checked at the Operations Office: U-235 was one of the small coastal U-boats, certainly not capable of reaching Japan.

Apart from the mixed cargo of war material being loaded, U-234 was also scheduled to carry a human cargo to Japan. Crammed into her already tight accommodation were twelve passengers, a mixed group of military and civilian experts. The two Japanese were Colonel Genzo Shosi, aeronautical officer (Japanese Army Airforce) and Captain Hideo Tomonaga, submarine architect (Japanese Navy). Seven were members of the German armed forces: Oberst Fritz von Sandrath, specialist in air defence (Luftwaffe); Lieutenant Erich Menzel, specialist in radar and aide to Kessler (Luftwaffe); Fregattenkapitain Gerhard Falck, Naval architect, responsible for the lead containers; Korvettenkapitan Dr Ing Heinz Schlicke, specialist in radar and other electronic equipment; Kapitanleutnant Heinrich Hellendorn, specialist in naval anti-aircraft gunnery; Kapitanleutnant Richard Bulla, specialist in air-sea co-operation; Oberstleutnant Geshwaderichter Kay Nieschling, military judge appointed to investigate the Sorge spy affair in Tokyo. Finally, there were two civilians: August Bringewald, Messerschmitt design engineer specializing in the Me163 rocket interceptor and Me262 jet fighter, and Franz Ruf, Messerschmitt procurement specialist, particularly in production facilities for rocket and jet aircraft. General Ulrich Kessler, newly appointed air attaché in Tokyo (Luftwaffe), was to join the boat in Norway.

On 25 March 1945, with loading completed in the shelter of the U-boat pens at Kiel and while the rest of the city was subject to another of the almost constant air attacks, U-234 slipped out of her anchorage to meet three of the latest type XXIII U-boats and their escort.

The plan was that this little armada would attempt to reach the comparative safety of the Norwegian port of Kristiansand. The escorts would leave as soon as they were in open water.

Using their surface speed as much as possible and taking advantage of the neutral seas off Sweden, the four U-boats arrived in Horton fjord two days later. They had survived several air attacks from marauding Allied aircraft as well as collisions with groups of ships heading back to Germany; the situation everywhere was becoming chaotic as the last few days of the Third Reich dragged on.

For the next few days U-234 was busy with training exercises in preparation for the next leg of the voyage. There was also maintenance and final repairs of equipment to be carried out. Unfortunately on 29 March, during a training exercise, another U-boat, U-1301, collided with U-234 below the conning tower on the port side, puncturing one of the fuel tanks, which resulted in the loss of 16 tons of heavy oil. With no dry docks available locally (the nearest was Bergen, which meant a three-day journey), Captain Fehler decided to have the boat repaired by his own crew members. Finding a quiet fjord near Kristiansand, and with the forward tanks flooded to raise the stern, the damaged structure was repaired and a new piece of steel was welded over the 5 ft sq gash. This work took the best part of a week and following the arrival of General Kessler, who must have had grave misgivings about ever taking up his post in Tokyo, the fuel tanks were topped up and the boat prepared to leave on its lone journey.

On the morning of 14 April 1945 Hirschfeld's signal room received the following radio message from Germany: 'U-234. Only sail on the orders of the highest level. Führer HQ.' This was followed a few hours later by: 'U-234. Sail only on my order. Sail at once on your own initiative. Doenitz.' Quickly arranging for an escort to clear any mines in their path, and with a final topping up of the fuel tanks, U-234 at last headed out to sea on the afternoon of 16 April 1945.

Time was quickly running out for the U-boat, on a voyage that would have taken two months, and time was also running out for the Third Reich. It was four days to Hitler's birthday, but the celebrations deep in the *Führerbunker* had lost some of their appeal. The Russians were inside Berlin and all the 'old guard' present (Goering, Goebbels, Himmler, Ribbentrop and Bormannn), as well as the last of the surviving military leaders (Keitel, Jodl, Doenitz and Krebs) knew the real situation. As they made their way from the 'party' – Goering with a caravan of trucks laden with booty from his dynamited Karinhall (his country house) – this was the last time most of them saw their Führer alive.

U-234 headed north up the Norwegian coast, which was still in German hands, and kept as close as possible to land. Fortunately it was equipped with the very latest in radar and radar-detection equipment, and on board was Schlicke, the radar expert, as well as the U-boat's own electronic experts. By this time Allied aircraft were free to roam unhindered by the Luftwaffe and the crew survived several near misses from the submarine hunters. A few days later they were through the Iceland–Faroes gap and into the Atlantic, heading south-east on the surface at full speed, 17 knots. The radar aerials kept a wide sweep through 360° of sky for the elusive aircraft. The crew and passengers began to relax; they had survived the worst part of the voyage and they were now only a small grey dot in the vast Atlantic.

On 1 May the signals room in U-234 picked up the first announcement of Hitler's death and the appointment of Grand Admiral Doenitz as his successor, but there were no messages for U-234 as she ploughed on through the Atlantic rollers. Nothing disturbed the glowing radar screens down below. However, on the evening of 4 May, Hirschfeld received a message from U-boat Command to the effect that all German submarines were to observe a ceasefire with effect from 0800 hours German time on the following morning, 5 May. All attacks were forbidden and any pursuit of enemy ships was to be abandoned immediately. Furthermore, all 'attack U-boats' were to return to Norwegian harbours. Captain

Fehler noted the words. U-234 was not an 'attack U-boat' and so they could continue on their present heading.

On 8 May 1945 a message was picked up notifying them of Germany's surrender. New orders prohibited the sending of coded messages and ordered the destruction of all old ciphers and the surrender of all current and forward-dated code books. Later that day, the U-boat Commander in Bergen, Captain Rosing, sent a signal to U-234 in the Japanese cipher: 'U-234. Continue your voyage or return to Bergen. FdU.' When Hirschfeld showed Captain Fehler the message Fehler replied: 'Well, I'm definitely not going back.'

Fehler may have decided to press on, but there was now a basic dilemma. The radio room had been monitoring all the wavelengths for information, including US broadcasts. On board the U-234 there was no means of verifying any of the information, but two days earlier, on 6 May, it had picked up a US news bulletin which had declared that Japan now considered itself free and unhindered by all treaties and contracts with the German Reich and would continue to fight on alone. On 8 May a message was picked up reporting that Japan had severed all relations with Germany and therefore German citizens in Japan were considered to be aliens and would be arrested.

U-234 was now in mid-Atlantic, her precious cargo was intact and she was all set for Japan. But what sort of reception would she receive? Captain Fehler informed his officers that he intended to surrender the submarine at the earliest opportunity. The two Japanese officers were placed under arrest and confined to their quarters, which was the only course open to Fehler.

Radio messages were now received from US stations to all German submarines that: all torpedo detonators were to be removed and jettisoned but the disarmed torpedoes were to be retained; all AA ammunition was to be jettisoned and the guns secured, facing astern; a black flag was to be set at the extended periscope tube; navigation lights were to be illuminated; the exact navigational position was to be reported and all further movements were to be made while surfaced. For all sea areas a port of surrender was given, and for U-234 this meant Halifax, Nova Scotia. Despite these instructions and orders Captain Fehler was still undecided, and a meeting between his officers and the passengers revealed disagreement on what action to take. Kessler and von Sandrath wanted to proceed to Japan; others wanted to sail to the South Pacific; Judge Nieschling and other keen Nazis wanted to surrender.

On 13 May Hirschfeld sent out the following message to Halifax: 'Halifax. Here is U-234.' The answer came almost immediately: 'U-234 give your position.' Once this had been transmitted they were given a course for Halifax and ordered to respond with their location every four hours. In fact, Captain Fehler had no intention of complying. For reasons of his own he intended to surrender in a US port. In the meantime, the Japanese officers, deprived of their weapons, had taken an overdose of sleeping pills and the submarine's doctor reported to Fehler that they were in a coma.

The air waves were now red hot with messages from Halifax concerning the obvious non-compliance with their orders and Fehler gave instructions to transmit false reports of their position. Within a few hours, however, it was clear that all signals from U-234 were being jammed and shortly afterwards the aft look-out reported a warship approaching quickly on the port quarter. It was the American destroyer USS *Sutton* and when it was within range U-234 was ordered to head for the Gulf of Maine and ignore all further communications from Halifax. It was now clear the USS *Sutton* had been the source of the jamming, and with the destroyer astern they now headed for Maine, on the surface and with a black flag attached to the periscope.

Fehler was now concerned about the Japanese. He knew that if they were still alive when they landed, the Americans would try to revive them. He instructed the doctor to ensure that they died peacefully and a few hours later he reported that they were dead. The bodies were sewn into weighted hammocks and despite *Sutton*'s signals as to why the U-boat had stopped, they were slipped into the sea after a short ceremony. The position was 47°07' N 42°25' W, approximately 1,000 miles from land. Soon afterwards a prize-crew from the *Sutton* came on board and on Saturday 19 May, the submarine entered Portsmouth harbour, New Hampshire.

U-234 was the last of three German U-boats that had surrendered at Portsmouth but this time there were much tighter security restrictions on the crew and their cargo. Nevertheless the local press reported the U-boat's arrival and a few days later provided some details of the crew, passengers and cargo. Mention was made of rockets, jet planes and German secret weapons, and in the general euphoria at the ending of the war in Europe, it made good reading. When the contents of the forward storage tubes were investigated and found to be lead containers the remainder of the cargo was unloaded and some days later, following the arrival of a number of US scientists, the lead boxes were finally removed. Hirschfeld and other crew members witnessed the arrival of these specialists, with their various instruments, and their concern at the radioactivity emitting from the forward storage tubes.

For 'personal considerations' the boxes were unloaded by the crew, as the Americans were reluctant to do it themselves. Wolfgang Hirschfeld subsequently wrote two books concerning the voyage of U-234, with his recollections of what happened. Later the US government acknowledged that part of the cargo onboard U-234 was 'Uranium oxide (10 cases, 56 kg, marked, For Japanese Army).' Although this confirms a connection with nuclear physics, neither the substance nor the quantity of the cargo directly relates to the evidence of the crew, in particular Hirschfeld, who has put down his recollections in print and provided information for the two television programmes about U-234, the latest being a joint German/Japanese production in 1993. Despite this speculation, and requests made to the US naval authorities, the reply has always been that matters relating to nuclear affairs are still subject to official secrecy.

The story of U-234 is left for the time being. The next question is: if the contents of the lead boxes came from a nuclear reactor, who built it and where?

CHAPTER TWELVE

The Nuclear Question

The extent to which German nuclear work progressed during the war has always been centred on two main issues: Did Germany produce a working nuclear reactor and did their top nuclear physicists really understand what was required to build an atomic bomb? These two concerns and the characters involved have resulted in a multitude of books, articles and media programmes by historians and physicists in Germany, the USA, the UK and Canada from 1945 to the present time. The debate continues, especially with regard to the role of the most influential of the German physicists. Did they really not understand how to make 'the bomb', or was it some devious ruse, in an attempt to ensure that Hitler never had a nuclear weapon?

To most people the term nuclear weapon means only one thing – the atomic bomb. Yet there is an alternative, mentioned on page 13 – to use the by-products of a reactor, in the form of radioactive dust. In any case, the German nuclear physicists provided the last ingredient for Hitler's miracle weapon. Throughout the war there was one main group which administered, directed and carried out nuclear research in the Third Reich, and in particular it was involved in the military application of the work. Those in the government with access to Hitler and the other leaders were Schumann, Gerlach, Esau and Ohnesorge and those actually involved with the work were Heisenberg, Harteck, Diebner, Bothe, Dopel, Wirtz, Hahn, Weizsacker, Bopp and Houtermans. Of those involved, possibly Werner Heisenberg's name has become synonymous with the German wartime nuclear work.

Heisenberg, a German physicist of world renown before the war started, had in 1933 received the Nobel Prize for Physics. However, his association with the ideas of Einstein became unacceptable amid the anti-Jewish feelings that were gathering strength after Hitler came to power in 1933. In particular, two previous Nobel Prize winners in Germany, Philip Lenard in 1905 and Johannes Stark in 1919, were among the leading exponents of the Aryan physics dogma that appealed to Hitler and his followers in the Nazi Party.

Heisenberg came under increasing official pressure to disassociate himself from any connection with the Jewish physicists, especially when he was being considered for the vacant chair of Theoretical Physics at the University of Munich. In 1939 Heisenberg was only 38, and he was certainly ambitious. He travelled abroad, especially to the USA, where many of the world's most notable nuclear physicists were now living. These included some of his compatriots, but

Heisenberg saw his future back in Germany. For the Munich post, Heisenberg was interviewed several times by Himmler's SS, travelling to the Berlin SS headquarters from Leipzig, where he was a professor at the university. When the Munich post went to Wilhelm Müller in 1939, Heisenberg could consider himself lucky that the intervention of well-known figures in the world of science eventually led to his re-acceptance into the scientific community of the Third Reich. Heisenberg in the meantime returned to Leipzig, disappointed but not deterred. As a believer in German nationalism, but not in the National Socialist Party, he was determined to stay at the forefront of the rapidly rising world of nuclear physics.

In December 1938, at the Kaiser Wilhelm Institute (KWI) for Chemistry in Berlin, Hahn and Strassman had demonstrated the fission of uranium U.235, and the report of this discovery spread like wildfire around the world. The implications of the announcement were appreciated particularly quickly in Europe, the USA, Russia and Japan. Some physicists may have been talking about the peaceful uses of this potential source of energy, but in 1939 the world was preparing itself for conflict and there were obviously other uses for it, especially military.

Other reports followed very quickly. The French physicists, Joliot-Curie, von Halban and Kowarski stated what was probably obvious: the fission process was most likely part of a chain reaction, which if allowed to continue, would result in a massive, instantaneous release of energy. In Germany, physicist Wilhelm Hanle delivered a lecture at Göttingen on the possibilities of harnessing this energy in a graphite-uranium pile, and a report of this lecture was eventually forwarded to Abraham Esau, Head of Physics at the Reich Research Council. Two other independent groups of scientists who were interested in the new world of the atom also attracted the attention of the military. Nikolaus Riehl, a physicist at the metals company Auer and an ex-student of Hahn, wrote to the Army Ordnance Office, while the Professor of Chemistry at Hamburg University, Paul Harteck and a colleague, Wilhelm Groth, wrote to the War Ministry.

Harteck's letter in particular, written on 24 April 1939, pointed out very clearly the potential for nuclear physics to provide explosives with unimaginable force; hence the country that possessed such material would have a dominant position throughout the world. This was not exactly the sort of letter one might expect from a chemistry professor, an academic with no obvious military interests. But this was Germany in 1939. Only five days later Hitler delivered his most important and last peacetime speech to the Reichstag, in response to a telegram from President Roosevelt. Roosevelt's telegram asked for assurances from Hitler and Mussolini that they had no military intentions towards the 31 countries listed in it, including Poland, France and Great Britain.

This speech, described by William Shirer as Hitler's masterpiece, poured scorn on Roosevelt's attempt to put the blame on to Germany for the present insecurity in the world. Hitler stated that Germany was only seeking to regain its rightful place in the world, denied for so long by the 448 articles of the Versailles Treaty, the infamous Diktat.

Despite this oratory, Hitler fooled no one. Germany was gearing itself for war, all the talk was of war and the new armaments factories were buzzing with activity. The Army Ordnance Office was not only directing the secret armaments work of Krupp, Rheinmetall-Borsig and others during the years of the Versailles Treaty, it was also funding the rocket work of Dornberger and his team. Although in early 1939 they had produced nothing significant, it was obvious that any new material which might conceivably have a military application for the new Reich would only be encouraged. Many Germans, including members of the scientific community, had been aggrieved at the harshness of the Versailles Treaty, and what Hitler was doing in public had restored the confidence and status of Germany as a world power and evoked strong nationalistic feeling.

The various reports from the nuclear physicists were now reviewed by Erich Schumann, Head of Research at the Ordnance Office, Kurt Diebner, (who was carrying out uranium research for the Army at the Kummersdorf range, also Dornberger's first 'home') and Esau. The subject was new and the issues were complicated. It obviously needed further discussion and from April to October 1939 a series of meetings and conferences was held, at which all the ranking physicists, including Heisenburg, were present.

The future for the new nuclear science was still not entirely clear. A door had been opened by the discovery of fission, but no experimental work had been carried out to verify the concept of a chain reaction. No atomic pile had been built and hence there was no confirmation that once the reaction had started it could be controlled and would not lead to a catastrophic release of energy. In short there was still an enormous amount of work to be done, not only as far as any military use was concerned, but to confirm the theories that had been put forward.

The way ahead decided by the Ordnance Office was that they would distribute packages of work on nuclear research to the leading organizations in the field. The intention was that with regular reviews of the progress, a balanced consensus would be available within a short period of time, so that a decision could be made on the military possibilities of nuclear power. The work was distributed as follows: University of Leipzig (Heisenberg and Dopel); University of Hamburg (Harteck); Army Research Centre, Gottow (Diebner); Kaiser Wilhelm Institute for Medical Research, Heidelberg (Bothe); Kaiser Wilhelm Institute for Physics, Dahlem, Berlin (von Weizsacker, Wirtz, Diebner and Bopp).

The focal point for this research would be the KWI in Dahlem. As the work involved military research, and hence was state secret, the resident director there, Peter Debye, a Dutchman, was asked to either accept German citizenship or resign. In the event he resigned and Kurt Diebner was appointed as his replacement.

All this research was directed towards one initial goal: was it practicable to build a nuclear reactor capable of producing energy and material suitable for a military weapon? Heisenberg's work was completed within two months and submitted to Schumann, and by the end of 1941 all the work necessary to reach a decision had been handed over to the Ordnance Office. An overall report was issued by Kurt Diebner and this recommended that, with the cooperation of industry, work should proceed to build a reactor and to produce fissionable materials. The report recognized, however, that in the short term the possibility of building a bomb was remote.

By 1941 and the issue of this report, Heisenberg appears to have become the unofficial, self-appointed spokesman for all those working on nuclear matters for the Army. This report for the Army Ordnance Office had put forward two conceptual designs for a reactor. The first was the Heavy Water Reactor, which used natural uranium, with heavy water (deuterium oxide) as a 'moderator'. That is, for the neutrons to be captured at the right speed, they needed to be slowed down or 'moderated'. Heavy water was specified because its neutron-absorbing properties, which might kill the reaction, had been removed and so refined natural uranium oxide could be used. Ordinary 'light' water could be used as a moderator but as it still contained neutron-absorbing chemicals, it meant that enriched uranium had to be used in the reactor. Natural uranium oxide is composed of 99.28% of the non-fissionable U.238 and 0.71% of the fissionable U.235. In order to use 'light' water in a reactor the proportion of the fissionable U.235 in the uranium oxide would have to be increased (or enriched) to approximately 3%.

It was basically a swings and roundabouts situation. Heavy water was very difficult and expensive to obtain, requiring huge amounts of electricity, but natural uranium oxide was relatively cheap and, in reasonable amounts, easily obtainable. Ordinary light water was obviously easily obtainable but it was anticipated that to produce U.235 in order to enrich the uranium oxide would be very difficult and expensive, and several methods were still being investigated for obtaining U.235. Heavy water was already being produced both in Germany and, in larger quantities, in Norway, using their ample hydro-electric power. Heisenberg also mentioned using pure carbon as a moderator, with the neutron-absorbing impurities removed, and refined natural uranium oxide as the fuel.

The most favoured design was a reactor comprising layers of uranium oxide, sandwiched between layers of heavy water; between each sandwich would be a layer of pure carbon, and the whole would be surrounded by a neutron reflector of pure carbon. The total volume would be 1.6 cu yd and it would need 2–3 tons of uranium oxide, 132 gallons of heavy water and 1 ton of pure carbon. Heisenberg went on to discuss the advantages of using enriched uranium for a reactor and the possible energy released using the nuclear reaction as a weapon.

However, Schumann advised against a national industrial approach to build a reactor. Instead the project was to be transferred to the Kaiser Wilhelm Society, which controlled the various KWI establishments, and the work should be classified as 'basic research, important to the war effort'.

The lack of any real interest in nuclear fission, as Dornberger was finding out with his rocket projects, was influenced by the success of the conventional armed forces, such that by the summer of 1941 Germany either controlled or was allied with most of Europe; any other nations were neutral. This confidence in the conventional forces and what they had achieved with existing weapons is exemplified by Hitler's personal order, issued in March 1941, that any new military projects had to be completed within a specified timescale; otherwise they were not to be continued.

The USA had no such delusions in 1941 about the military situation. The Manhattan Project, under General Groves, was already underway. In March 1941 the first microscopic quantities of the highly fissionable new element plutonium, Pu.239, had been produced in the laboratory and a few days later it was confirmed that under neutron bombardment, plutonium atoms fissioned as readily as U.235. The American politicians and military leaders had been made aware of the possibilities of using the new nuclear energy as a military weapon and they had been appraised by the new experts of what the next steps should be. There were five basic choices available. To separate U.235 in order to provide enriched uranium for a reactor (by 3%) or for a bomb (by 70%) the feasible methods were: centrifuge; gas diffusion; electromagnetic. To obtain plutonium for a bomb the feasible methods were: nuclear pile, graphite moderated, using enriched uranium; nuclear pile, heavy water moderated, using natural uranium. The cyclotron was really only a laboratory method. The Americans pressed on with a single-minded purpose, concentrating on what appeared to be the most promising method of enrichment, gaseous diffusion (proved later to be correct), and the building of a reactor specifically for the production of plutonium.

In Germany the nuclear researchers who did not share all of Heisenburg's views, must have been showing signs of impatience at the lack of progress. Paul Harteck, possibly the most dynamic of those not directly associated with Heisenberg, had realized that when Heisenberg had discussed the question of reactor temperatures, it was feasible that a reactor could be designed which produced no heat and therefore no power; yet it would still produce irradiated material, in the form of spent fuel and radioactive isotopes, plus plutonium, which they were also aware of as well as its possible use in a nuclear weapon.

This reactor would have to be moderated at a very low temperature and one method suggested by Harteck was to use solid carbon dioxide (dry ice) at –80°C, which was cheap and easily obtainable. Harteck was an excellent experimental physicist as well as a theoretician and as such had established many contacts with the big chemical firms, including IG Farben. As early as April 1940 he had obtained an assurance from its research director, Dr Herold, that it would supply 15 tons of dry ice, early in May. Obtaining uranium oxide was a more serious problem and Harteck, not fully aware of the supply situation, asked Diebner at the KWI if there were 300 kg available. Harteck's request eventually found its way to Heisenberg, as Diebner knew that he was expecting a large delivery of the oxide from the War Department as part of his ongoing work for Schumann. However, despite several requests from Harteck, Heisenberg was evasive, suggesting that he delay his low-temperature-reactor experiment until he had ensured that all the correct preparations had been made; otherwise it would be a waste of valuable material. By June, Harteck had only 185 kg of uranium oxide – 50 kg from Diebner and 135 kg from the Auer Company, a metal-refining organization. Nothing came from Heisenberg.

The results which Harteck was able to obtain from this experiment proved little. However, Wirtz, one of the KWI Dahlem group, stated that if this experiment had been successful, Harteck would have been able to obtain some of the basic coefficients, especially in respect of positive neutron multiplication. This would have enabled him to calculate more accurately the critical size of his low-temperature reactor.

Heisenberg's reluctance to supply Harteck with uranium oxide is surprising when it is considered that at that time he himself was not carrying out any work directly involving large amounts of this material. In fact his only two reports issued to Schumann at the Army Ordnance Office in August and December 1940 were based on laboratory experiments using only small amounts of uranium oxide. Heisenberg's reasons for having a ton of the oxide at Leipzig were not explained, but, the only other use of potentially large amounts of uranium oxide at the time was for an experimental pile attempted by Wirtz, Fischer and Bopp at KWI, Dahlem. The supply problem was about to be resolved, however.

The German offensive against the Low Countries had led to the rapid conquest of Holland and Belgium, and when King Leopold III surrendered on 28 May 1940 it resulted in a uranium windfall. For some time the Union Minière had obtained uranium from its mines at Katanga in the Belgian Congo, and their refining plant and warehouse at Oolen in Belgium still had over 1,000 tons of mixed uranium products, which they had not been able to ship to the USA, before the Germans arrived. When this news eventually filtered through to the German nuclear researchers, Harteck started to plan a much larger experimental pile, using 20 tons of refined uranium oxide and 30 tons of dry ice.

The plans for this second, more ambitious, experiment, once they were known, drew criticism from Heisenberg and others who claimed that the experiment was too large and that a more gradual approach was necessary; otherwise it would be wasteful of resources.

It is not difficult to realize that Harteck, who was predominantly an experimentalist, would meet opposition from the other nuclear researchers, especially Heisenberg, who was essentially a theoretician. Here they were carrying on with their basic research and there was Harteck, trying to leap-frog over everyone.

While Heisenberg and Dopel were working on the use of heavy water as a moderator, Bothe and Jensen at KWI, Heidelberg, were working on the use of graphite. A report issued by Bothe in 1941 stated that the purest graphite they could obtain resulted in too high a rate of neutron capture and hence Heisenberg's theoretical model of a reactor would not work. Two other workers, Professors Joos and Hanle from Göttingen, showed that Bothe had not detected the neutron absorbers boron and cadmium in the carbon used: when he had reduced the material to ash, after the experiment, these two highly efficient neutron absorbers had been lost into the atmosphere. Joos and Hanle went on to describe how reactor-grade graphite could be obtained.

If any real headway was to be made with a reactor the Army Ordnance Office, still in control of nuclear research under its research director Erich Schumann, now had to choose between heavy water and graphite as a moderator. To produce the required quantities of reactor-grade graphite would embarrass the supply situation for other essential materials required in its production. The alternative, heavy water, was a different matter. Unlike graphite, it could be used indefinitely without deteriorating, and a source of supply had just become available in Norway.

The Norsk-Hydro plant at Rjukan produced heavy water as a by-product of its hydro-electric-powered chemical works and supplies had been coming to Germany since 1940. These were relatively small amounts, 100 kg per month, but this could obviously be increased if there was a change in the priority rating. On this basis, heavy water was chosen as the moderator and work on graphite slowed down. Nevertheless, Joos and Hanle also showed that graphite would act as a neutron reflector, if placed on the outer fringes of the pile, thereby improving the fission process. If Heisenberg and his colleagues were not aware of the reflector advantages of graphite, it did eventually become apparent – in January 1945 it was used for this purpose in their final experiments.

Another aspect being investigated by the Heisenberg group, and in particular von Weizsacker, was the possibility that the fission process inside a reactor may proceed to another, perhaps even more fissionable, element than uranium U.235. As far back as July 1940 von Weizsacker had produced a report which put forward this thesis, based on work carried out in the USA in 1939. Von Weizsacker's report went on to state that this new element, known then as Eka Re.239, could possibly be used as a nuclear explosive, in preference to enriched U.235, which would require a huge industrial effort to produce the many kilos needed for a bomb. Perhaps Heisenberg and his colleagues thought that as the possibility of building a working reactor was so remote, the topic of this mystery new element, now known as plutonium, could be discussed in safety.

Apart from the readily fissionable isotope of plutonium, Pu.239, produced in reactors as part of the fission process, simultaneously there are several other plutonium isotopes produced and they are all extremely radioactive. With one exception, Pu.243, they all have very long half-lives (that is, their radioactivity decays to half its original value within the half-life timescale). Thus, the potential existed not only to use the fissionable Pu.239 as a bomb, but also to use the highly radioactive plutonium isotopes mixed with sand as another variation on the nuclear weapon idea.

In the meantime, Heisenberg's influence and reinstatement in the scientific world was confirmed in the spring of 1942 when he was appointed Director of the KWI for Physics in Dahlem, which also included a chair at the University of Berlin. Unfortunately, that meant removing the current director, Kurt Diebner, but it was a question of 'politics' behind the scenes. Heisenberg's recognition was part of an ongoing power struggle, whose aims were to reinstate German physics. In the 1930s any connection with the Jewish community had meant being sent into the scientific wilderness or worse. The Ministry of Education, directed by Bernhard Rust, was one of the prime targets of these changes, owing to the powerful influence that it could exert on any scientific project. Early in 1942, the Reich Research Council, the most important part of the ministry in terms of research funding, was transferred to the growing empire of Hermann Goering, as part of his responsibilities as Commissioner of the Four Year Plan.

Another figure now appeared on the nuclear scene, Albert Speer. Speer had been appointed Minister of Armaments and Munitions after the unexpected death of Dr Fritz Todt as a result of a flying accident, in February 1942. Speer was not interested in the political and scientific infighting that was going on around Hitler. He was more concerned with ensuring that Germany had the full benefit from any new developments that were taking place, particularly in science. This included nuclear power and Heisenberg gave a talk on this topic to Speer and other military and political leaders in June 1942. Heisenberg reaffirmed what the Army had said some months previously, that any possibility of producing nuclear weapons was beyond the timescale of the present conflict; they were something for the future.

From 1942 to 1943, as far as Heisenberg's public statements were concerned, the chances of building a working reactor were becoming remote. As has been mentioned, there is still considerable debate going on as to whether Heisenberg deliberately misinformed the German leaders about the difficulties of building a reactor and a bomb or whether he and his associates did not understand some of the fundamental issues involving such projects. Heisenberg was now spending part of his time lecturing in German-controlled countries and in Switzerland, and the scope of his nuclear work became less orientated towards reactors and more towards subjects with no military significance, such as cosmic rays.

However, there was other work going on with a military interest and associated with the KWI. A contract was placed by the Army in February 1943 with the Biophysics Department at Frankfurt to study the biological effects of radiation, with regard to the possibility of it being used as a weapon. In addition, Field Marshal Milch was organizing Luftwaffe scientists to investigate the feasibility of using X-rays and gamma radiation as a defence against enemy aircraft. Also, Professor Bothe at Heidelberg had reported in 1943 that investigations were being carried out to determine the possibility of using radioactive elements with a short half-life as a nuclear weapon.

The acceptance of heavy water as the most suitable moderator appeared to stimulate Allied interest in the Norsk-Hydro plant, and attacks on the facility became more frequent. In February 1943 a team of Norwegian saboteurs from the UK destroyed 350 kgs of heavy water and put the process out of action for three months. Other raids by the USAF caused some disruption to supplies and in February 1944 the last major shipment of heavy water in Norway was destroyed on a ferry, while *en route* to Germany. The supplies available in Germany amounted to 2,500 kg, which would have been barely enough for a single concentrated reactor experiment (had all the interested parties been able to agree on a common method of approach).

In May 1943 Heisenberg, lecturing to the German Academy of Aeronautical Research, referred to progress towards a reactor design: 'The next state is to build a reactor using about 1,500 kg of heavy water and 3,000 kg of uranium metal in layers of metal plates.' He expected that this might be built in the summer of 1943 and that it would provide definite conclusions as to the ultimate properties of the working reactor. This was the basis for the principle reactor design, as Heisenberg saw it, and remained so from 1944 onwards when experiments were carried out using graphite as a reflector with only 1,500 kg of uranium.

There were other organizations, not connected with the KWI, which were interested in nuclear power, and one of the most unlikely of these was the Deutschen Reichspost (German Post Office). This concerned itself not only with the task of ensuring that the mail was delivered on time, but with research completely unconnected with this function.

The flexibility of its approach to research may derive from experiments of the 1920s, when these early pioneers attempted to build mail-carrying rockets to show that there was a practical purpose to their work. However, as early as September 1941 a report had been issued by the Forschungsanstalt der Deutschen Reichspost (Post Office Research Institute) under Baron Manfred von Ardenne. In it Professor Fritz Houtermans described how a chain reaction could be initiated by the use of a liquid carbon moderator in a low temperature reactor; although no power would be produced, radioactive isotopes would be obtained and these would have wide applications in other fields. This conclusion, that the low-temperature reactor was the simplest method of obtaining the by-products of the fission process, had been reached independently of the work carried out by Harteck. As a matter of routine, Heisenberg received a copy of this report, as did fellow researchers. A copy was also sent personally by von Ardenne to Paul Harteck at Hamburg.

Although von Ardenne did not have a formal scientific background, in the 1930s he had quickly become interested in the field of telecommunications, especially television. He had a large laboratory built in the grounds of his house in Lichterfeld-Ost, Berlin, and added an underground bunker complex. His entrepreneurial skills brought him considerable success with larger industrial concerns, resulting in contracts from Krupp and Lorenz (of radar fame). In 1937 a permanent contract was signed between von Ardenne's Institute, as it was now known, and the Post Office, run by Dr Wilhelm Ohnesorge. This contract was for development work on radar and television, and was amended in 1940 to include nuclear physics.

By 1940 von Ardenne had several physicists working for him. Probably the most capable of these was Houtermans, who had been an assistant professor at Berlin in 1933, followed by spells in England and Russia. Sent back to Germany in 1940, following one of Stalin's purges, he was arrested by the Gestapo but was paroled on the personal intervention of Professor von Laue, the 1914 Nobel Prize winner in physics. Houtermans was almost a natural recruit for von Ardenne's new organization; he did not fit in with the mainstream nuclear workers, but many of the conclusions presented in his 1941 report mirrored those put forward by the Establishment. As in Harteck's thesis, these included the concept of the low-temperature reactor, by which a moderator of heavy water or graphite was unnecessary. His version would use a carbon compound, methane, which is liquid at $-164°C$ to $-186°C$, as a moderator. He also covered the subject of plutonium.

The actual design of the reactor was included in Houtermans' report; it was a sphere lined with a reflector of natural uranium. He estimated that his reactor would produce an amount of radioactive isotopes equivalent to 10,000–100,000 cyclotrons. No mention was made of nuclear weapons. Von Ardenne was probably more interested in the commercial aspects of relatively large and cheap amounts of isotopes for use in industry and medicine.

Following Heisenberg's review of this report, he visited von Ardenne's laboratory with von Weizsacker on 28 November 1941. Details of their conversations were not recorded but it is clear that Heisenberg and von Weizsacker must have felt some concern when they discovered that a third party, outside their sphere of influence, was engaged on a line of research which they were apparently trying to stifle. But now there was nothing they could do: not only was the Post Office independent, its director, Wilhelm Ohnesorge, had contacts close to the Führer.

A few days later, on 10 December, Houtermans received a visit from none other than the 'father' of fission, Otto Hahn, together with three colleagues from the KWI for Chemistry. Again, there appears to be no record of the conversations, but the fact that Hahn and three others took the trouble to visit this relative unknown in the nuclear field, and certainly not a member of an established group, is significant. Houterman's report was reissued in 1944 and among the new acknowledgments was one to Professor Johannes Jensen, a leading researcher in Harteck's group, for his assistance on low temperature technology.

The bunker in the grounds of von Ardenne's house was ready for use at the end of 1942. It was a considerable size. The main section, 11 yd below ground, had a floor area of 11 yd × 11 yd and the reinforced concrete walls were 1.6 yd thick. Next door was a 250 KW transformer room and beyond that a room 2 yd × 3 yd. One of the original purposes of this underground laboratory, certainly as far as von Ardenne was concerned, was for the installation and use of a cyclotron (an apparatus for producing microscopic quantities of radioactive isotopes). However, according to postwar statements by von Ardenne (who worked for the Russians after the war on nuclear weapons), the cyclotron was never used. Instead it spent the war years gathering dust, until the Russians took Berlin in 1945. (Dr Ohnesorge may also have helped the Russians; he declined to join the West and spent his last years in East Berlin.)

It can be seen, therefore, that as far as the low-temperature reactor is concerned there is an established link between von Ardenne's Institute and Houtermans and Harteck. Harteck had received a copy of Houterman's 1941 report and it is more than likely that visits were exchanged. There is also no doubt that Heisenberg's assumption of the role of unofficial spokesman for all German nuclear research would not have been accepted by everyone, especially as no real headway seemed to have been made under this regime. They, too, were ambitious and may have felt too restrained by the current situation. Harteck, especially, would have recognized in the Post Office organization of Wilhelm Ohnesorge an independent outlet for some of his own ideas on low-temperature reactors, which had been frustrated since 1940, mainly by Heisenberg.

One of Harteck's supporters was Walther Gerlach, who was Professor of Physics at Munich. He had been appointed scientific head of the Reich Research Council in 1943, a post which had been created the previous year to achieve better industrial use of nuclear power. Its president was the Education Minister, Bernhard Rust.

Its first scientific head had been Professor Esau, President of the Reich Bureau of Standards, and it was hoped that the appointment of Gerlach would, among other things, reduce the competition between the various organizations carrying out nuclear research. One of those influential in removing Esau was Albert Speer, the new Minister of Armaments and Munitions, and it would have not taken him very long to realize that there was something seriously wrong with German nuclear work. There appeared to be no shortage of expertise and money, but no real progress had been made and time was running out for the Third Reich.

It is more than likely that the German leaders, including Speer, were aware of some, if not all, of the US developments in nuclear technology. For example, General Groves quotes the size of the Manhattan Project. The Oak Ridge works, where all the U.235 separation and enrichment equipment was located, had 82,000 people on its payroll by 1945, while the Handford pile, built by DuPont to supply the plutonium for the Nagasaki bomb, used over 10,000 sub-contractors; the total number of people working on the Manhattan Project was over 200,000. With such large numbers involved, there were bound to be leaks of information, especially from those who did not always have their country's best interests uppermost in their minds, whether unintentionally or for monetary gain. In addition, many of the physicists who in the 1930s had gone to the USA from Germany and other countries, still had family ties in these countries. Not until December 1943 was mail censored at Los Alamos. This was the centre of atomic-bomb development and was where Robert Oppenheimer, scientific head of the Manhatten Project, had his office.

With Gerlach's appointment, which was sponsored both by Speer and by Vogler, an associate of Krupp and head of one of Germany's biggest steel works as well as president of the KWI, there is no doubt that the intention was to get something moving. After the war, in 1947, von Heisenberg wrote that: 'Gerlach had taken over the Physics Section of the Reich Research Council [in 1943] and had endeavoured to promote more particularly the scientific side of the uranium problem, including not only the physical but the medical aspects. At the suggestion of Harteck, the intention had been announced for the building of a low-temperature pile. Such a pile, even of small dimensions, could be expected to produce profitable amounts of radioactive elements for tracer research.' What Heisenberg failed to mention was that the radioactive material from this reactor could obviously be put to another use: a nuclear weapon.

CHAPTER THIRTEEN

Gathering the Pieces

Von Heisenberg, unofficial spokesman and leader of the main group of nuclear researchers, was ensuring either by extremely devious and subtle sabotage or because he genuinely did not understand some of the basic principles of a nuclear device that Hitler did not have an atomic bomb. In addition, the members of the Harteck group of nuclear research workers, based at Hamburg, were interested in the low-temperature reactor. The Army Ordnance Office was funding work on rockets at Peenemünde, led by General Dornberger, and was undertaking its own nuclear research at Kummersdorf and Gottow under Kurt Diebner. The German Post Office, led by Dr Ohnesorge, was also supporting nuclear research and work by von Ardenne and Houtermans on low-temperature reactors. Finally, there was the voyage of U-234.

First, the Post Office would not seem a likely candidate for nuclear research, or in fact any research that did not directly relate to its normal postal functions, but the Deutschen Reichspost was different. The contract from Peenemünde (fig. 3), concerning the work on rocket fuels, has already been mentioned. This contract, dated 15 October 1942, also covered the subject of nuclear power as a possible means of rocket propulsion. The quality of the expertise available at the Post Office and its research institute may be illustrated by work they carried out involving telephones.

In 1940 the USA had set up an organization to scramble telephone messages between it and the UK, particularly between Roosevelt and Churchill. Developed by the American Telephone and Telegraph Company (ATT), the A3, as the device was known, changed its code parameters 36 times every 12 minutes and it was thought that the code was unbreakable. The German Post Office was aware of these messages crossing the Atlantic and decided to try to break the code as quickly as possible.

Working from the research institute's headquarters in Ringbahnstrasse, Berlin, and using telephone traffic intercepted at Bordeaux, the code parameters of the A3 were reconstructed and by the end of 1940 the Post Office was able to descramble the messages.

An organization was set up at Noordwijk aan Zee on the Dutch coast, where they could get the best reception, and all the conversations between Churchill and Roosevelt were intercepted, descrambled, translated into German and transmitted to Berlin.

In 1943, following Commando raids, the operation was moved inland to Valkenswaard, 5 km below Eindhoven, and later in 1944 it was moved to Bavaria, where reception was much poorer.

Ohnesorge was one of the 'in' members of Hitler's Cabinet and certainly he was one of the most enduring; he was appointed Minister of Posts in 1937 and remained there until the end of the war. Part of his acceptability was because of his friendship with Heinrich Hoffmann. Hoffmann, the only person allowed to photograph Hitler on a professional basis, had been a member of the leader's inner circle since the 1920s and had introduced Eva Braun to Hitler (she worked in Hoffmann's photographic shop). Ohnesorge, therefore, had a personal link with Hitler and with those closest to him, and this would obviously be of great value.

The Post Office nuclear research was discussed at Hitler's confidential table-talk and Hitler visited von Ardenne's laboratory on more than one occasion. At these visits even his bodyguard was barred from seeing the work being carried out. These recorded table-talk conversations include references to the new weapon, a uranium bomb, and that some of the assembly work on this weapon was being undertaken at the underground rocket factory at Nordhausen. One of the occasions when these weapons were mentioned was in August 1944, when the guest was the Romanian dictator, Marshal Antonescu. Hitler refers to four *Vergeltung* weapons, the fourth one being of such a potent effect that all human life would be exterminated within a radius of 2–2.5 miles of the point of impact.

Paul Harteck's interest in the low–temperature reactor has already been established. He had first attempted to construct a low-temperature pile but his efforts had been frustrated initially by the lack of uranium and later in the year, when Belgian ore was available, by resistance from Heisenberg and his colleagues. Interviewed in 1967 by Professor Ermenc (the transcript was published in 1989, four years after Harteck's death), Harteck stated that the primary purpose of the dry-ice reactor was the production of reactor waste for use in a radiological bombs, which would target the civilian population of enemy cities.

The three years from 1940 to 1943 would have caused considerable frustration for Harteck. Despite all the nuclear research being carried out at the various establishments of the KWI and associated universities, no real headway had been made with a weapon or a reactor. It is not surprising that when Professor Gerlach took over as Physics Director of the Reich Research Council in 1943, those nuclear physicists dissatisfied with the progress of nuclear technology should associate themselves with Gerlach, in the hope that things would improve. Among them was Harteck and his main efforts could again be directed towards the construction of a low-temperature reactor, to produce not an atomic bomb but a canister of radioactive materials; some of them would have half-lives of months and years.

Even Harteck would have no illusions about producing an atomic bomb. In 1943 there was no possibility of manufacturing enough bomb-grade U.235 (of about 70% purity), or enough plutonium (from a reactor); nor was it possible to acquire the separation process technology and equipment within the timescale, or carry out sufficient experiments with plutonium to determine the requirements for a bomb. Harteck's low temperature reactor, like all other types of reactors, would have produced the following types of radiation:

• ALPHA PARTICLES: these are produced during nuclear reactions induced by radiation or from the natural radioactive decay of heavy elements such as uranium or plutonium. A sheet of paper is sufficient to stop alpha radiation, but it is dangerous if contaminated material is inhaled or swallowed.
• BETA PARTICLES: these are emitted from isotopes of the various materials in the reactor during radioactive decay. They can be stopped by an inch or two of perspex or an inch of aluminium, but again they are dangerous if contaminated material is inhaled or swallowed.
• NEUTRONS: these are produced as a direct result of the fission process and hence are only present while the reactor is operating.
• GAMMA and X-RAYS: these are electromagnetic (like radio waves), and gamma radiation is emitted during the fission process and from radioactive isotopes during the decay process; X-rays are similar but are of lower strength. Gamma radiation is very penetrative, and to reduce the radiation intensity by a factor of 10, 2 in of lead or 9 in of concrete are required. The thickness of the shielding depends on the specific mass of the material used.

Therefore, alpha, beta and gamma radiation can be emitted from material removed from a reactor. All can cause radiation illness or death (depending on their radioactive strength) if they are inhaled or swallowed or, in the case of gamma rays, if the body is directly radiated.

All materials break down into various radioactive isotopes during the fission process, so for instance in uranium fuel, after 1,000 days of irradiation and no cooling, some of the isotopes in the fission products are:

	ISOTOPE	HALF-LIFE
Iodine	I-131	8 days
	I-134	52 months
	I-135	6.7 years
Caesium	Cs-137	33 years
Strontium	Sr-90	28 years
	Sr-89	54 days
Ruthenium	Ru-106	1 year

In addition, numerous isotopes are produced from materials affected by the fission process. These usually collect as radioactive waste and they can include isotopes of cobalt, nickel, manganese, iron, molybdenum, tin, etc. from metal items within the reactor system, sodium isotopes from water, carbon (including the famous carbon 14 which has a half-life of 5,700 years) and plutonium isotopes. Five of the plutonium isotopes have very long half-lives: Pu.238, 90 years; Pu.239, 24,400 years; Pu.240, 6,600 years; Pu.241, 13 years; Pu.242, 900,000 years.

Depending on the type of reactor and the materials with which the fission process had come into contact, it would be a relatively simple job to collect a package of radioactive material, although there would be safety problems for those collecting the material. Such a package, mixed with sand or ash, would produce a deadly parcel of radioactive material. Both from Harteck's interview with Ermenc and from Heisenberg's postwar writings it is clear that Harteck was engaged in the construction of a low-temperature reactor, using solid carbon dioxide (dry ice), at $-80°C$, as a moderator and coolant with natural refined uranium oxide as a fuel, and that this work was supported by Gerlach, who had influence and access to considerable resources.

The timing was important: it was the end of 1943 or early in 1944, when Allied bombing was resulting in the dispersal of many establishments of importance, or related, to the war effort and this included the nuclear work. Harteck's facility at Hamburg University was moved to Freiburg, Heisenberg moved to Hechingen and Hahn to nearby Tailfingen. The KWI in Dahlem and von Ardenne's laboratory both had access to underground bunkers and hence were not disturbed by the bombing. This disturbance of many of the established nuclear workshops may have been fortuitous, in that Diebner had also been forced to leave the Berlin area, where his Kummersdorf laboratory and workshops were situated, to relocate as much of his equipment as possible near Erfurt, only 80 miles from Harteck at Freiburg. Diebner, it must be remembered, had been appointed to be Director of the KWI for Physics in Dahlem in 1939, following the refusal of the then Director, Peter Debye, a Dutchman, to take German citizenship. This post, the most prestigious physics post in Germany, had been taken from him in 1942, when, for various reasons including politics, Heisenberg was appointed to the post. Diebner returned to his Army work at Gottow and Kummersdorf. Although he did not have the same status or the same abilities in the world of physics as Heisenberg – and he would have been the first to appreciate that – his removal from the KWI obviously would have caused some resentment, especially against Heisenberg.

Harteck of course had continually been frustrated and at odds with Heisenberg, ever since his first attempt to build a low-temperature reactor in 1940. However, all those interested in the low-temperature option now had the support of Gerlach, one of the few administrators who was also a competent and recognized physicist. Diebner, with his Army connections, was Gerlach's administration assistant. By 1944, with time running out, Gerlach must have realized that Germany's lack of progress in nuclear physics could not have been entirely the result of a lack of funds or official interest, especially considering the expertise that had been available since the 1930s. However, there was still time to build a nuclear weapon as conceived by Harteck.

Harteck's recognition of the potential advantages of heavy water as a reactor moderator had also led him, together with an assistant, Hans Suss, to devise a modification for the manufacturing process at the Norsk-Hydro works, which resulted in a 400% increase in production.

Although by 1944 there were no more supplies of heavy water being sent from Norway, there were approximately 2½ tons available in Germany, sufficient for at least one reactor experiment. In addition he had supported the work of Dr Wilhelm Grath to produce U.235 by the ultra-centrifuge method, that is, two or more centrifuges connected together.

Although the Americans concentrated on perfecting the gaseous diffusion method to produce their U.235 for the Hiroshima bomb, recent centrifuge technology has improved to such an extent that Japan and a European consortium from the UK, Holland and Germany are expecting that centrifuges will provide the most economical method of providing U.235 for reactors and military purposes in the 1990s. The German wartime experiments in uranium separation resulted in ten centrifuges being built, but the output of these was too small for a realistic programme of U.235 production; at least 10,000 centrifuges would have been required, and once again there was not enough time available. The centrifuge laboratory at Celle, 120 miles west of Berlin, was eventually moved to Hechingen, where it was discovered by the Americans.

Von Ardenne had also experimented with methods of uranium separation, concentrating on the modified mass spectrometer electromagnetic method; this was also one of the methods successfully developed by the Americans during the war and this equipment, designed by von Ardenne, was installed in the bunker at his house in Berlin.

Early in 1944, therefore, the stage was set for Harteck, to build a low temperature reactor, moderated and cooled by liquid pentene at −160°C. He had the support of Diebner, Gerlach and the Reich Research Council.

Also backing him were von Ardennes and Houtermans, and their contribution included the influence and resources of the Post Office. Their particular interest was isotope separation and the analysis of material from the reactor using equipment installed in von Ardenne's bunker. The objective was not to build an atomic bomb, as there was insufficient time for the reactor to produce enough plutonium; nor was there time to develop the plutonium technology to build a bomb. However, there was time for the reactor to produce enough radioactive material, in the form of spent fuel and isotopes, to assemble a radioactive package, which would weigh several kilogrammes. The reactor would have to have been operational for several months to produce sufficient radioactive material, and to give it more bulk this would be mixed with some other material such as fuel ash or fine sand, which would itself become radioactive. This would all be loaded in the modified V2, the resultant weapon being the V4. Throughout the period that the reactor was critical, small samples of the isotopes would be analysed in von Ardenne's underground laboratory, supervised by Houtermans. This constant checking of what was being produced by the fission process would reduce the amount of work required when the reactor was shut down, as they would have to know with some accuracy what the radioactive package was composed of, in terms of what isotopes there were, their radioactive energy and their half-life. The researchers had to ensure that the package would still have sufficient radioactivity to remain lethal, following its transfer to Nordhausen and then to the launching site in France.

From 1943 onwards Hitler and the other leaders mentioned in private conversations and public speeches that there was a new weapon, the V4, which was capable of exterminating all human life within a radius of approximately 2 miles from the point of impact. But this new weapon was never described as some new form of explosive; instead it was implied that it was a new form of warfare. A Frenchman now living in the UK has related to me a story that his father told him concerning work he was doing during the war in late 1943 and early 1944. His father was in charge of a drawing office in the dockyards at Boulogne and the drawing and printing facilities were used by the Germans to modify drawings of secret installations in the Pas de Calais. These included a very large concrete structure a few miles inland from Boulogne (undoubtably Watten), which contained a huge amount of piping and electrical circuits. Every copy of the drawings had to be accounted for and every night originals and copies were locked in the safe, for which the German officer responsible had the only key. Despite the strict security the father was on good terms with the Germans and on several occasions managed to obtain extra copies of drawings while the guards were distracted; these were then passed on to the resistance. The father remembers being told on several occasions that Germany was developing a new weapon, so powerful that 1 kg would destroy everything within a radius of 0.5 miles, 2 kg within 1 mile, and so on. The impression was given that this was no idle boasting, but a statement of fact from professional Army engineers.

The date 1943 recurs whenever the new miracle weapon is mentioned. It is also the date on the drawing of the modified V2 and although only two drawings of the same design modifications have survived, this is undoubtably as a result of the wartime and postwar chaos in Germany. With such a major modification to the standard V2 as this, it is likely that the task would have been given to at least three groups of designers, and each group given a brief description of the new specification, together with a deadline for the design solution. The new designs would have been assessed and the most promising would have gone ahead, with detailed drawings and models, followed by full-scale manufacture and testing. It is quite likely, therefore, that there are other schemes put down on paper, still in the archives and whose significance has never been realized.

Of the drawings which have survived, it is worthwhile studying the main changes, as shown in figs 1 and 2. First, to guard against an accidental detonation of the original high-explosive warhead, and as this was to be replaced by something more deadly, it was omitted. Second, as the rocket usually made a large crater on impact, and a proximity fuse to detonate it above the ground was not available, the new payload was placed as far back as possible in the structure, to ensure maximum dispersal of the radioactive contents. Finally, the new payload compartment was designed for quick assembly to the remainder of the V2 fuselage and this new compartment was a very strong and rigid structure which would easily detach itself from the rocket and remain intact with its payload, in the event of a misfire on the launching pad.

The duration of some of the radioactive half-lives of the material in the canister might be weeks or even days. Furthermore gamma radiation would have been present, and this was capable of penetrating the thin walls of the canister and compartment. Hence, there was obviously some urgency to assemble the modified V2 as soon as possible. It is more than likely that forced labour would have to used for the final assembly of the compartment to the rocket, when there was the greatest danger of radiation.

The modified V2 had a reduced range compared with the standard version and the date (15 October 1942) on the contract from Peenemünde to the Post Office Research Institute, to investigate the possibility of producing an improved rocket fuel, now becomes significant.

It means that as early as 1942 the question of modifying the V2 was being investigated. It also implies that the Nazi leaders anticipated that a quantity of radioactive material would be available some time in 1943 or 1944.

All the complex sites built in France and their construction dates now enter into the equation. For instance the revolutionary new silos near Cherbourg were started in 1942, as was Couville, while the other complex sites such as Watten were started later (in 1943), but with far greater urgency. The same dates and the same sense of urgency also apply to the underground manufacturing and assembly facility of Nordhausen, which was started in August 1943. As at Watten it was built and run with a mixture of slave labour and skilled forced labour, under the control of Himmler's SS.

In 1944 the researchers joined forces to provide the deadly radioactive cargo for the new rocket. Harteck's group from Hamburg University, Diebner's Army group from Kummersdorf and Gottow, von Ardenne and Houtermans of the Post Office (with the agreement and support of Gerlach), all moved south to Erfurt. In the cellar of a school, they assembled the low-temperature reactor that Harteck had wanted to build four years earlier.

Erfurt is only 48 miles from Nordhausen, on a straight road. It would have taken only minutes to get the nuclear package safely underground for its final checks and for the sand or ash to be mixed in. It would then have been loaded into the special rail transportation container. Two days later, travelling only at night and with great secrecy, the container would have arrived at the launching site in France. Only minutes before launch the radioactive canister would have been transferred to the rocket.

At the end of 1944 Gerlach wrote to Martin Bormann, by then one of Hitler's confidants, that the project they were working on might be 'decisive for the war'. As ever, Gerlach played the part of the cautious scientist, unwilling to categorically state that they had the 'miracle weapon' that could end the war.

Heisenberg was continuing with his experiments. In collaboration with Wirtz, Weizsacker and others, he built a laboratory in some caves on the outskirts of the village of Haigerloch, near Hechingen in southern Germany. Here, in February and March 1945, they attempted to bring their final reactor design to criticality.

The reactor, sunk into the floor of one of the caves, comprised an outer concrete pit, which measured approximately 10 ft in diameter and was 6 ft deep. This pit was lined with a graphite reflector, and the inner reactor vessel, 7 ft in diameter, contained 1.5 tons of uranium cubes, suspended by chains from the lid of the vessel. From the centre of the lid, via a tube, a radium–beryllium radioactive source was lowered into the centre of the uranium assembly and heavy water was slowly pumped into the outer vessel through the central tube.

The experiment was terminated on 1 March 1945, without criticality being achieved (that is, there was not enough fissionable material to sustain a chain reaction and the dimensions of the pile would have required substantial increases to achieve a critical state).

It is difficult to believe that this was a serious attempt to achieve a critical reaction, as there were several basic flaws in the design of the reactor, especially with regard to radiation safety. There was no biological shielding provided of any sort to protect against the neutron and gamma radiation that would have occurred, once criticality was reached.

The intention had been to manually lower a neutron-absorbing cadmium rod into the centre of the pile, in order to control the criticality once it had been reached. In this case the operative would have had to climb on to the top of the lid to lower this control rod, with no radiological protection whatsoever. If Heisenberg and his group aimed to demonstrate exactly how far behind they were in the practical application of nuclear physics they could not have arranged a better example.

The futility of this experiment appears to have impressed the American ALSOS organization, which followed quickly behind the advancing Allied troops, to capture as much rocket, medical and nuclear material and those involved, before the Russians. General Groves (in charge of the Manhattan bomb project) founded ALSOS (Greek for 'groves'). Its scientific chief, Samuel Goudsmit, was himself a nuclear physicist, and he was already acquainted with Heisenberg through work carried out before the war. ALSOS and Goudsmit were quickly on the scene at Haigerloch to organize the dismantling and removal of the equipment and documentation to the USA.

As Professor R.V. Jones, one of Churchill's wartime scientific advisers, stated in his book *Most Secret War*, all the German nuclear files were to have gone to the USA after a short stay in the UK, but at the last moment and without any discussion, the order was changed and not a single document on the German nuclear effort was seen by the British experts. Eventually, copies of some of the files were sent to the UK, but how complete they were and what had been amended, was only known to the Americans. Like the U-234 cargo, it is still 'classified' information.

One result of the technical shortcomings shown in the design of the final, Heisenberg experiment was that it contributed to Goudsmit's belief that the nuclear work in Germany was a long way behind that of the USA and that Heisenberg and his colleagues did not understand some of the basic principles of making an atomic bomb. They appeared to believe that they would have to drop a complete reactor as a nuclear weapon.

As the crux of Hitler's nuclear weapon hinges on the low-temperature reactor, with the involvement of Harteck and others, it is a strange coincidence that in 1989 a book was published of interviews which took place 20 years earlier (in 1967 and 1970), with, among others, Heisenberg, Harteck and Kowarski (who actually built a low-temperature reactor in Canada after the war). In these interviews, questions are pointedly asked about the low-temperature reactor, Heisenberg's opposition to Harteck's original low-temperature experiments and how much Heisenberg really understood about the technology of building a reactor and a bomb.

These interviews benefited from the fact that none of the individuals had access to previous questions and answers. The interviewer, Ermenc, describes himself in a letter as a non-expert on nuclear matters but from the astute way in which the questions are posed, this appears to be a considerable understatement.

Heisenberg's responses to questions about his opposition to Harteck's early low-temperature experiments (which ensured that they were never completed), his appreciation of the technicalities of building a reactor and a bomb, and his opinion of the work of von Ardenne, Houtermans and the Post Office, are full of contradictions. Heisenberg plays down his opposition to Harteck's work, giving the impression that there were no disagreements, even to the point of declaring that 'there was never any friction between the physicists and physical chemists' (of which Harteck was the leading authority).

This contrasts with Harteck's claim that the physicists adversely affected his work: 'A few egoists pushed others aside.' When referring to Heisenberg's self-appointed leadership of the nuclear researchers, he commented: 'But how can you be a leader in such technological matters when you have never run an experiment in your whole life? That's ridiculous. . . . That was poor judgement, it is almost unbelievable.'

On the other hand, Heisenberg became extremely angry when Ermenc referred to the statements in Margaret Gowing's book (*Britain and Atomic Energy 1939–1945*) on the official UK history of nuclear power, that during the war he did not understand three of the basic nuclear facts relating to reactors and bombs. This contrasts completely with the lack of wartime progress of Heisenberg's 'group', in both reactors and bombs. It also belies his apparent disbelief, when he first heard the news, that the USA had dropped atomic bombs on Japan.

Ermenc's questions on the work carried out by von Ardenne, Houtermans and the Post Office were quickly passed over by Heisenberg, giving the impression that they were of no real consequence. Even Harteck has little to say about Houtermans and yet it is known that they kept in touch, especially about their low-temperature reactor work. Harteck's final comments on this particular subject were: 'Much highly radioactive material could have been made which could have been thrown around. That would have been very bad.' For the UK.

But it was Kowarski who put both Heisenberg's and Harteck's comments in their proper context. He dismissed Heisenberg's opposition to Harteck's work as irrelevant, suggesting that the size of the experiment and the use of 'dirty' uranium oxide, were no problem. Of the shortcomings in Heisenberg's work he comments: 'There were quite a few inexplicable blunders . . . Perhaps he did not quite understand some of the details of experimental nuclear work. In particular his clinging to layer [reactor] arrangements for such a long time is strange.' Kowarski concludes: 'There were some strange things in this whole business which I could never understand. One of my favourite perplexities is that the Germans on the whole, made the same mistakes that we did.' By 'we', Kowarski was referring to himself, Joliot-Curie and von Halban, whereas the Germans had at least 100 top-class nuclear physicists at work in the same area.

Professor Ermenc refuses to be drawn on the reasons for his pursuit of the low-temperature theme, 25 years ago, but the relevance today is more than significant.

CHAPTER FOURTEEN

The Last Act

On 19 May 1945 the German submarine U–234 arrived in the USA, docking in Portsmouth, New Hampshire, approximately 250 miles north of New York. Onboard was a cargo of nuclear material; of that there is no question. The US authorities have admitted that part of the cargo comprised uranium oxide, the reported weight of which varies from 56 kg to 560 kg, depending on how the unloading list is interpreted. All other details remain classified. If, as stated by the US, it was only uranium oxide, why was it transported in lead containers (U–234 crew member Hirschfeld is certain about the containers), when wooden barrels would have been sufficient for the low levels of radiation present (Union Minière used wooden barrels at their plant in Belgium)?

The Japanese were carrying out their own nuclear research, funded by the government through the Army and the Navy, and supplies of uranium oxide were available during the war from both Korea and Burma. Although their nuclear work was not as advanced as that of the USA or Germany, they had at least two nuclear physicists who had an international reputation, Yoshio Nishina and Ryokichi Sagane. Nishina in particular had reached the stage of calculating the degree of enrichment and the actual amount of U.235 required for a bomb. In his Tokyo laboratory he was attempting to produce uranium hexafluoride, for use in a thermal diffusion process for uranium separation. Thermal diffusion, like all the separation processes (gaseous diffusion, centrifuge, electromagnetic), uses only uranium hexafluoride (produced from the natural oxide by a chemical process), to separate U.235 from the uranium hexaflouride in order to produce the reactor or bomb-grade enriched U.235. In addition, Japan had five cyclotrons in use (the laboratory method for producing microscopic amounts of plutonium). Two were at the Institute for Physical and Chemical Research in Tokyo, two were at Osaka University and one was at Kyoto University.

The first US reactor, designed by Enrico Fermi and built under the west stands at Stagg Field, Chicago University, had gone 'critical' on 2 December 1942. From that date onwards the USA became a 'nuclear power', and only a colossal blunder or mistake would have prevented the advancement from the first critical reaction to the production of enough highly enriched uranium for a uranium bomb, and then using the plutonium from the larger reactors at Clinton and Handford for the Nagasaki bomb.

In Germany the possible use of nuclear energy for military purposes had been reported to the Army in 1941 and at that time the German and American nuclear work was virtually at the same stage of development. Based on the fact that in France construction of both the simple and complex sites started in 1942, planning for the operational use of the V2 in a conventional role and as a nuclear weapon (V4) must have begun in 1941 at the latest and probably in 1940.

The means of delivering these weapons was to be either by conventional aircraft, the long range Me264 and Ju390, or the new rockets. As even the most promising of the two aircraft, the six-engined Ju390, had many shortcomings, it was anticipated that rockets would provide the only practical and economical method of delivering a nuclear payload. The new rocket technology required the development of far-sighted plans for the operational use of these weapons, especially as the ultimate size of the rockets was merely an estimate. The only definite piece of information was the size of the first operational rocket, the V2, and hence provision was made at the complex sites for the storage, servicing and launching of rockets from 45 ft to 100 ft in length.

A concurrent programme was also required for a separate offensive using the V2 with a conventional high-explosive warhead. The sites required for this operation would be far simpler, with little or no protection for those working on the rockets. For all the complex sites, (Brécourt, Silos, Sottevast, etc.), provisions would have to be made for the storage of radioactive material or the actual production of this material at the site. In 1941 it was far from clear which function the sites would serve, but it was clear that they would be required regardless of how the nuclear technology developed.

The production and assembly of the rockets and final assembly of the radioactive payload would also require protected underground facilities and the most suitable location was the existing tunnel complex at Nordhausen, which would merely need to be enlarged to provide the necessary space.

Despite the success of the conventional military forces, to the extent that by the autumn of 1941 it might have appeared that in the immediate future nuclear weapons and rockets would not be required, the German Army, and in particular Hitler, had a history of supporting innovation and the unconventional. Very often this was even against the advice of at least one group of experts. Examples were Krupp's Big Bertha and the Paris Gun, as well as synthetic nitrates, petrol and rubber, so this support was usually shown to be well founded. The rocket and nuclear programme, therefore, went ahead, although on a system of low priorities for strategic materials.

The two years from 1941 to 1943 were significant for the distinct slowing down of process in nuclear research, rocket development and site building. These two almost 'lost' years suddenly became critical following the unexpected failure (at least to Hitler) of the conventional armed forces and in particular their failure in Russia. It then became clear that possibly the only hope for a decisive military solution in Germany's favour lay with the unconventional methods of warfare.

Hitler must have considered his judgement vindicated when, although proved wrong against Russia, in a wider context he still had the ability to complete the development and use of the 'miracle' weapon. The sudden realization that considerable work still needed to be done to produce this weapon resulted in a sudden change to the priority ratings for rockets, the larger rocket sites and

Nordhausen. Nuclear technology had fallen too far behind for an atomic bomb to be feasible but there was another option available. Far quicker, and technically achievable, was the production of radioactive material, to be distributed over an enemy city in a modified V2. The construction work at Nordhausen and Watten was put under the control of the SS and forced through, using slave labour. The test launchings at Peenemünde jumped from 1 to 25 per month in an attempt to solve the existing problems with the V2 and to ensure that it was ready for reliable operational use.

The lack of nuclear progress must have caused much thought as to how the situation had come about. How had the world-class German nuclear physicists allowed themselves to fall so far behind the Americans? This was not a question of minor differences; there was a major disparity, and Hitler and his leaders had to accept that in three years, from 1941 to 1944, the Americans had gained an unassailable lead. Unless there had been some gross incompetence or subtle technical sabotage, it would have been very difficult to accept how this situation had arisen.

The outstanding problem with a radioactive payload of the size intended for the V4 was one of safety, as any accident on German or friendly territory would result in the contamination of a huge area and possibly thousands of deaths. The problem was the same with the chemical weapons they had available, Tabun and Sarin. Any accident with these could have similar consequences. The other problem associated with the radioactive package was one of numbers. The reactor would have to operate for several months to produce enough radioactive material, and in the present military situation on the East and West fronts, there was insufficient time to produce radiocactive material for more than one rocket. As a result there would be no second chance.

There was also the question of retaliation from the UK or the USA, which was much more serious if there was no chance of a second nuclear strike. Germany was still without a means of reaching the USA with any real chance of success, whereas the USA could use any number of bases in the UK, North Africa, the Middle East and Russia, without having to put her own population at risk from nuclear accidents or retaliation.

Although all was not lost, the inactivity of the period from 1940 to 1943 was doubly infuriating. With limited radioactive material available the viability of the modified V2 was in doubt due to rocket reliability problems and reduced range; the A9/A10 version capable of reaching America was too far from completion to be of any use within the required deadline. It was an exasperating situation knowing that they now had the 'miracle' weapon, about which so much publicity had been given, both in unofficial rumours and hints and then when it became a fact, in speeches by Goebbels, Speer and other leaders. Hitler himself had publicly referred to it, putting his own credibility at risk. He still valued opinion, not just in Germany but in the rest of the world, including the last real ally and Axis partner, Japan.

With most of Britain turned into a radioactive wasteland and lost as an Allied base, it would be impossible for the USA to continue a major offensive against Germany, other than limited air raids from other countries, and Hitler would once more be able to turn all his resources against Russia. As in a bizarre game of chance, he had a hand that was almost but not quite unbeatable and in this game the stakes were enormous; the winner would take all and for the loser it would mean oblivion. Every day that was spent trying to determine which way to move was another day lost, and another day which brought the Russians that much closer to Berlin.

THE JAPANESE CONNECTION

But there was one other choice and this was something that had been discussed early in 1944 as a contingency plan, but it would really be the final move in the game. Himmler had initiated the first moves and once general agreement had been obtained, the formal aspects were left to the Foreign Office and Dr Karl Ritter, Ambassador for Special Assignments in the Foreign Ministry. Details were finalized on 28 December 1944. This final move lay in the East: Japan.

If the use of the miracle weapon in Europe was unacceptable for a variety of reasons, the only other possibility was Japan. It did have a nuclear programme and the Americans were sure to be aware of this, but they probably did not know the details, especially how far advanced the Japanese work was and how much assistance had been provided by Germany. If this single, unique cargo of German radioactive material could be transported to Japan in time, there would be one last chance to stop the USA and halt the war, at least in the West. It would also appear not to involve Germany so if there was any retaliation it would only be directed at Japan. Hitler was probably aware that the USA's nuclear strike capability was still limited to one or two weapons.

As far as Japan was concerned it was an ideal opportunity to use equipment that was available at that time and which might have been designed specifically for such a project. Before the war, plans had been made for the bombing of strategic enemy targets which were likely to be beyond the range of normal land- or carrier-based aircraft: the US mainland and the Panama Canal. These plans had resulted in an order being placed for 18 Type STO class I.400 submarines, each capable of carrying three aircraft in watertight hangars on the deck. The aircraft would be launched by catapult along rails ending at the bows.

These submarines were the largest in any navy, with an overall length of 400 ft, submerged displacement of 6,500 tons, surface range of 30,000 miles and a crew of 144. (This compares with U–234's length of 294 ft, displacement of 2,200 tons and crew of 52.) The I.400 class incorporated all the latest developments and benefited from German technical cooperation, being equipped with a *Schnorchel*; also, the hull used a similar rubber coating to the one undergoing experiments in Germany, in an attempt to make the hull less responsive to ASDIC and radar.

There was a problem during the construction of these submarines because of their size, and to keep the draft within acceptable limits the pressure hull was divided into two cylinders side by side. This, together with the deteriorating war situation, resulted in the order being curtailed and only three were actually completed: I.400, I.401 and I.402. I.402 was converted into a tanker; I.400 was commissioned on 30 December 1944 (Lieutenant Commander Nambu) and I.401 on 8 January 1945 (Commander Kusaka). To redress the reduction in production,

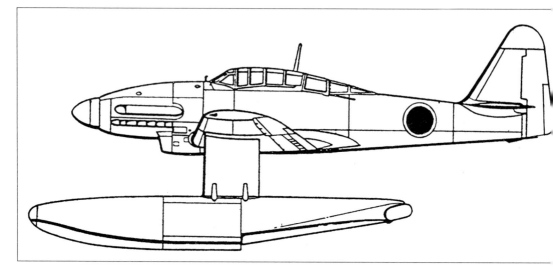

14. Japanese Aichi M6A1 Seiran (Mountain Haze) float-plane as used on aircraft carrying submarines I.400 and I.401 and on two modified type AM submarines, I.13 and I.14. Wings, fin and tailplane were folded for storage in circular watertight hangars on deck. The aircraft could be readied within 10 minutes for catapult launch.

two existing type AM large patrol submarines were converted to carry two of the special aircraft. I.13 and I.14 were both of 4,700 tons displacement, and the modifications to I.13 were completed on 16 December 1944 (Commander Ohashi) and to I.14 on 14 March 1945 (Commander Shimizu).

The aircraft were designed to a very high specification by the Aichi Watch and Electric Machinery Company of Nagoya, which was already a supplier of successful aircraft to the Imperial Navy, having been contracted in June 1942. The first prototype of the Aichi M6A1 Seiran (Mountain Haze) was completed in November 1943 and eventually 20 production aircraft were completed by 1945. The Seiran was a two-seater all-metal low-wing monoplane with twin floats and had the highest performance in terms of maximum speed and payload of any float-plane in the Second World War. It carried a 1,760 lb bomb-load over a maximum range of 740 miles at almost 300 mph. Successful trials showed that the aircraft could be removed from its hangar and readied for flight in less than 10 minutes by four trained personnel.

On completion of commissioning, all four submarines joined the 1st Submarine Division under Captain Tatsunosuke, as part of the 6th Fleet operating from the Kure naval base. I.13, I.400 and I.401 immediately commenced training in the western area of the Inland Sea, and were joined by I.14 on 15 March. On 12 April I.401 was slightly damaged by a US air-laid mine near Iyonada and returned to Kure for repairs. From April to July, the movements of the four submarines now became critical in relation to the voyage of U-234. U-234 left Kiel on 25 March 1945 and by the middle of April was through the Iceland–Faroes gap and into the Atlantic. From previous voyages by Japanese submarines, and in particular I.8, which took 64 days in September 1943 to return to Penang from Brest, U-234 could be expected to reach Penang or Singapore by early June. She could then either unload her cargo there for transportation by air over the remaining 3,500 miles to Japan, which would take two or three days, or proceed directly by sea to Japan, which would take an extra two weeks. The U-234's cargo could therefore arrive in Japan by late June or mid-July 1945. Whichever option was chosen, U-234 would have been in radio contact with Japan some days before reaching Japanese-controlled territory.

Although by 17 May the local New Hampshire press in the USA was publicizing the forthcoming arrival of a German submarine, U-234, in

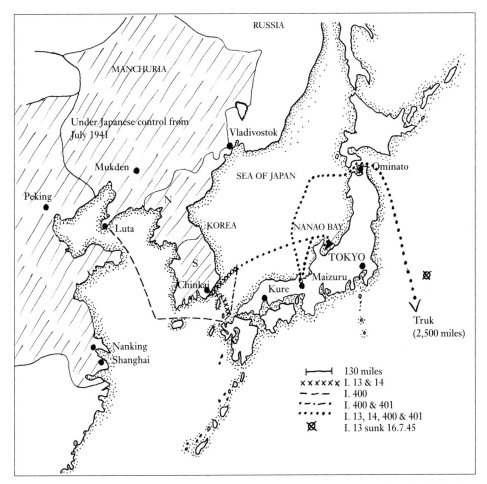

17. Details of the movements of the Japanese aircraft-carrying submarines I. 13, 14, 400 and 401 from 14.4.45 to 23.7.45. This is the critical period when U-234 was planned to be en route for Japan with an expected arrival in Penang/Singapore in early June 1945. It was on 12 June that the orders for these submarines were changed from a strategic raid on the Panama Canal to a tactical mission against the US fleet.

Portsmouth, German U-boats were now surrendering in large numbers to the Allies. Hence, even if the information reached Japan immediately, confirmation would still be required that it was in fact U-234. Because there was no radio contact with U-234 it is unlikely that this confirmation would have been obtained until at least the end of May or early in June.

The movements of the four submarines now become of major interest. I.401 returned to Kure naval base on 12 April for repairs and remained there until 1 June. In the meantime I.400 had left Kure on 14 April for Luta (Dairen) on the Kwantung Peninsula, part of the vast area of Manchuria taken from China and a major port for raw materials being transported back to Japan. (China and Korea were major suppliers of Japan's essential raw materials. Nowadays these countries are among the world's largest producers of uranium (along with Canada, the USA and Russia), at over 5,000 tons per year.) This was a return voyage of some 2,000 miles and I.400 arrived on 20 April, returning to Kure on 27 April. The reason for this visit was given as refuelling and the original commander of I.400, Nobukiyo Nambu, has recently confirmed that this was the case. However, the seas around Japan had become extremely hazardous for any sort of naval activity. I.401 was still being repaired at Kure, and to send the sole survivor of the class on a 2,000 mile round trip simply to load fuel seems strange. This was especially so since Luta was not the only source of fuel available. On 27 May I.13 and I.14 left Kure for the Nanao Bay naval base on Japan's west coast, stopping *en route* to refuel at the Korean port of Chinkai, next to Pusan. This means that there was a much closer alternative to Luta, and the proximity of the large port of Pusan would virtually guarantee fuel being available.

The question of the fuel supply available to the navy and how the last dwindling stocks were used provides a relevant and highly significant part to the last part of this story. By the beginning of April all four submarines had returned to the Kure naval base. On 6 April the pride and last remaining capital ship of the Imperial Navy, the 73,000 ton *Yamato*, the largest battleship afloat, was despatched from Kure on a suicide mission in a vain attempt to stop the American landings at Okinawa, only 700 miles away. This was a suicide mission because *Yamato* was sent out with only enough fuel for a one-way trip. There was fuel remaining at Kure, certainly enough to have brought *Yamato* back from Okinawa, but the mission it was being saved for was so important to Japan that the battleship could be sacrificed. The very last drop of diesel fuel left at Kure went into the tanks of the now repaired I.401, over 1,300 tons of it, before she left for Nanao Bay on 1 June, followed by I.400 on 2 June, arriving on the 4th and 5th respectively.

On 3 June the Seiran float-planes of the 631st Naval Flying Corps arrived at Nanao Bay and following the arrival of I.400 all four submarines commenced operational training, each with a full complement of aircraft. The official reason for this training is still that it was intended as a prelude to an attack on the Panama Canal lock gates, as originally planned in 1942, but the situation in 1945 was very different from 1942.

The plans for an attack on the Panama Canal had originally been approved by Admiral Yamamoto, Commander-in-Chief of the Imperial Navy, and in 1942 it

Japanese submarines (left to right): I. 400, I. 401, I. 14 anchored in Tokyo Bay after the surrender. The hangars for the Aichi Seiran float-planes and the launching rails for the catapults are clearly visible. I. 400 and I. 401 carried three Seiran and I. 14 two, and at 6,500 tons and 4,700 tons respectively they were the largest submarines in any navy during the war. I. 13, the sister ship to I. 14, was sunk by US ships on 16 July 1945, en route to Truk. (Imperial War Museum)

was quite conceivable that putting the canal out of action for several months would have had a serious effect on the Allied supplies reaching the Pacific; this was especially so at a time when the Allies were suffering defeat after defeat at the hands of Japan. However, in 1945 the likelihood of such an attack being of any major advantage to Japan's standing in the war was negligible.

Admiral Yamamoto had died in April 1943 when his Mitsubishi 'Betty' had been shot down by US P-38 Lightning fighters. In any circumstances it would be normal for plans such as the raid on the Panama Canal to be periodically reviewed to confirm their continued feasibility and military value. With the death of Yamamoto in 1943, his successor, Admiral Toyoda, would be certain to carry out a critical review of all the plans approved by his predecessor. If the canal project was just about kept alive during 1943 and 1944, by late 1944 another project had been made known to Japan by its Axis ally Germany. The plan appealed to Japan's military leaders, who were now considering any move, no matter how desperate, to bring about a change in their fortunes.

The new project required virtually the same resources as those for a raid on the Panama Canal. The target was San Fransisco, which is actually closer to Japan, so very few changes to the strategy would be required. The biggest modification would be that the bomb-load of the Seirans would now comprise Hitler's radioactive material, and this could certainly change the outcome of the war.

It is probable that the exercises in Nanao Bay were in preparation for this plan; geographically and in terms of size Nanao Bay, 30 miles wide, is much closer to San Fransisco Bay, 12 miles wide, than it is to Panama Bay, 130 miles wide. The exercises lasted until 12 June and on this date there was a sudden and significant change to the plans. The Panama Canal project was abandoned and instead plans were put into place for an attack on units of the US fleet at the Ulithi Atol, 1,000 miles to the west of the island of Truk, which was still in Japanese hands. The importance of this date cannot be overemphasized as it would have been at approximately this time that U-234 would have been expected to arrive at Penang or Singapore, and the lack of any previous radio contact would only have confirmed what had probably been suspected for some days, that U-234's radioactive cargo was destined never to arrive in Japan.

The discovery of this cargo by the US at Portsmouth now had fatal repercussions for Japan and sealed the fate of the inhabitants of two of its largest cities, Hiroshima and Nagasaki. An indication of how fundamental the changes in plans was is shown by the modifications that were now carried out to I.13 and I.14. On 20 June these two submarines unloaded their Seirans at Nanao Bay and proceeded directly to the Maizuru Naval Base. They arrived on 22 June, and work started to convert their hangars into storage compartments for two Nakajima C6N1 Saiun (Painted Cloud) reconnaissance aircraft. The Saiun was the fastest carrier-launched reconnaissance aircraft of the Second World War, with a maximum speed of 390 mph and a range of 2,500 miles. In addition, some versions could carry one torpedo offset to starboard under the fuselage. I.13 and I.14 were each to carry two of these aircraft to Truk, from where they would carry out reconnaissance flights to Ulithi, 1,000 miles to the west. What does not seem to have been considered is the fact that as a Japanese base and one-time headquarters for the Pacific Fleet, Truk had been devastated by attacks from US carrier-based aircraft and had been virtually unusable since February 1944.

On 2 July, with the modifications completed, I.13 and I.14 left Maizuru for the Ominato Naval Base at the northern-most tip of Honshu. They arrived on 4 July. The same day they each loaded two Saiuns and on 11 July I.13 left Ominato for Truk. However, five days later she was attacked and sunk some 400 miles to the west of Tokyo by a US hunter-killer group, led by the escort carrier CVE *Anzio*. On 13 July I.400 and I.401 left Nanao Bay for Maizuru, where they spent seven days taking on food and ammunition and topping up fuel. They left on 20 July for Ominato, arriving on 23 July. In the meantime I.14 had left Ominato on 14 July, arriving at Truk without incident on 4 August, and the two Saiuns were unloaded. On 23 and 24 July respectively, I.400 and I.401 left Ominato for Ulithi. The date set for the attack was 17 August, but on 15 August, seven days after the Nagasaki bomb, Japan capitulated and the attack was cancelled. The submarines were ordered back to Japan, and surrendered to US naval forces between 27 and 29 August. All three submarines were eventually shipped to the US for evaluation.

If U-234 had arrived in Japan as planned, the operation on the US west coast would have been carried out two or three hundred miles from the coast. The aircraft would have been catapult-launched from the submarine within range of San Francisco or Los Angeles, dropped their bomb-load, returned to land on the sea, the crew picked up and the aircraft abandoned. The weapon would have consisted of the radioactive material, packed around a filling of normal high-explosive. Dropped over a large city it would have had the impact of an atomic bomb without the huge blast, but the radiation would have had a similarly deadly effect. It would also have been completely unexpected. The west coast of the USA had seen virtually nothing of the war and so the surprise and panic would have been even greater. The USA would not have known how much more radioactive material was available or that the material had come from Germany; hence there would be no retaliation against Germany.

All this would have meant that Germany would lose control of the precious radioactive cargo once it arrived in Japan, but there was no choice and even now it might have been left too late; Japan was two to three months away by submarine when Germany surrendered. But what happened to the all-important cargo? When it was finally unloaded from U-234 and unpacked at the end of May, the question suddenly facing the political and military leaders in the USA was: had there been other cargos of radioactive material from Germany, or was this the only one? If there had been others, was Japan at that very moment planning to drop a radioactive bomb over American west-coast cities? It was known that both Japanese and German submarines had made successful voyages between the two countries, carrying strategic war material, and this spasmodic but regular traffic had been going on since 1942. Before U-234, there had been U-195, U-219, U-511, U-532 and for the Imperial Navy, I.8, I.30, I.34 and I.39, but not all these boats completed the round trip.

The Americans were urgently trying to find a cure for radiation poisoning, but as in Germany there was no such remedy available. To the American politicians, the concept of the distribution of a large amount of radioactive dust on a city like Los Angeles or San Francisco was unthinkable. They could recall the prewar panic that had occurred in New York in 1938 following the mock radio announcement that alien spacecraft had landed, but this was the real thing, not H.G. Well's *War of the Worlds* fiction.

The first US atomic bomb was not yet ready but the programme was going ahead, now at full speed. The Alamogordo plutonium test bomb was dropped on 16 July and this was the first and only confirmation that the theoretical calculations were correct. Only three weeks later the uranium 'thin-man' bomb was dropped on Hiroshima, followed two days later by the plutonium 'fat-man' bomb on Nagasaki. Years later, the USA had tested hundreds of nuclear devices to confirm its theoretical studies, but in 1945, when the science of nuclear weapons was brand new, it decided to use two bombs. The only evidence it had that the bombs would work was based on the results of just one experiment, at Alamogordo, and this was relevant to only one of the bombs used on Japan. The actions of the USA were clearly a spontaneous response to the discovery that Japan might have a nuclear weapon, and from the desperate Kamikaze measures being adopted by Japan, there was no doubt that it would be used.

But if there was no nuclear weapon threat, by 1945 Japan's ability to carry on the conventional war was limited by the lack of strategic materials, especially oil and petrol. Many of the islands were still occupied by Japanese garrisons but the important islands, those which the provided air bases for the B-29 Superfortresses, had been captured.

The main Japanese islands could have been pounded into oblivion and Tokyo was already largely in ruins, without any more costly assaults. The dropping of the atomic bombs by the USA was therefore unnecessary, unless it feared that Japan had a nuclear weapon.

One last point that is worth considering is how close the attack on Hiroshima came to never happening. The US heavy cruiser *Indianapolis* unloaded the Hiroshima bomb at Tinian in the Mariana Islands, from where the B-29 *Enola Gay* would carry it to Japan. On 26 May 1945 the *Indianapolis* set off on the return journey to the Philippines, but she never arrived. On 30 May the cruiser's path crossed that of I.58, a modern 2,000 ton radar-equipped long-distance patrol submarine of the Japanese Imperial Navy, commanded by Moshitsura Hashimoto. On a bright, moonlit night, travelling without an escort, the *Indianapolis* was hit by three torpedoes on the starboard side. She sank within minutes, with the loss of over 900 lives. It was three days before she was missed and only then did rescue ships come looking for the survivors.

APPENDIX A

Allied Photographic Interpretation Reports

THE V2 OFFENSIVE FROM HOLLAND

Item 1   ACIU telex and report on the first operational rocket site identified in Holland.

Item 2   API history of the V2 during attacks against England, 8 September 1944 to 27 March 1945.

Note   These British reports refer to the rocket offensive against England using standard V2s with high-explosive warheads. The offensive was under the control of the SS and the rockets were fired by SS Batteries 444, 485 and 836, commanded by SS General Dr Hans Kammler.

Abbreviations
ACIU   Allied Central Interpretation Unit
API   Allied Photographic Interpretation
SHAEF   Supreme Headquarters Allied Expeditionary Force
M/T   Motor Transport
HQFC   Headquarters Fighter Command
AL   Army Liason
Crossbow   Code name for Allied offensive against V-weapon sites

INTERPRETATION REPORT NO. BS 1039

CROSSBOW

Sortie: 106G/4538 of 26th February 1945, Scale 1:8,200. Hague/Duindight (GSGS 4427/372).

INTRODUCTION

The first operational rocket launching site to be definitely identified on air photographs is seen at 68059498. The following preliminary report, while giving

---

```
XAH V MDM MDM 22/27   P    P
T A2 V SECTION SHAEF MAIN (AIR)(ATTN W/CDR PRICE)

FROM MEDMENHAM 272230A

 TO HQFC( S I R O)     A I 2(H)      A2 V SECTION SHAEF MAIN (AIR)

    ATTN W/CDR PRICE       NO 6 A L SECTION RAF NORTH WEALD) ATTN

    MAJOR EAST

 QQX BT

A T 821 27 FEB   PRINTS 3279 AND 3260   OF 106 G/4538 (26TH FEBRUATY
1945 - SCALE 1:8200) SHOW ROCKET IN LAUNCHING POSITION WITH
ATTENDANT MEILERWAGEN, TRACTOR AND FUELLING VEHICLES AT
GSGS4083/30/D.67959505 EMPTY MEILERWAGEN IMMEDIATELY N W OF HOUSE
AT 68109494 AND CONSIDERABLE WHEELED TRACK ACTIVITY INDICATES AREA
BOUNDED BY D.676950 - D.680953 - D.684959 - D.680945 IN CONSTANT
USE AS LAUNCHING AREA   REPORT AND PHOTOS FOLLOW

BT 272230A

AS
CC 26TH FEBRUARY   CC IN ADD TO WA NORTH WEALD

HANKIN AR
XAH R 0010/28 A. WEBB AR
```

a certain amount of detail, must be considered as provisional and is therefore subject to modifications and additions in the light of more detailed interpretation. This will be provided by a further report which will be accompanied by a plan.

1. A rocket is visible in the vertical launching position, with attendant vehicles in a tree-lined ride through the wood immediately S.E. of the race track.
2. The base of the rocket appears to measure 12 ft × 12 ft. Immediately adjoining it is an object, possibly the *Meilerwagen*, 37 ft long, the rear portion of which (16 ft) appears broader than the forward portion (21 ft), no useful measurement of the width being possible. A light-toned line 10 ft long, which may be a tow bar, leads to what is thought to be a tractor 23 ft × 8 ft. It is noted that the ZGKW vehicle on the preliminary recognition sheet, dated 14th August 1944, is given as 22 ft × 8 ft, and this is though to be the tractor for the *Meilerwagen*.
3. Almost parallel to the possible *Meilerwagen* is an object approximately 29 ft × 6 ft, alongside which is a further object 35 ft × 6 ft, though this latter may be two objects end to end. The lengths 29 ft and 35 ft should be treated with reserve since definition of the N.W. end of each is obscured by the shadow cast

by the rocket. On the S.W. side of the rocket is a small white-toned object 11 ft x 4 ft, with possible small projections at each end.

4. Very characteristic tracks leading from the main LEIDEN road across the field to the S.E. up to and through this ride and in a turning loop at its N.W. end just outside the wood. Similar sets of tracks lead off to the S.W. and also to the E. the latter ending close to a large house at 68109494 where there is an object approx. 40 ft × 6 ft which is thought to be another *Meilerwagen*. Two light-toned bars across the object, 22 ft apart, may be rocket supports and the impression is gained that the vehicle may be articulated, since its longitudinal axis does not appear perfectly straight.

5. An exhaustive search in the immediate neighbourhood has not confirmed any further launching site.

6. The area is also covered on 106G/4540 of 26.2.45 Prints 3373–3375. This sortie was flown at almost exactly the same time as that under review; it is slightly inferior in scale and no further information can be obtained from it. No previous cover of critical date and quality is available at this unit, but from present cover there appears to be no reason to assume that any special preparation of the surface of the launching site has been effected.

Prints distributed 3279, 3280, of 106G/4538

TOP SECRET	STANDARD DISTRIBUTION 55B	
	External	39
	Internal	12
ACIU	CIC HQFC	1
GBR/RR/IW/A	No. 6 AL Section	1
	RAF North Weald (Attn Major East)	1

API HISTORY OF V2 DURING ATTACKS AGAINST ENGLAND

8 SEPTEMBER 1944 TO 27 MARCH 1945

This report is largely compiled from the findings of Photographic Interpretation as given in BS Reports. Statistical information in the Foreword is based on Reports regularly supplied to ACIU by the Operational Research Centre at HQFC.

FOREWORD

Statistical appreciation of attack.

LAUNCHING SITES AND FORWARD STORAGE

(i) Photographic recognition material to hand before Sept. 8th 1944.

(ii) Additional information following ground check of known launching site on

Walcheren Island – photographic proof of launching from wooded areas – attacks on Norwich.

(iii) Forward storage in the Haagsche Bosch – ACIU liason with HQFC and AL Squadrons – resultant bombing.

(iv) First photograph of launching preparations – (Duindigt) – small storage area at Ravolijn.

(v) Continental PI findings in areas firing against Antwerp.

ROCKET ASSEMBLY

Niedersachswerfen – identification of 'triple-flats'.

RAILWAY ROCKET TRANSPORT

Railway incidence implies Niedersachswerfen as a sole V2 assembly plant.

RELATION OF PHOTOGRAPHIC INTERPRETATION AND TARGETING

Relative PI responsibilities of ACIU and SHAEF.

FOREWORD

The first A-4 long-range rocket or V-2, as it was popularly called, fell in England on September 8th 1944 and the last incident, No. 1115, was on March 27th 1945. The total of known launchings recorded from all sources was 1346, this indicating that 231 were abortive. For the whole 29 weeks of the attack against England London was the sole target, except for a short period from September 25th to October 12th 1944 when attention was diverted to the Norwich Area, this being undoubtedly due to the British advance to Arnhem and the consequent threat to the German line. The Gaasterland area N.E. of the Zuider Zee was responsible for the majority of launchings during this period, though there is some radar evidence implicating either Torschalling or Vlieland in the Friesians and the Apeldoorn area. The stabilisation of the line along the Waal, however, again transferred operations to The Hague which continued to be the sole area used for launching operations against England until the final cessation of attacks.

The first 16 weeks of the attack yielded 382 incidents, the remaining 13 weeks containing 733 recorded incidents. As might be expected the rough tendency was for succeeding weekly totals to mount steadily, the highest daily total (16) being reached on four occasions. An approximate weekly percentage quotient of accuracy, taking Greater London as the target, only twice attained 50% and fluctuated considerably from week to week. It must be remembered in this connection that the A-4 long-range rocket was working at extreme range and that its accuracy over shorter ranges, as when fired against Antwerp from other Continental firing areas, was considerably better. Rockets had first been reported from ground sources and later confirmed by air photos and ground checks in dumps at the Forêt de Nieppe.

LAUNCHING SITES AND FORWARD STORAGE

(i) There was a fair amount of photographic rocket recognition to hand when the campaign started, this having been supplied by photographs of the Bois de Baugy. The 'herring-bone' dumps in Germany may have been intended for a similar purpose. Experimental launching operations photographed on the foreshore at Peenemünde had indicated that little or no ground preparation was necessary when launching rockets, though captured documents showed that two roads in Normandy (at Le Molay and the Château de Cloay) had been reinforced with concrete in a particular way in order to facilitate the placing of vehicles for fuelling the rockets. This, too, was confirmed by a ground check, but vertical photographs showed that situated under trees and camouflaged as they were, those two examples could not reasonably have been picked up by Photo Interpretation. An intensive search of wide areas in France, Belgium and Holland yielded negative results regarding the discovery of other such sites if indeed they existed.

(ii) Such was the situation when the first incident was recorded. The launching areas were soon roughly defined but the trees were still in full leaf and effectively shielded this type of activity; nor was there any evidence of rocket activity of any description in open country or on road or rail. The confirmed launching of a few projectiles from Walcheren Island during the morning of September 16th 1944 was thoroughly investigated off excellent vertical photographs taken incidentally in the afternoon of the same day. There were no visible indications at all that such operations had been carried out and there was little natural cover to hide any such traces. A ground check quickly followed the British occupation of the island and the actual launching sites, after being pointed out by the inhabitants, were thoroughly examined. Three points could now be postulated – (a) that any level 'hardstanding' was suitable for launching purposes – (b) that all launching apparatus was fully mobile – and (c) that no traces were necessarily left, due to the actual 'taking-off' of the rocket from an open space. It was now clear that no launching site on open ground could be confirmed from photographic evidence alone, unless the rockets were to be seen actually in the vertical position with attendant M/T concentration. The chances of a reconnaissance aircraft flying over the actual pinpoint and taking satisfactory photographs at the right time were rather slim considering in addition that many rockets were launched in the hours of darkness. Activities in densely wooded areas would naturally be completely undetected by photos until following launching operation. This latter point was proved when the first evidence of launching activity was confirmed by aerial photography among thick woods in Gaasterland in N.E. Holland. Cover of October 5th 1944 revealed that a large bowl shaped 'clearing' among the trees near Rijs was of recent origin. Its appearance was consistent with the burning calculated to take place if a rocket were launched from among the drying twigs and leaves of trees in Autumn. A further cover flown on November 5th 1944 showed that yet another 'clearing' had arrived. Radar evidence indicated that both these areas were being used for rocket launching and these two instances were accepted as providing visible evidence of the existence of rocket launching activity. Though this was interesting, such information could not assist tactical counter-measures unless constant use of such areas could be proved. Following the transference of launching activity back to The Hague after the Arnhem operation, cover of the known launching areas was regularly flown and interpreted right up to the very end of the rocket campaign.

(iii) It was not until December 29th 1944 that rockets were first photographically revealed away from the experimental areas. A continental sortie showed at least 13 long-range rockets in the Haagsche Bosch, a wooded park situated centrally in The Hague. They were in the horizontal position and were evidently on *Meilerwagen* dispersed on either side of roads and partly under tree cover. The leaves had now fallen and the striped appearance of the projectile due to 'dazzle-painting' being used as a camouflage medium, only tended to draw still more attention. This type of camouflage had previously successfully hindered the definite identification of such objects as actual rockets, and both at Peenemünde – where rockets both light and dark in tone, but not dazzle-painted had positively been identified – and at Blizna, such striped objects, due possibly to the angle of the sun and consequent lack of good shadows, had been tentatively identified as 'rocket cradles'. Photographic cover of The Hague during December 1944 and early January 1945 was not very satisfactory, due to unfavourable weather conditions, but rockets in varying numbers were identified in the Haagsche Bosch on various dates. A comprehensive report on all covers showing rockets between February 3rd and 9th 1945 in this area was issued, complete with full indications of pinpoints round which activity seemed to centre most. As a result of this HQFC placed the Haagsche Bosch on priority and adopted these pinpoints as aiming points. It should here be mentioned that the task of bombing rocket targets in Holland was undertaken by Fighter Command, who initially bombed targets on ground and radar evidence alone. Mustangs of an Army Liaison Squadron accompanied attacking Spitfires for photographic reconnaissance purposes and it was arranged that ACIU should receive copies of such cover. Excellent in quality and scale (weather conditions permitting) it provided all the material for the comprehensive report already mentioned, and as a result of this growing liaison, definite photographic information began to exercise an effect for the first time on rocket target priority in The Hague.

(iv) The first operational rocket launching site was identified off photographs of February 26th 1945. It was situated on a rough roadway running through a scattered wood S.E. of the racecourse at Duindigt in the north-eastern outskirts of The Hague proper. The area had not been satisfactorily covered during January and February but a special job had necessitated cover of the whole of W. Holland in an effort to locate long-range flying-bomb sites known to be projected or under construction for renewed attacks on London. While primarily searching for these a long-range rocket was discovered in the vertical launching position, apparently being fuelled by attendant motor vehicles. The relative placing of the vehicles approximated to that already noticed at Peenemünde, indicated on captured documents and obviously prepared for at the concreted areas at the Château de Cloay and at Le Molay. An unloaded *Meilerwagen* and a great amount of wheeled track activity in the neighbourhood indicated that the area was in constant use for launching purposes, while very large craters in the surrounding square mile testified eloquently to the danger of abortive launchings. The attention that Fighter Command had paid to the Haagsche Bosch was now seen to have caused the enemy to abandon the area for forward rocket storage and no rockets were ever again observed in the wood. HQFC was kept fully informed of this and, indeed, any information adjudged to be of operational use by ACIU was signalled whenever photographic cover was interpreted. Duindigt racecourse and the surrounding areas were immediately placed on the target list and given top priority. Bombing of the Haagsche Bosch had resulted in the almost complete cessation of attacks for two days, one incident only being recorded on February 24th and none on the 25th, (12 had been launched on the 23rd and 9 were launched on the 26th). It was feasible to assume that forward storage and/or maintenance plans had been dislocated by the bombing, for Duindigt gave ample evidence that actual launching operations had been unhindered for some considerable length of time.

The search for new storage areas revealed that a small area at Ravolijn north of and close to Duindigt, contained three rockets on *Meilerwagen*. They were dispersed under tree cover in the immediate vicinity of a house known to be used for hospital purposes. This target, too, was immediately given priority by HQFC and was bombed along with Duindigt. Three other rockets were observed at Duindigt during this period, all in the vertical launching position and all on the same rough roadway as previously, while rockets on *Meilerwagen* were also visible. The bombing of Duindigt and Ravolijn following ACIU information quickly caused their abandonment and once again the rate of fire on London slackened temporarily. It is worthy of note that the bombing of the Haagsche Bosch in the 25th week, and of Duindigt and Ravolijn in the 27th week of the campaign, was almost certainly responsible for the two relatively low totals of recorded incidents during those weeks, these being the only two such totals in an otherwise rising scale. An unremitting search of all available cover was continued until the cessation of attacks but no further storage or launching areas were discovered, and it is possible that rockets were finally stored on a day-to-day basis under cover in suitable buildings. This may explain the location of the only other long-range rocket photographically recorded in The Hague area. Cover of March 9th 1945 showed the missile loaded on a *Meilerwagen* in a tree lined street in the heart of the town, near to an open area called Zorgvliot. This area was variously reported as being used for launching purposes, though there were never any visible signs of such activity observed on photographs.

(v) In addition to the above rocket campaign against London parallel activity against Antwerp, though of far greater intensity, was being carried out in other firing areas notably around Hellendoorn, Enschede and the district east of Born and a few examples of wooded sites were discovered presenting the same appearance as at Rijs in Gaasterland. The long-range rocket was only seen twice on aerial photographs of these areas – once near Rock where a single rocket on a

Meilerwagen was being manoeuvred off the road into a wooded area containing a clearing thought to be used for launching purposes, and again near Hillscheid, east of Bonn, where projectiles on *Meilerwagen* were seen in transit through wooded country. In both cases camouflaged railway stock was visible at a neighbouring railhead, which most probably was used for off-loading directly on to *Meilerwagen* for transit to launching sites.

ROCKET ASSEMBLY

Following a ground report indicating that there were underground workings at Niedersachswerfen near Nordhausen connected with secret weapon activity full cover of the area was flown in September and October 1944 and two underground complexes were revealed on a scale obviously providing extensive facilities for storage and manufacture. One feature alone at this time gave colour to the suspicions that the long-range rocket was included in the list of materials manufactured or assembled, and even then the evidence was solely deduced from a theory built up around an unusual type of rolling stock.

The varying numbers of rockets seen on cover of the Haagsche Bosch up to February had indicated that forward supplies for use against England were probably kept on a day-to-day basis in this area, being delivered by rail to Leiden and The Hague from back storage dumps and/or assembly plants. Two types of rolling stock could reasonably be expected to be identified in connection with rocket activity, fuel wagons and wagons carrying the actual projectiles. The former type had been seen at Peenemünde but information regarding the latter was non-existent. It was known that the rocket itself was segmented and could easily have been transported in normal rolling stock if not fully assembled before despatch to the firing areas, but on the other hand, if fully assembled, the total overall length (45 ft 10 in) and shape, as well as the relative fragility of such a load, would demand either a specially constructed truck or the adaption of existing stock. In any case it was expected that such wagons would be fairly quickly picked up off photographs when any degree of rocket rail transport had been attained. Rakes of wagons on 'flats' were observed on sidings outside the tunnels at Niedersachswerfen apparently consisting of sets of three trucks linked together and travelling as single units, a combination not fully explained by any known railway transport demand. They were fully sheeted and their loads were thus effectively hidden, but a theory was evolved based on the peculiar shadows thrown by these sheeted loads and it was stated that very probably rockets were carried by such 'triple-flats', as they were primarily called, two missiles per unit of three wagons with noses overlapping on the centre wagon. Confirmation was quickly forthcoming from a P/W interrogation report and this type of 'triple-flat' was added to photographic material and also supplied to Continental PI Units.

RAILWAY ROCKET TRANSPORT

As the weeks of the rocket campaign continued, the plotting of the steadily mounting total of photographic incidences of the recognition of both fuel wagons and of 'triple-flat' units began to form a pattern indicating that Niedersachswerfen was the central if not the only assembly plant for the long-range rocket. It was known that the manufacture of rocket components was widely dispersed throughout Germany but their rail transport need arouse no suspicion as ordinary rolling stock could be used; the despatch of the fully assembled rocket however was much more difficult.

Taking Niedersachswerfen as the hub, two spokes could be seen radiating to N.W. and S.W. representing the two main railway systems supplying the northern and southern group rocket launching areas, and along these lines fell almost all the recorded pinpoints of positively identified rocket rail traffic. All known 'herring-bone' ammunition dumps were also regularly interpreted but no positive photographic evidence was forthcoming that such layouts, often annexes to well-established national ammunition dumps, were used for rocket storage with the exception of that at Siegelsbach, where 'triple-flat' units were identified although it was impossible to say whether they were loaded. The plan followed in supplying The Hague apparently entailed actual rail movement by night, the units being stabled by day, under cover at goods yards in Leiden and The Hague itself.

This precaution against discovery, particularly by photographic reconnaissance units, was rigidly adhered to in Holland until the mounting instability of the enemy position in March 1945 caused a general relaxation. Rakes of 'triple-flats' were then identified in quick succession in stations in Leiden, The Hague, Rotterdam and Amsterdam. Good photographs at this time showed that the triple units were not indeed composed of actual 'flats' as had been thought at first, but were made up of wagons with the ends removed. Some form of top covering was provided and the whole was covered by a type of camouflaged netting which presented a distinctive finely striped pattern. But it was not until April 10th that the rockets themselves were actually observed on triple units, uncamouflaged and unsheeted except for the usual broad banding of dazzle-painting on the rocket body and fins. Cover of some dead-end sidings at Wilhelmshafen showed twenty triple units in three rakes, one of which was severely damaged by fire. Other units were still loaded and sheeted but several were unsheeted disclosing rockets, assembled and loaded in position on the wagons exactly as had been deduced from the first examples seen at Niedersachswerfen. Cover taken four days later showed that all rocket material and transport on these sidings had been totally destroyed by fire. The agent was unknown but there was some evidence to indicate bomb damage.

RELATION OF PHOTOGRAPHIC INTERPRETATION AND TARGETING

During the rocket campaign, and incidentally during the flying bomb attacks against Continental targets and later against London, responsibility for interpreting sorties of Crossbow areas flown by 106 Group, US7 Group lay with ACIU while a special section (V Section) was instituted at SHAEF in November 1944, to coordinate examination of all sorties flown by PR Squadrons based on the Continent. It could broadly be stated that ACIU dealt with the areas involved in firing against England and with experimental and suspected assembly and supply installations, while SHAEF examined areas chiefly containing V-weapon activity levelled against Continental targets (e.g., Antwerp). Naturally there was a good deal of overlapping in photographic cover but such was independently examined as soon as possible by either SHAEF or ACIU. The fleeting nature of rocket launching sites militated against their being given any degree of priority in a targeting programme and it was realised that attacks on storage and supply targets were the two winter measure (action for the winter months) promising the greatest degree of success.

Photographic confirmation of rocket activity in target areas was slow in coming due to difficulties already stated. In the closing weeks of the campaign a policy of rail interdiction was adopted as sufficient information had been accumulated by then to indicate the main railway lines used for supply. 2nd TAF and Fighter Command both switched bombing policies, and railway targets became almost the sole objectives, though it is difficult to estimate the degree of success that would eventually have crowned their efforts as the cutting off of Holland by 21st Army Group in any case completely stopped all supply and summarily put an end to the rocket campaign. Before concentrating on rail interdiction HQFC had 20 rocket targets ranging from launching areas down to billets and offices used by rocket administration and technical personnel. The first eighteen had been laid on following ground information and several of these by their very own nature, could not be confirmed by aerial photography. Others, however, the Haagsche Bosch and railway stations in Leiden and The Hague, were fully confirmed as being concerned with rocket activity, while Duindigt and Ravolijn were taken up as high priority targets solely due to photographic findings.

GBR/PW
23.5.45

APPENDIX B

U-234 Cargo List

CARGO UNLOADING LIST FOR U-234 AT PORTSMOUTH, NEW HAMPSHIRE, ON AND FROM 23 MAY 1945.

Source: US National Archives, Box RG-38, Box 13. Document OP-20-3-G1-A, Dated 23 May 1945.

Injection pumps.
Documents.
Atabrin – 465 kg.
Aircraft warning device.
Direction finding (DF) set.
All-wave receiver.
Searchlight drawings.
Planospheric lenses.
Uranium oxide (10 cases, 56 kg, marked for Japanese Army).
Coils (presumably electrical coils).
Benzyl cellulose.
Silk ribbons.
Recoilless anti-tank munition plus igniter.
Junkers drawings (many).
Vacuum tubes.
Computer parts for fire-control computer.
Drawings for Me-323.
Thallium metal (106 kg).
23 cases of various munitions.
Steel (6,110 kg).
Fuses (for munitions).
Lead (11,151 kg).
Zinc.
Mercury (1,926 kg).
etc., etc.

In the Keel
Belts for machine guns (38 kg).

1,474 bars of lead (55,758 kg).
564 bottles of mercury (22,186 kg).

Grand Total 162,352.9 kg

Glossary

APOGEE   The highest point of a trajectory.

ASDIC   Allied Submarine Detection Investigation Committee, used to describe equipment for indicating underwater objects by high-speed sound waves.

ATOM   The smallest particles of which all matter is composed. An atom cannot be broken down by chemical means into anything simpler.

BALLISTIC MISSILE   Generally used to describe a missile which is guided or controlled for the first part of its flight but which afterwards continues along a natural uncontrolled trajectory.

CENTRIFUGE   A mechanical device for producing uranium U.235, consisting basically of a spinning cylinder rotating about its longitudinal axis and containing **uranium** hexafluoride. Centrifuges are grouped together into cascades, sometimes with several thousand in each.

CHAIN REACTION   A self-sustaining nuclear reaction in which the release of **neutrons** results in the splitting of further nuclei, leading to a succession of **fissions** and an increasing number of **neutrons**.

CYCLOTRON   Laboratory method for producing microscopic quantities of **radioactive isotopes**.

DOPPLER EFFECT   The returning frequency of sound or magnetic waves directed at a moving object is proportional to the speed at which the object is moving away from the transmitter. It results in an apparent change in frequency, especially of sound waves, to an observer.

ELECTROMAGNETIC SEPARATION   A modification of the mass-spectrometer technique for the detection, identification and measurement of **isotopes**, in which larger scale equipment is used to produce **uranium** U.235.

ELEMENT	A substance that cannot be split chemically into simpler substances. The **atoms** of a particular element each have the same number of protons in their nuclei.
ENRICHED URANIUM	Natural **uranium** consists of two main **isotopes**, U.235 and U.238, in proportions of 0.72% and 99.28% respectively. U.235 fissions more readily than U.238 and therefore to produce weapons, or for some types of nuclear reactors, the concentration of U.235 is increased to around 70% for weapons and 3% for reactor fuel, the U.235 being produced by the **centrifuge**, **electromagnetic** or **gaseous diffusion** methods.
FISSION	The release of large amounts of energy by the splitting-up of atomic nuclei into two fragments. The energy per fission of U.235 is composed approximately of 83% kinetic energy of the fission fragments and 17% as energy of the **neutrons**, beta particles and gamma rays.
GASEOUS DIFFUSION	The main commerical method for the large scale separation of U.235 from **uranium**, in which uranium hexafluoride is caused to diffuse through a special porous barrier. This method was used by America in its original weapons and reactor programme. It is now being superceded by advances in **centrifuge** technology.
GYROSCOPE	A mechanical device employing a spinning mass (flywheel) in which the spin axis tends to remain fixed in space, the flywheel being mounted within gymbals which allow it one or two degrees of freedom.
HALF-LIFE	**Radioactive** decay is a nuclear process which affects all radioactive sources and the rate of decrease in radiation is proportional to the number of **atoms** present. To provide a more usable appreciation of this decay the term 'half-life' is used to describe the period of time in which the radioactivity of a source will have reduced to half its original value.
HTP	High Test Peroxide, concentrated hydrogen peroxide which when used with a suitable catalyst (calcium or potassium permanganate), produces superheated steam. The system is often used to drive auxiliary power supplies in rockets. In a very diluted form it is used as a bleaching agent for hair (peroxide blonde).
ICBM	Inter Continental Ballistic Missile, usually applied to a missile with a range of over 5,000 miles.

ISOTOPE	Atoms of an **element** with the same atomic number but with different numbers of **neutrons** in their nuclei. Isotopes occur naturally but can also be produced artificially as a result of nuclear reactions, all artificial isotopes being **radioactive**. Many elements, including **uranium**, have both natural and artificial isotopes.
INLAND SEA	Japan comprises four main islands, Kyushu, Honshu, Shikoku and Hokkaido. Between the largest island, Honshu, and smallest, Shikoku, is a stretch of water called the Inland Sea. It has two outlets into the Pacific and one into the Sea of Japan.
KAMIKAZE	From the Japanese meaning 'Divine Wind', it is usually applied to suicide attacks from the air.
MACH NUMBER	The ratio of the speed of a body divided by the speed of sound in the air through which the body is moving. Mach 1.0 implies that the body is moving at the speed of sound. The speed of sound is approximately 750 mph at sea level.
MODERATOR	In a nuclear reactor the probability of the **fission** of U.235 by slow neutrons is much higher than that of U.238 by fast neutrons. Hence the neutrons are deliberately slowed down by a suitable moderator such as heavy water (deuterium), carbon or hydrogen in the form of light (normal) water. Such slowed down neutrons are called thermal neutrons and hence reactors with moderators are called thermal reactors.
NEUTRONS	The nucleus of a reactor consists of two primary particles, protons (with a positive charge) and neutrons (with no charge). The **fission** of U.235 produces 99.25% prompt or fast neutrons and the remainder delayed or slow neutrons, the fast neutrons being slowed down by a **moderator** to ensure more neutron collisions and hence more **fissions**.
PLUTONIUM	A range of artificial **isotopes** which are only produced in quantity in nuclear reactors. The most important plutonium isotope is Pu.239 which **fissions** readily and has a **half-life** of 24,000 years. All plutonium **isotopes** are highly **radioactive**.
RADIATION	The emission of radiant energy as particles or waves.
RADIOACTIVITY	The spontaneous emission of **radiation** from the nuclei of **atoms** of certain substances. This **radiation** comes in three main types: alpha particles, beta particles and

gamma rays, the latter two of which are the most harmful to body tissues.

SCABBING

When a missile impacts a target (such as a concrete structure), the stresses generated can result in a large portion of material being ejected from the back face of the target, even though penetration has not occurred.

SCHNORCHEL

Used initially by German U-boats, this Dutch invention allowed a submarine's diesel engines to be run while the boat was partially submerged. It comprised a telescopic tube with a ball valve at the head, which could be extended above the surface of the sea from the conning tower, in similar fashion to the periscope, allowing the engines to breathe air. The *Schnorchel* thus enabled a submarine to proceed under diesel power below the surface, while at the same time recharging the boat's battery cells which were used for submerged propulsion below *Schnorchel* depth, and facilitated ventilation with fresh air of the boat's interior crew spaces while surfaced during stormy weather.

SILO

A circular emplacement, usually constructed of reinforced concrete and sunk into the ground. Arranged in scattered groups with one rocket per silo.

SPALLING

When a missile impacts a concrete structure, spalling occurs when material is ejected from the impacted surface without penetration necessarily occurring.

TEST VEHICLES

Used to describe rockets or any missile, launched to obtain data or to confirm design information, as opposed to those being used operationally.

URANIUM

Uranium is a naturally occurring metal and as mined contains three isotopes, U.234 (0.005%), U.235 (0.72%) and U.238 (99.28%). U.235 is readily **fissionable** by slow moving **neutrons** compared to the fast **fission** contribution from U.238. However, U.238 is responsible for **plutonium** production via resonance absorption during the nuclear reaction. Numerous artificial **uranium isotopes** have been produced from nuclear reactions.

Selected Bibliography

Bormann, M.	*Bormann – Vemerke, Hitler's Secret Conversations, 1941–1944*, Signet Books, New York, 1961.
Bower, T.	*The Paperclip Conspiracy*, Michael Joseph, London, 1987.
Brooks, G.	*Hitler's Nuclear Weapons*, Leo Cooper, London, 1992.
Collier, B.	*The Defence of the United Kingdom*, HMSO, London, 1957.
Dornberger, W.	*V2*, The Scientific Book Club, London, 1952.
Ermenc, J.J.	*Atom Bomb Scientists, Memoirs 1939–1945*, Greenwood Publishing Group Inc., Westport, 1989.
Gantz, K.F.	*The United States Air Force Report on the Ballistic Missile*, Doubleday & Co., New York, 1958.
Groves, L.	*Now It Can Be Told*, Harper & Row, New York, 1961.
Guillaume, A.	*The German Russian War, 1941–1945*, War Office, London, 1956.
Gwaltney, R.C.	*Missile Generation and Protection in Light Water Cooled Power Reactor Plants*, US Atomic Energy Commission, 1968.
Hirschfeld,W.	*Das Letzte Boot – Atlantik Farewell*, Universitas Verlag, Munich, 1989.
Irving, D.	*The Mare's Nest*, William Kimber, London, 1964.
Jones, R.V.	*Most Secret War*, Hamish Hamilton, London, 1978.
Manchester, W.	*The Arms of Krupp, 1587–1968*, Michael Joseph, London, 1964.
Picker, H.	*Hitler's Tischgesprache im Fuhrerhauptquartier*, Seewald Verlag, Stuttgart, 1976.
Rohwer, J. and Hummelchen, G.	*The Chronology of the War at Sea, 1939–1945*. Vol. 2: 1943–1945, Ian Allan. 1974.
Shirer, W.L.	*The Rise and Fall of the Third Reich*, Secker & Warburg, London, 1961.
Speer, A.	*Inside the Third Reich*, Weidenfeld & Nicolson, London, 1970.
Walker, M.	*German National Socialism and the Quest for Nuclear Power*, Cambridge University Press, New York, 1989.
——	'Heisenberg, Goudsmit and the German Atomic Bomb', *Physics Today*, American Institute of Physics, January 1990.
——	'National Socialism and German Physics', *Journal of Contemporary History*, Vol. 24, SAGE, 1989.

Relevant Archives

Bundesarchiv/Militaarchiv, Koblenz, Potsdam and Freiburg, Germany: correspondence on V2 programme; Todt Organisation drawings of Watten and Wizernes; details concerning the transfer of expertise and materials vital to the war effort between Germany and Japan.

Karlsruhe Atomic Research Centre: German wartime nuclear reports.

US National Archives, Washington DC: information on U-234, including unloading list.

Public Record Office, Kew, London: documentary and photographic records from German and Allied sources of V2 programme, including V2 drawings.

Imperial War Museum, London: documentary and photographic records from German, Japanese and Allied sources.

National Institute for Defense Studies, Tokyo, Japan: information on movements of I. 13, I. 14, I. 400 and I. 401 and naval fuel situation.

U-Boot Archiv, Cuxhaven-Altenbruch: information on U-234.

Index